Taking the 12 Steps Up- and Down-Kilimanjaro

JAN 3, 2019

Taking the 12 Steps Up- and Down-Kilimanjaro

For Sonia, with many thanks & all God's blessings for your serving your growing success & your own health, happiness, prosperity & joy !!!

Robert P.

Robert P.

A Pleasant Oliver Media LLC Publication

Published in the United States by Pleasant Oliver Media LLC

Designed and printed in the United States by CreateSpace,
a DBA of On-Line Publishing LLC

Cover design by L.T. and R.P.
Photograph of African Crowned Eagle copyright Robert Flack. Used with permission.

First U.S. Edition

Library of Congress Cataloging in-Publication Data
Robert P.
Taking the 12 Steps Up—and Down—Kilimanjaro / Robert P.
Paperback ISBNs: ISBN-13: 9780692954508, ISBN-10: 0692954503
eBook ISBN:
1. 12 Step Fellowships. 2. Kilimanjaro. 3. Recovery from addiction
Library of Congress Catalog: XXXXXXXXXXXXXX
Dewey Decimal Number:
Library of Congress Control Number: 2017960326
Pleasant Oliver Media, Reston, VA

Dedication

To Samia, Humphrey, Rodrik, Chef Ely, Noel, Kihago, and the other 56 "Tough Guys" from Wilderness Travel who made it possible for me to take the 12 Steps up and down Mount Kilimanjaro on my own two feet and survive the Serengeti Plain.

Gratitudes

Most books call this part "Acknowledgements" to thank those people who helped the author publish the book. Much more accurate, from my 12 Step point of view, is the term "Gratitudes." I am so deeply grateful to everyone and every organization who made taking the 12 Steps up and down Mount Kilimanjaro the most meaningful experience of my life. The names of my beloved L.T., my family, and my "recovery family" in my 12 Step Programs will remain anonymous for obvious reasons.

First, my most sincere thanks to the staff of Alcoholics Anonymous for their kind permission to quote the 12 Steps and 12 Traditions and a brief quote from *Alcoholics Anonymous*, 4th Edition, throughout the work.

Of equal importance, I could not have asked for a more supportive, knowledgeable, compassionate company or group of people than everyone with whom I worked at **Wilderness Travel. Contact Info:** 1102 Ninth Street, Berkeley, CA 94710. **Phones**: Toll free: 1-800-368-2794, Local: 1-510-558-2488, Fax: 1-510-558-2489. **Email** info@wildernesstravel.com. **Web www. wildernesstravel.com**

Thank you to all at Wilderness Travel. And a very special Thank You! for permission to give direct credit to Samia, Humphrey, Rodrik, Ely, Kihago, Neal and the entire group of "tough guys" who made my successful trek possible. Without them, I would not have lasted beyond the first day.

Next, my sincere thanks to my manuscript reviewers: my OA sponsor, Jerry Z.; my Al-Anon sponsor, John H.; my therapist, Michael W.; and my beloved L.T. Each of you made significant improvements to this work, and I am forever grateful. L.T. has been so much more than a reviewer; she has been my chief cheerleader. She has showered enormous compassion **on me** throughout the daunting task of completing this book and establishing Pleasant Oliver Media LLC as an indie publishing company. Most important, she has taught me how to smile and has showed me what unconditional acceptance and true love really mean.

To my "recovery family," my band of brothers and sisters whom I love like my own flesh and blood. We carry each other in our hearts and on our shoulders every day: Alan C., Tim P., Jane L., Deborah C., Anne M., Eric vS.,

David L., Jeff D., Jeff Da., Jerry Z., John H., Rich R., Darcy D., Patricia, Meg, Bill, Emilie, and many, many more. My most sincere gratitude for your love, support, experience, strength, and hope that you share with me through our all of our good times and bad.

To my family members—my late brother C.P., my sisters M. R.-T. and N.P.—and my late parents, L.O.P. and M.O.P.—Pops and Momma. Despite our struggles, I know in my soul that you loved me and were doing the best you could.

To Bill W. and Dr. Bob, the founders of Alcoholics Anonymous; Anne W. and Lois S., the founders of Al-Anon; Roseanne S., the primary founder of Overeaters Anonymous; and John H., the leading founder of Debtors Anonymous. Thank you for your incredible sacrifices, your genius, your perseverance, as well as your pain and desperation, that inspired you to create and offer the world the 12 Step Way of Life. The challenging roads less traveled you all took have led to the most effective way for me, and millions like me, to recover from our addictions and to live lives beyond our wildest dreams. I know deep in my soul that without my 12 Step programs, I would have died in abject misery many years ago.

Last and most important, to my Higher Power, without you, I am lost; with you, despite all my shortcomings and mistakes, I live a life of health, happiness, prosperity, abundance, joy, love, and service. I am among the most blessed on this earth, and you are the Source of all my Good.

Tithe to the Sources of My Good

Each year, the author will donate 10 percent of the net proceeds from the sales of all versions of this work to Overeaters Anonymous, Debtors Anonymous, Al-Anon Family Groups, Inc., and Alcoholics Anonymous up to the amount of their annual donation limits. Any amounts that exceed the group's annual donation limits will be divided among various charities endorsed by Wilderness Travel and to reputable Kilimanjaro and Serengeti conservation organizations.

The Twelve Steps of Alcoholics Anonymous

- We admitted we were powerless over alcohol—that our lives had become unmanageable.
- Came to believe that a Power greater than ourselves could restore us to sanity.
- Made a decision to turn our will and our lives over to the care of God *as we understood Him.*
- Made a searching and fearless moral inventory of ourselves.
- Admitted to God, to ourselves, and to another human being the exact nature of our wrongs.
- Were entirely ready to have God remove all these defects of character.
- Humbly asked Him to remove our shortcomings.
- Made a list of all persons we had harmed, and became willing to make amends to them all.
- Made direct amends to such people wherever possible, except when to do so would injure them or others.
- Continued to take personal inventory and when we were wrong promptly admitted it.
- Sought through prayer and meditation to improve our conscious contact with God *as we understood Him,* praying only for knowledge of His will for us and the power to carry that out.
- Having had a spiritual awakening as the result of these steps, we tried to carry this message to alcoholics, and to practice these principles in all our affairs.

Table of Contents

Glossary of Abbreviations and Terms

Links to Some of the Largest 12 Step Groups
AA – Alcoholics Anonymous – www.aa.org
Adult Children of Alcoholics – www.adultchildren.org
Al-Anon – Al-Anon Family Groups, Inc. – www.al-anon.alateen.org
DA – Debtors Anonymous – www.debtorsanonymous.org
GA – Gamblers Anonymous – www.gamblersanonymous.org
OA – Overeaters Anonymous – www.oa.org

Wikipedia has a list of dozens of other 12 Step groups and links to their websites at this link:
https://en.wikipedia.org/wiki/List_of_twelve-step_groups

Abbreviations for Accepted Program and My Favorite Phrases
ACOA – Adult Child of an Alcoholic
FMG – Father/Mother God, my personal concept of my Higher Power
H, H, P, A, and J – Health, Happiness, Prosperity, Abundance, and Joy
HP – Higher Power
ODAT – One Day At A Time
TW, NM, BD – Thy Will, Not Mine, Be Done
TYFMGFAMMMMMB – Thank You, Father-Mother God, for all my many, many, many, many blessings (or variations on the number of "M's" I include)

PROLOG

Why Would I Do Such a Thing?

"If an ass goes traveling, he'll not come home a horse."
THOMAS FULLER

I decided to climb Mt. Kilimanjaro—all 19,343 feet of it, give or take a foot or two of ice—to celebrate my 60th birthday and my 20th anniversary in the second of my three 12 Step recovery programs. Why would I, in long-term recovery from multiple addictions—alcohol, food, compulsive debting, co-dependent relationships, and more—risk my abstinence, my sobriety, and my solvency and perhaps my physical, mental, and emotional health to climb a very high mountain in very late middle age?

After all, I had been a member of Overeaters Anonymous since 1976, Alcoholics Anonymous since 1986, Debtors Anonymous since 1990, and Al-Anon since 2008 for my recovery from my own multiple addictions and the impact of those of my multi-generational family of addicts. From the late 1980s until the early 1990s, I also attended meetings of Co-Dependents Anonymous (CoDA), Adult Children of Alcoholics Anonymous (ACoA), and Food Addicts in Recovery Anonymous (FAA) for periods ranging from a few months to several years. I claimed progress, not perfection, in my recovery and a thorough dedication to the 12 Step Way of Life. Did this middle-aged "ass" really believe he would come down that mountain a "horse"? What did I have to prove?

I will tell you many reasons, all true, but the last reason is the truest of all.

Brief Introduction to the 12 Step Way of Life

Before I explain my reasons, let me briefly define 12 Step recovery programs for those readers who are not familiar with them. All 12 Step programs (at my last count, more than 130 for any addiction one can think of!) are based on the 12 Steps and 12 Traditions of Alcoholics Anonymous that Bill W., Dr. Bob S., and the early AA pioneers developed between 1935 and 1950. The 12 Step recovery process can be summed up this way, according to the American Psychological Association:

- admitting that one cannot control one's alcoholism, addiction or compulsion [I would add 'or obsession' – Step One];
- recognizing a higher power that can give strength [and I add 'give you a reprieve from, but not cure, the compulsion' – Steps 2 and 3];
- examining past errors with the help of a sponsor (experienced member) [I would add 'admitting those errors to yourself, your HP, and another person' – Steps 4, 5, 6, and 7];
- making amends for these errors [I add 'after becoming ready for and asking your HP to remove them, and listing the names of those you harmed' – Steps 8 and 9];
- learning to live a new life with a new code of behavior [I add '*one day at a time*' – Steps 9, 10 and 11]; and
- helping others who suffer from the same alcoholism, addictions or compulsions [I add, 'by carrying and living the message of recovery' – Step 12].
  (Source: https://en.wikipedia.org/wiki/Twelve-step_program)

The 12 Step Way of Life means that you do your best to live according to the principles embodied in the Steps and Traditions *in all your affairs*, not just within your 12 Step groups and close friends. Those principles include these especially important to me: honesty, service, integrity, humility, faith, and perseverance, as well as hope, courage, willingness to change, self-discipline, love, and spirituality.

Some people get hung up on the Higher Power or G-O-D thing, especially atheists and agnostics. However, and this is critical: You do NOT have to believe in ANY religion, G-O-D figure, spiritual practice, etc. In fact, many 12 Step program members find that the 12 Step group itself and its Steps and

Traditions show, by the positive results of their members, that the groups can serve as a perfectly adequate Higher Power.

The doubters see other members stay sober, clean, and abstinent from their addictions, and live happy, healthy lives. The members' ability to transform their lives through the 12 Step Way of Life helps show the doubters that the group has found a solution to their serious disease that the doubters have not found. The doubters have been unable to "cure" their diseases for their entire lives, so when they see a group of people with successful recovery, they often conclude that the group itself can serve as their Higher Power. No G-O-D required.

Many other members define G-O-D as "Good Orderly Direction," exactly what you get when you live in 12 Step recovery. No religion, sect, cult, or other form of formal belief required.

See the Glossary at the front of the book for definitions of abbreviations I use throughout the book and hot links (if you are using an e-reader) to a number of groups' websites. You can find a 12 Step program for any addiction by surfing the Internet as well.

Many people do not agree with these programs and principles, and many others who have "tried" to work the programs and dropped out for their own reasons. Bless them. All those who have been able to find their own way to recovery from and avoid acting out their addictions, have my support. I pray only that all people in the world afflicted with addiction be relieved from it by whatever means works for them.

However, all I can say is that for more than 40 years, I have tried every other way to "cure" my addictions—stop overeating, stop debting, stop drinking, and stop screwing up relationships—you can imagine. The *ONLY* way I have gained any semblance of sanity, and in fact, been granted the gift of an incredibly wonderful life, has been participating in 12 Step programs and living the 12 Step Way of Life.

I am going to share my experience, strength, and hope gained during my challenging personal journey taking the 12 Steps Up and Down Mount Kilimanjaro. As we tell folks in meetings, "Take what you like and leave the rest." It's my simple mission to carry the message to those who still suffer, especially those "multiple winners" like me who have more than one addiction. This memoir is an important way for me to give service and carry the message.

Thank you for allowing me to share my journey, its challenges, and its life-changing lessons with you. By reading and interacting with this book and our web site, you help me recover as well.

Reasons for Taking the Steps Up and Down Kilimanjaro

Please keep my mission and these program basics in mind as I explore with you why I did such a crazy thing as climb this amazing mountain.

First sighting of Mt. Kilimanjaro from 40 miles away! Awestruck!

Maybe I read too much Ernest Hemingway when I was a teenager. His story, *The Snows of Kilimanjaro*, and the dead leopard in the snow have stuck in my mind for more than 50 years. By the way, I did not see any dead leopards, though I saw a lot of defeated, dead-tired climbers heading back down the mountain.

Maybe I needed another thrill; after all, like many recovering addicts, I still can act like an adrenalin junkie. When I turned 55, I went skydiving—a wonderful thrill to see the world from a bird's eye view, but a very short thrill measured in minutes.

Maybe I just wanted something spectacular to top the skydiving. After I went skydiving, my boss at the time, a former US Air Force officer and F-4 jet pilot, began to introduce me as 'This is Robert. He jumps out of perfectly good airplanes" with both an incredulous and admiring tone in his voice.

Maybe I was feeling bored when I first came up with the idea. Life had been too good most of the time, so maybe it was time to ratchet up the ante a notch or two.

Maybe it was because Kilimanjaro is called the "Mother Mountain." For thousands of years, she has been the source of the cascades of water that flow down her sides every year. This water nourishes the crops and waters the herds that the tribes, who live on her side and at her base, rely on for their food. Oh yes, Kili is most certainly a "SHE" in every sense of the concept!

Maybe I just needed a challenge to get into good physical shape; I was working as a staff officer for a government agency, sitting on my "brains" 9 to 10 hours a day and rarely seeing the light of day.

Maybe I needed to do something to show I was still alive. Maybe I was just deep down scared of getting old. Climbing "Kili," as I love to call it, would prove to myself and the world that I wasn't over the hill and that I would not have to face my mortality quite yet.

I knew in my heart that climbing Kili would test my inner resources to the utmost and challenge the quality of my recovery. It would give me the ultimate opportunity to practice what I had been preaching for more than three decades: Living the 12 Step Way of Life one day at a time under the most extreme circumstances. I had long preached, and practiced, however imperfectly: "No matter what: Don't drink, don't overeat, don't debt, don't act out your addictions..."

I knew—or thought I knew—that climbing that mountain would give me the ultimate challenge: Could I take the 12 Steps Up—and Down—Mt. Kilimanjaro? How would the experience affect my recovery and me both as a man and as a recovering addict?

Began as a Joke

My journey up the mountain began as a joke right after I went skydiving on my 55th birthday. For months after that, my friends and family kept asking me, "What are you going to do for your 60th to top that!?" I joked with them about a variety of extreme ideas—walk the Appalachian Trail (would take too long), run a marathon (I hate to run), or bicycle the C&O Canal (Chesapeake & Ohio) and the Allegheny Trail more than 300 miles from Washington, DC to Pittsburgh, PA (would take too long and be monotonous). By the way, all of these and much more are still on my 'bucket list' of things to do before I die—if I feel like it.

Climbing Kilimanjaro came to my mind about a year later because I had taken an easy tourist safari to Africa for my 56th birthday. I had become fascinated with seeing more of the continent and its incredible wildlife. My original idea was to climb Kili in 5 or 6 days and then go on another safari with my wife (my second, more on that later). I had a strong yen to see the leopards, cheetahs, and rhinos we had missed on our first trip as well as visit the Ngorongoro Crater and the famous Serengeti Plains that seemed fairly close to Kili on the map.

Unfortunately at the time—but in the end, fortunately—this idea quickly became a symptom of the subtle problems with my second marriage.

Addiction is Like Playing Whack-A-Mole

One recovery lesson I learned the hard way: Addiction is like playing "whack-a-mole." That's a carnival arcade game: When you whack the head of one mole, another pops up from a different hole. The object is to whack as many mole heads as possible in the allowed time. If you are good at whacking moles quickly, your "prize" at a carnival is likely to be a cheap toy or stuffed animal.

Similarly, recovering from one addiction has no effect on, and may in fact encourage, another addiction to gather strength and exert enormous pressure on your sanity. "Whack" one addiction, and another is likely to pop up. In my experience, I have seen dozens of recovered alcoholics become obese and become ill with, even die of, heart disease or diabetes. I always see recovering alcoholics standing outside AA meetings smoking cigarettes; just a slower way to kill yourself with another addiction. In my case, I substituted freedom from alcohol and food obsession for the new prisons of compulsive debting and ir-rational co-dependency.

By the way, "practicing" multiple addictions at the same time is formally called "cross-addiction" by the medical and psychiatric professionals. I like to keep it simple: Cross-addiction and multiple addictions are the same thing:

an addict acting out more than one addiction at the same time. At my worst, I was eating compulsively, binge drinking, spending compulsively, and wrecking relationships. I "qualify" for membership in this much-too-large club of tens of millions who have other addictions: drugs, sex, gambling, risk-taking, cluttering/hoarding, nicotine, etc., etc.

The problem—and tremendous opportunity—of multiple addictions is that you have to work each recovery program separately. To paraphrase one of my favorite slogans of old-timers in multiple programs: ***The credits don't transfer***. In other words, you cannot recover from one addiction by working the 12 Steps for a different one. You have to work the Steps, live the Traditions, and use the Tools for each addiction. You have to make recovery your way of life. Right now, I attend between three and five meetings a week for my three active programs—OA, DA, and Alanon.

My personal—and very painful—"whack-a-mole" experience ground on for the last 13 years of my 16-year first marriage. To say it was crazy would be the understatement of this book. During almost all those years, my wife and were freelance writers who wrote and lived together 24/7/365.

With our mental and emotional instability—and despite my successful recovery in OA, we moved 19 times in those 13 years. Whenever we had a crisis in our relationship or our work, we blamed where we lived or our clients and moved, wasting thousands of dollars in deposits, relocation costs, and disruption to our business. It was a wildly unstable marriage, although we presented an extremely good facade. One of our editors even called us 'the young Rothschilds,' not a compliment by the way.

Even when we were in the worst throes of our addiction to debting, we had always taken severe risks in our work as freelance writers—missing deadlines, juggling far too many assignments, using different aliases to get more work, using one credit card to pay off another, and worse. We lived constantly on the edge of failure and bankruptcy. I felt terrified and shell-shocked most of the time—when I didn't feel enraged and abandoned.

It became a financial disaster that rolled downhill faster and faster with each year. We went from a bankruptcy on $12,500 in debt in the mid-1970s to more than $100,000 into debt by the late 1980s; however, we had been very successful freelance writers. In less than 13 years, we wrote 15 books, two dozen book-length market research reports, and thousands of articles. During those years, we spent as much time together as people married four or five times as long. At the same time, because of my 12-Step work in OA, I maintained a 50-pound weight loss most of the time and got sober in AA during those 13 years before we separated.

Weight great, sober great, debting insane. Whack-a-Mole! The credits did not transfer!

My second marriage was a huge relief compared to my first: My wife was financially sound and patient, and she had two stepchildren who were fundamentally good people—even as teenagers! When we were dating, I began my recovery in DA and participated in other programs to learn how to enjoy healthy relationships. Our relationship was healthy and happy for a number of years, primarily while we were getting the kids through high school and college, and I was working as a writing instructor and continuing to freelance. Like many middle-aged married couples, we were happily busy, so busy we could ignore our fundamental issues.

However, when the idea of climbing Kili came up before my 56th birthday, my wife (married 13 years at the time) strongly objected to my mere mention of climbing it. Even three years before my 60th birthday, every time I brought up the subject, she would say with obvious hostility, "That's your trip, I'm not going." I would reply, "I'm not asking you to go. You could go to Zanzibar to the beach for a week while I climb the mountain and then meet me, so we could go to the Serengeti." Then she would reply, "I don't want to do that." We went around and around like that for months.

She never simply said, "It's your trip, and I'm not interested. But if it's your dream and you want to celebrate your 60th birthday doing that, I support you in your dream."

The climbing Kilimanjaro issue, of course, was one of many small fissures that gradually widened into multiple chasms. They finally widened so far that we could no longer close the gaps; they led to our separation soon after my 58th birthday. We endured the formal divorce process as I began the 18 months I seriously prepared to climb Kili. The separation and divorce—and how poorly I managed it—caused intense pain for my wife, my adult stepchildren, their families, and me.

Simply, during our nine-month separation, I understood that I was pursuing my dream of climbing Kilimanjaro to give myself something extremely challenging and positive in which to immerse myself during (more like distract myself from the pain of) an excruciating time.

What Makes Kilimanjaro Both "Easy" and Very Difficult

More than 20,000 people—mostly college students and millennials from Europe—try to climb the "Mother Mountain" each year. Less than half make it to the top because they take the less expensive, shorter routes. Most turn around because the climb is too strenuous, and the air is too thin-literally; they are struck with altitude sickness; or they are not physically, emotionally, or mentally prepared for its challenges.

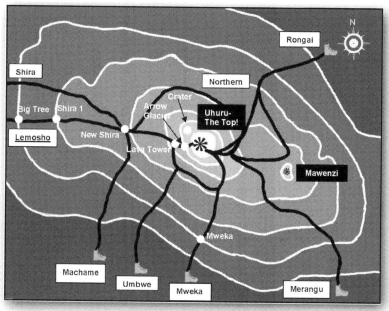

This map is an overview of all the tourist routes up and down the mountain. Each gateway is indicated by a boot symbol. To the far left (southwest corner) is the Lemosho Trail (underlined). The Lemosho is the eight-day-up, two-day down route that we took. The map shows our camp sites: Big Tree, Shira One, New Shira, Lava Tower, Arrow Glacier, and Furtwangler Glacier on the way up and Mweka Camp on the way down. The other trails that begin at the bottom of the map are the 5- and 6-day routes that most hikers take and fail to make to the top.

Yet, Kili is considered the easiest of the "Big 7," that is, the tallest mountain on each of the seven continents. Why does Kili appear so deceptively easy, yet so few make it to the top? It looks easy because it stands out as a magnificent sight on a very wide, very flat plain; the view is utterly enticing. During the summer months beneath the equator, there is little to no snowfall or serious rain. The icepack and glaciers seem charming and easy to reach from the plain—in fact, they are melting and retreating rapidly.

The ascent appears to be just a long hike up what appears to be gradual slopes. It is not a tough technical climb. In those tougher climbs, you endure ice, snow, high winds, and sub-zero temperatures up craggy, spiny slopes, such as Mt. Everest at 29,029 feet in Nepal, Mt. Denali in Alaska at 20,310 feet, or even Mt. Rainier at 14,411 feet that dominates the skyline in Seattle, Washington.

Kili's "good looks" are deceiving because altitude is the killer. I took the long 10-day Lemosho route up the southwest crest—eight days up and two days down—because I learned that this route offers about a 90 percent chance of success. But it is the most expensive route.

Most climbers try to climb the four cheaper, shorter routes (Machame, Umbwe, Mweka, and Marangu) straight up the middle. They take five or six days up and down the steepest slopes, including a 4,000-foot slog through the middle of the night to the peak.

Most people fail because they do not stop and acclimatize to the loss of air. At the peak, you are breathing much less than half the air you normally breathe at sea level. Every step of the way, you gradually have less and less air to breathe. Yet, the loss is so gradual that you don't realize you are in trouble until you begin to come down with the pernicious disease of altitude sickness:

- Stage One: Headaches, nausea, insomnia, loss of appetite, and general fatigue;
- Stage Two: Diarrhea, vomiting, dehydration, worsening headaches, etc.; and
- Stage Three: Edema, that is, you begin bleeding in your brains and/or lungs and you can die if you don't get down the mountain and obtain medical treatment as quickly as possible.

The "kicker" is that altitude sickness can strike anyone at any time regardless of the physical condition you are in. However, drinking booze, eating too much unhealthy food, and staying up late will make it easier for altitude sickness to hit you as well.

Worst of all, with their ignorance of the serious perils of altitude sickness and often their sense of invincibility, many young climbers try to hike very fast. That is the easiest way to get sick because they change altitude faster than their lungs and brains can cope.

Closest to the Truth

Knowing all this hidden danger—which I thought I understood before I got to Kili—Ha!—why did I really take on this challenge at my age? The reason closest to the "Truth" with a capital "T" is Grief with a capital "G." Deep, gut-wrenching pain from my second divorce that caused a lifetime of unresolved grief to burst forth and almost cripple my ability to act. I completely lost my relationship with two stepchildren I love as my own. I helped raise them for 15 years through high school, college, graduate school, and marriage. I helped pay their way through college, helped put my stepdaughter through graduate school, and encouraged both of them through their serious relationships into their marriages. I even had one of the greatest honors of my life—my stepdaughter asked me to preside over her wedding ceremony. It was one of the best days of my life, and I felt the deepest feelings of love and gratitude I had ever felt to that time.

And I blew it. I utterly botched how I managed my separation and divorce. I alienated my wife and stepchildren so badly that to this day, my stepchildren have never replied to my four Ninth Step letters of apology. They rebuffed with silence my every overture to make amends. Neither of them has spoken to me voluntarily in many years. I felt intense grief for several years; now, I just feel a dull pain in the back of my mind and a dull ache in my heart.

After my separation in September 2008 and their rejection, I was stricken with overwhelming grief and numbness and despair. Through therapy and my 12 Step work, I had to go back and grieve my entire life because of my multiple-addicted family of origin. I have lived to see seven generations of addicts: Going backward, there were three generations of parents, uncles and aunts, grandparents, and great-grandparents who were born between 1870 and 1923. Of all those ancestors, I know that at least one great-grandmother was grossly obese, at least one grandfather died of several diseases related to alcoholism, and multiple aunts and uncles died of alcohol-related diseases.

Since my birth in the middle of the 20th century, I have watched four more generations become addicts from both "nature and nurture": 13 marriages among myself and three siblings; the death of my younger brother due to obesity-related diseases; and cousins, nieces and nephews with alcohol, drug, and/or obesity addictions; and serious signs of obesity among great nieces. Just for starters. These seven generations span 135 years—since Rutherford B. Hayes was president and the telephone was brand new until today with our smartphones, instant global communication, the ubiquitous Internet, space travel, and all-electric cars.

But I have found for myself only one long-term solution to addiction: the 12 Step Way of Life gained by working the 12 Steps and living the 12 Traditions one day at a time. I honestly do not know if any of my 32 first cousins and their dozens of children and grandchildren has joined any 12 Step group. I am the only one of four children in my family who has lived the 12 Step way of life.

Add my family history to the pain of sabotaging my career for 30 years in insidious ways, primarily during my first marriage, and of losing both marriages and my stepchildren. The result of all this unresolved pain was that my suppressed grief had been waiting for decades to erupt.

The Grieving, Defenseless Two Years to Prepare to Climb

As I grieved and felt defenseless for almost two years, I turned to climbing Kilimanjaro to force myself to exercise. Exercise is one of the only ways the hormones in my addict brain stay arranged in a healthy way. I needed a huge goal that would give me something positive to do every day and distract me from my agony and the two horrific jobs I blundered into, deluding myself all the while I was going to be great in both.

First, when I was doing what is called a "joint duty assignment" at a different agency, I botched what I thought would become the job of a lifetime. Unfortunately, it turned out that jealous coworkers undercut my effort and actively sought to ensure that I looked incompetent. In my bereaved state, I believed I did not deserve to defend myself against the bureaucratic subterfuge of senior staff members who were supposed to help me.

Cleaning Up My Side of the Street

A year later, when I returned to my home agency, I was put to work editing federal budget books, something I literally knew nothing about. I was named to a lead a "team" of two—an inexperienced contractor and me—to edit a critical budget book and perfect it within six weeks of my arrival. It usually takes months. I felt bewildered, betrayed by my new bosses, and resentful. The people who were supposed to train and mentor me did almost nothing to help and actively undercut my efforts. It was terrible.

In each situation, I had to go back and take Steps Four through Nine to work through my anger and resentments, prepare for and ask my FMG to remove my shortcomings, and make amends to the people I harmed during these rough years. My best amends in both was to release my resentments and work as hard as I could to do a good job, regardless of their attitude or actions toward me. We call it "cleaning up my side of the street."

I turned to preparing to climb Kili—and swing dancing—as my salvation from hours of tears, intense frustration, and deep depression. I worked out with two trainers (thank you Daryl and Adam!!!) at least twice a week, went swing dancing once or twice a week, took dance lessons for a year, hiked in the Shenandoah Mountains frequently, and spent a week in Colorado hiking at 10,000 to 12,500 feet to test my response to higher altitudes.

The Power of the "3 Cs" Plus One

For my spiritual survival, I began to attend Al-Anon at the suggestion of a dear friend who had been in AA for about 15 years and Al-Anon even longer. I began to attend Al-Anon meetings, especially two men's meetings, at least once or twice a week. Most importantly, I learned the power of the Al-Anon "3 Cs," to which I added a fourth:

> *I cannot **cause** others' addiction or problems, I can't **control** them—the people or their problems, I can't **change** them, and I can't **cure** them.*

I reached out to my men friends in all my programs, and for the first time in my life, grew deep and true friendships with men. I had always either depended on my female teachers or been co-dependent with my girlfriends (of which there were few) and my wives.

My regular attendance at Al-Anon men's meetings showed me how to develop a healthy, happy relationship with a woman—through several painful "trial-and-error" relationships along the way. Today, I enjoy the most loving, mutually supportive, and understanding relationship of my life. But we found each other months after my climb. It took a while for the long-term, positive lessons of climbing the "Mother Mountain" to seep into and create a strong, healthy influence on my addict brain.

In the 18 months before I climbed Kili, I practiced more prayer and meditation than ever before. For the first time, I consistently got on my knees every morning and every evening to take the Third and Eleventh Steps: to turn my will and my life over to my Higher Power's care and to pray **only** for knowledge of my HP's will and the power to do it.

In short, little did I know when I began thinking about this climb at age 57 that Kili, the "Mother Mountain," would exact a very high price throughout the journey—long before, during, and after the actual climb. In exchange, "She" would teach me dozens of valuable lessons in recovery—lessons I continue to practice and learn—and would give me the most valuable gift I've ever received—the gift of true compassion.

That gift was bestowed on me by three human angels in our crew—Samia, Humphrey, and Rodrik, despite the "best efforts" of every one of my character defects to sabotage my goal. Samia was the team leader who was making his 197th— yep, that's right, 197th—ascent; Humphrey, an assistant team leader; and Rodrik, the short, very strong team member who was my personal "tough guy" for 10 days.

Their deep care, serious concern, and constant consideration allowed me to reach the top of the mountain on my own two feet when I surely did not deserve that privilege: I repeatedly ignored their wise advice. I treated them and my fellow climbers rudely and upset the camp's collegial atmosphere. And I became physically, mentally, and emotionally exhausted, draining my spiritual reserves and making me susceptible to acting out.

Despite the best I could do to sabotage my goal of reaching the top and to push myself into serious relapse, these three incredible men literally carried my load when they didn't have to do so. When they had every right to send me down the mountain, they encouraged me and kept me moving forward. Their kindness, freely given, humbled me and taught me what it means to give and receive real compassion.

Ultimately, this book is a *Remembrance*—

- A personal celebration of my adventure-of-a-lifetime accomplishment;
- A recollection of lessons learned, pain survived, and shortcomings overcome;

- A commemoration of the slow letting-go of my character defects that continues each day;
- A sacrament to the 12 Step way of life;
- A heartfelt tribute to Samia, Humphrey, Rodrik, Kihago, Ely, Neal, and the **56 other team members** who made it all possible (Yes! That is the right number!); and
- An amends to myself, my fellow travelers, my supervisors, my family, and all those toward whom I have had so little compassion during my blessed life.

I mean the title "Taking the 12 Steps Up—and Down—Mt. Kilimanjaro" in every sense:

- Taking the 12 Steps, that is, "carrying" them in my head and my heart as I climbed up and down
- Working the Steps every day
- Living the Steps through my actions

Perhaps a more accurate title would have been *"Carried by My Higher Powers Up—and Down—Kilimanjaro."*

Join Me on My Journey

I invite you, both my fellow travelers in recovery and those interested in this great mountain hiking adventure, to walk with me step by step—literal and 12 Steps—day by day throughout this book. I'll also leaven my experience, strength, and hope by describing many of the incredible plants and animals we saw and Kili's unique geology and ecology. I'll share the lessons I learned about the frailties and strengths of human nature and the marvels of the natural world.

In this memoir, each day of the climb is described in one chapter of the book. Each day's entry begins with reflections on my thoughts during each long, cold, often sleepless night before the dawn. Then, it describes our experience as we progressed—***pole pole***, that is Swahili for "slowly, slowly," up the mountain. (You pronounce the phrase "po-lay po-lay" with a long "o" sound.)

At the end of each day's entry, I'll review the lessons I learned—at least temporarily. I'll reflect on which of the 12 Steps I worked that day and how well I believe I worked them. Each day, I will describe the challenges of increasing cold, exhaustion, mental fatigue, and my increasing dependence on my Higher Powers—human and spiritual—as the days wore on and I wore out.

First Lessons

Lesson One on Journeys: Every journey up and down a mountain begins with one step—and continues with the second.

Lesson Two on Teams: "The team is ONLY as strong as the support the strongest members give the weakest." Notice the 180-degree difference between this attitude and the more common attitude in the U.S. that "A chain is only as strong as its weakest link." Our team leader Samia made this, for me, life-changing statement during his first talk with my group. His statement means that the strongest have a moral and ethical duty to support the weakest and help make sure they can reach the team's goals, too. Mutual support and responsibility of the strong to carry the weak are very different from our "dog-eat-dog" philosophy. Without their compassionate values, I would never have made it to the top.

The second lesson is the heart of why 12 Step programs—lived correctly—work so well. It is the service of our time, energy, experience, strength, hope, and compassion that we give freely to our fellow sufferers that carries us through and bestows upon us our HP's miracles of recovery.

I hope my service in sharing my experience, strength, and hope may help you hike a bit more easily the often challenging, but ultimately "happy road of destiny," that we are invited to follow—one day, one step at a time.

Ultimately, maybe I was just an ass who wanted to go traveling and see if he could come back a horse. I hope I came down the mountain an improved ass; I know I came down a much more humble and more grateful ass; I know I didn't come down a horse. The rest of this book is about how this recovering ass came down the mountain as a somewhat improved ass by doing my halting best one day at a time to work and live the 12 Steps.

PART 1

Twelve Days and the Twelve Steps Compassion Had On Me on Kilimanjaro Days 1-12, June 19-June 30

* Compassion—dictionary.com says com·pas·sion
1. a feeling of deep sympathy and sorrow for another who is stricken by misfortune, accompanied by a strong desire to alleviate the suffering.

Origin: 1300–50; Middle English (< Anglo-French) < Late Latin *compassiōn-* (stem of *compassiō*). See com-, passion

Synonyms - commiseration, mercy, tenderness, heart, clemency. See sympathy.

Source: Dictionary.com Unabridged
Based on the Random House Dictionary, © Random House, Inc. 2011.

SATURDAY, JUNE 19

Day One, Step One

"Pole, pole—slowly, slowly."
SAMIA, THE TEAM LEADER, HIS FIRST
DIRECTION AND CONSTANT REFRAIN

Step One - Admitted we were powerless over (alcohol, food, debting, spending, relationships, self-sabotage, etc.), and that our lives had become unmanageable.

The day began with the first of many signs that I was going to go through an incredible experience for the next 17 days. I was sitting in the ornate white dining room of L'Ambassade hotel at 341 Herengracht Canal in Amsterdam at 7:15 a.m. I was gazing out its 12-feet-high window, pondering how weird it was going to be to land in as different a city as I could imagine in just 12 hours—Arusha, Tanzania. I looked up and a perfect rainbow arched across my view, its multiple hues framed like a painting with a gilded frame and a black cloud background.

I smiled, said a silent prayer of thanks to my Higher Power (whom I choose to call Father-Mother God and just HP or FMG for the rest of this book.) I watched the rainbow for many minutes until the sun shifted and it faded. I felt I had received the most startlingly clear sign that my HP was looking out for me and that everything was going to be okay.

I had never taken a trip of this magnitude by myself. I had visited 30 other countries on six continents, including Africa and Antarctica, but my wife at the time had always been with me. Frankly, she had made most of the arrangements for each trip. This adventure climbing Kilimanjaro was the first time I had ever done all the planning and physical preparation myself. Honestly, the tour company **Wilderness Travel** did most of the preparation—planning the climb itinerary, assembling the crew, coordinating all of the logistics and schedules. But I did have to get in shape—18 months of working out several days a week; swing dancing twice a week; and hiking in the Rockies, the Shenandoahs, and the Berkshires. I also had to arrange the plane flights and the hotels and tours for my visit to Amsterdam on my own. Finally! A bit of independence at age 59 years, 11 months, and 24 days, but who was counting?!

By the way, for you "curious" sorts, I behaved myself in Amsterdam and was a very "good boy"—no booze, no drugs, no brothels. I just enjoyed walking the old city, seeing the historic canals and colorful houseboats, and dodging all the bicycle riders everywhere. I took an on-water canal tour to visit the Van Gogh and Rijksmuseum Museums. I did the most important thing of all—I remained abstinent from all my addictions, especially by avoiding the 3 Bs—bread, booze, and bon-bons—and eating healthy food according to my daily food plan.

It was an exciting time to be in Amsterdam because the World Cup Soccer matches were being played in South Africa. It was the year the Netherlands lost to Spain 1-nil in the championship game. The game this day was the semi-final when the Netherlands played Japan. All the bars and cafes were packed with raucous people. Most were dressed in Dutch orange and blue watching the match on large TV screens. Many others in their offices were listening on radios I could hear through their windows.

With a warm day and all the café and bar doors open to the streets, I heard people whooping or groaning at every attack and every missed shot-on-goal as I walked beside the canals. Banners of the Dutch flag were hung along the ornate railings of the bridges spanning the canals and across the narrow streets from street lamp to street lamp. The Netherlands won this tight game, 1-nil, against Japan. They scored a goal in the 53rd minute and withstood a fierce Japanese push into the overtime period. With screams of joy, it seemed like an entire nation of happy people poured out of the bars and into the streets. I was amused and thrilled to see European soccer mania up close and personal, and I have rooted for the Netherlands team ever since. Unlike in the U.S. and many other countries, the Dutch were just happy people, enjoying a great victory;

no trashing cars, no violence, and no crowds losing their minds. Just joyful people relishing their victory.

Setting Foot in Tanzania

The 12-hour flight from Amsterdam to Kilimanjaro International Airport, outside Arusha, Tanzania was utterly uneventful, as every good flight should be. Crammed into a middle seat between two large guys, I found a way to sleep most of the flight. I arrived late in the afternoon (still June 19). The airport was crowded and noisy; compared to a U.S. airport, it was chaotic as vendors hawked their trinkets and crafts to tourists, taxi drivers hustled fares, and throngs of people waited for or sent off loved ones. No Transportation Security Agency (TSA) shakedown or x-ray machines or taking off your shoes, belts, etc. going in, and virtually no questions asked at Customs leaving the terminal. U.S. airports may be cleaner, quieter, and more orderly, but I felt perfectly safe from terrorists. I did keep a close hand on my wallet, though, because I had been warned that pickpockets were around.

Six members of our small tour group of eight arrived about the same time. We were met by Wilderness Travel guides, locals who had done this routine dozens of times before. Pleasant, polite, and efficient. We waited in our van for the other two members to arrive, but they missed their flight from Amsterdam and were not going to arrive until the next morning.

Here's a quick snapshot of the first six of us to arrive. *(Disclaimer—The names of all of the tour members have been changed to protect their identity and my anonymity. I asked for and received permission from Wilderness Travel to use the company name and the names of their team leaders and "tough guys" who took care of us for 10 days on the climb and our five equally crucial days on the Serengeti plain.)*

Heinrich, 58, was a short, bearded Austrian-born sculptor who had already climbed the more than 18,000 feet to the Mount Everest base camp. Etienne, 60, was a thin, attractive blonde from California who lived at 8,500 feet and jogged regularly at 11,000 feet (remember this for a week from now), and a family—Steve, a 40-something dad with his 21-year-old daughter Felicia and his 15-year-old Jason. This climb was Steve's college graduation present to Felicia, a competitive swimmer for a well-known California college team. Jason, a tall blond teenager, played in his high school band and enjoyed music. Last and least, me, the 59-year, 11-month, 19-day-old grieving ass who was sort of in decent shape and who had climbed the previous summer to 12,500 feet in Colorado. More on all these fine folks later.

First Surprise

Since it was already dark when we landed, I thought we would be taken to a nice hotel after our long flight before we drove to the starting point the next morning some 50 miles away. Ha! Our guys drove us in a van for an hour and a half from the airport through small towns and villages lining Highway A-23, a modern two-lane highway, to a camp in Arusha National Park.

After we drove for the first 30 minutes, we turned off the paved road onto a gravel—to be polite—road and bumped through the edge of Arusha National Park to the Momella Gate. Momella Gate is on the east side of Arusha National (By the way, Mount Kilimanjaro is its own national park.) The Arusha park protects the second highest mountain in Tanzania, 15,500-foot tall Mount Meru, also a volcanic cone considered sacred by the Tanzanians. Mt. Meru plays a beautiful and mysterious role in my climb up Kilimanjaro, so look for much more on the stunning "relationship" between Meru and Kili on Days 5 through 8 of my journey.

The Welcoming Party

By now, it was late at night and very dark. At the Momella Gate entrance, we woke the sleeping guard who raised the "security gate"—a long wooden pole on a rope pulley across a dirt road. As soon as we drove through the gate and under an arch that said "Welcome to Africa," we met our first "welcoming party"—two twin giraffe calves and their very tall "mama" or cow. We spooked them from the side of the road, and all we saw was their hind ends and long, patterned back legs running into the tall grass. They had been feeding by the side of the road, less than 100 feet away from the guard hut at the gate.

As we drove along a very bumpy, deeply gullied dirt road through a rain forest, we saw two more giraffe calves and a cow, a small herd of zebra, some Cape buffalo—every one of them hundreds of pounds of horned, stupid, dangerous mean—and somehow, one very familiar looking rabbit!

When we arrived very late at our stop for the night, Moira Camp, I learned I had a "luxury" tent to myself. For being 50 miles in the middle of a rain forest, it was very comfortable; it had a double bed, its own toilet, and its own sort-of shower. It was at least 50 to 100 feet away from the closest tent. The tents for the team leader, the local guides, and our camp tent where we socialized, had tea, and ate breakfast were even farther away. But I could tell I had plenty of company nearby—screeches and squalls and calls of long-tailed, black and white Coloebus monkeys nesting in the moss-laden trees surrounding our campsite.

The unusual black-and-white Coloebus monkeys lived in the trees around our camp and sometimes broke in and ransacked them for food. We kept our tents sealed tight!

Rules One and Two, Lesson One, and Step One

After we arrived, we first met with our team leader Samia over cups of hot tea in the chilly "mess tent." He briefly laid out our itinerary and gave us two rules I will never forget—because I broke both of them again and again—to my pain and chagrin:

Rule One: "Pole, pole!"—pronounced "po-lay, po-lay," with a long "o" sound, or "Slowly, slowly." He said if we wanted to make it to the top, we had to walk very slowly and follow the leader's pace. At the peak, I would be breathing less than half of the air I breathed in Virginia where I lived just above sea level.

Rule Two and Step One: "Do what I tell you to do and you will be fine. If you don't follow instructions, you will hurt yourself." At that moment, I took Step One for this trip—Samia became my "land-based," human Higher Power for the next 10 days because his statement was absolutely true: When I followed his instructions to the letter, I was healthy and fine; when I didn't, I suffered. The rest of this story pretty much compares what happened when I truly surrendered to Samia's guidance and what happened when I foolishly took back my own will. For the next 10 days, my Higher Powers were Samia; the team of "tough guys," really our human angels who took care of us; and of course, my spiritual H.P. What happened should be familiar to anyone who has ever relapsed in a 12 Step program or tried to recover from their addictions on their own; the results are almost always not pretty.

By the way, I will run out of adjectives telling you how much Samia and the tough guys meant to me and what their example taught me during this daunting physical, spiritual, emotional, and mental challenge to my recovery.

First Lesson

I had practiced the first lesson when I was contracting the trip because it is the key to my sobriety, my abstinence and my sanity throughout the adventure: **ASK FOR WHAT YOU NEED!** And I needed alcohol-free, wheat-free, low-sugar meals three times a day, so I put this special requirement on my application at the beginning. I am humbled and grateful to say that from the first night, the cooks prepared special foods for me every day. They not only did so without complaint, but also went far out of their way to make sure I could eat what they planned to cook.

First "Smart Robert Choices"

I learned from our briefing and the first night in my tent that I had done a few things right preparing for my climb. Throughout this story, I will call these "smart Robert choices" as I recall the things I did right and "rash Robert regrets" when I describe my mistakes. I have plenty of both to share with you. Today's "smart Robert choices" included bringing the following:

- Warm ankle-high booties! It is chilly and damp in the rain forest at night. It is ferociously cold at 18,800 feet near the summit.
- My beat-up safari jacket with 14 pockets I bought for my first trip to Africa trip in 2006. You can never have too many pockets on an adventure like this. Yes, I looked like some English colonial "Bwana man," but who cared?!
- Headlamp—It wins the prize award for the dumbest looking, but most useful attachment you can have at night in the middle of nowhere.
- Long sleeve shirts—various fabrics, including cotton, fleece, insulated, and microfiber.
- Long johns—wicking 100 percent polyester tops and bottoms
- Layers and layers of clothes—I put them on before daybreak each day, peeled them off as the temperature and I climbed each day, and put them back on when the temperatures plunged to below freezing at night.

After our first dinner, I was escorted to my tent and found myself in a unique situation: Going to sleep in an African rain forest surrounded by wild animals in a small tent all by myself. Something I had never done before, even if others were only 50 feet away. By the way, if a Cape buffalo, hippopotamus, or elephant decides to tromp by or through your tent in the middle of the night, it doesn't matter how close your nearest neighbor happens to be.

Fortunately, this late night, I fell asleep in an amazingly quiet forest. The Coloebus monkeys quickly got used to our presence—after all, someone was in the tent at least once a week. I was expecting lots of animal and bird calls and noises, but they are smarter than that. The big cats—lions and leopards, especially—come out at night to hunt. The monkeys and baboons know to stay quiet so they stay safe in their roosts in the crooks between tree branches and trunks.

With heavy droplets of dew plunking on my tent, I wrote my first diary entry at 12:50 a.m. on the very early morning of June 20, more than 19 hours after I saw the rainbow in Amsterdam. My final note:

"TY *(Thank you)*, FMG *(Father-Mother God)* for safe travel. I'm in the rain forest in a tent by myself—never done this before—ever—So FMG—I know you are with me—every moment, every step-FAITH-SLEEP."

Step One Lessons of the Day

I quickly and willingly admitted I was powerless over the rain forest, the animals, everything about the adventure. But I still had to take action. My life was certainly unmanageable as I had no clue what I was doing. I did realize that by surrendering to my HP, Samia, the team, and the process, I could experience many good things with a few simple actions:

- Expect the unexpected—I will receive many pleasant surprises along the way.
- Ask for what I need to be successful and I am likely to receive it—maybe not the way I want it, but the way I actually need it.
- Take every step of the way with an "attitude of gratitude."

SUNDAY, JUNE 20

Day Two, Step Two

"Every journey begins with a single step...
and continues with the next one."
FROM MY KILIMANJARO JOURNAL

Step Two - Came to believe that a Power greater than myself could restore me to sanity.

Today was the day my earthly Higher Power—Samia—sized us up to find out what kind of shape we were in, how well we took orders, and how well the eight of us would work as a team. In essence, baby steps. A lot like how HP and our 12 Step meetings introduce us to recovery. I came into the meeting rooms for the first time afraid, defiant, beaten down, hopeless yet hopeful, confused, wary, expectant, and ashamed. Add your own experience of how you felt attending your first meeting.

That's how I felt this day through our first hike with Samia. The day began with half a dozen Coloebus monkeys chattering in the trees outside my tent that woke me up about daybreak—more like a lighting of the gray fog that hung over the camp. In the lush, thick green forest, the scene evoked images from a ghost story about campers who wake up and find themselves in a very different place than where they had been the night before. I stood outside my tent, shrouded in swirling mist. Dew dripped from moss hanging languidly from tree limbs. I was overshadowed by huge trees. There was no sunlight. Just a gray gloom with a brighter gray to the east, but no ray of hope peeking between the trees' thick limbs.

Shrouded in ghostly fog and mist, this morning reminded me we are indeed in a rain forest.

At my "door," in fact the zipper to my tent, I found that a wash stand with a small aluminum pan of warm water had magically appeared. With the exception of a "shower" this afternoon, a similar small pan of lukewarm water—twice a day—would be all I had to wash up and brush my teeth for the next 10 days. But I didn't know that at the time. I thought, "Oh good, I can brush my teeth now and get more water and brush my teeth, maybe shave and take a shower later."

Didn't happen that way. The rainforest is very wet, but fresh, potable water is hard to come by. Every precious drop we used had to be taken every day from nearby streams—sometimes mere dripping springs on the mountainside—in beat-up, 5-gallon plastic buckets. It was filtered through—well, you really don't want to know what the filters looked like, but they worked!—so we could drink it. I also had brought along plenty of water purifying tablets as Wilderness Travel had advised. We were told to put them in our water bottles and shake them up. I carried three quart-sized bottles in my backpack every day. Again, Samia and his team knew what they were doing because none of us ever got sick from drinking the water. Again, our earthly HP knew better than we did.

After a quick, hardy group breakfast, we drove in Land Rovers along a rel-atively smooth dirt road through the rain forest to the Maio waterfalls. It is a set of three small, but lovely waterfalls that cascade one after the other through the forest into a small pool next to an equally small, grassy flood plain. After we arrived at the falls and took the obligatory "ooh-ah" tourist pictures, we began our first hike with Samia.

During our hike, it rained a steady mist and drizzle all morning until noon. We wore rain gear and ponchos and just kept trucking. We hiked up an easy trail to the top of the highest waterfall and back down. We saw hyena tracks and Cape buffalo dung piles and tracks. Our constant companions at every stop, the curious Coloebus monkeys clambered through the trees to peer down at us.

The most interesting and beautiful sight that morning was dozens of iridescent swallowtail butterflies flitting from one bright orange, cone-shaped flower to another on the flood plain. The plant is called "dangerously" enough the "Red Hot Poker" (or *Kniphofia thomosonii* for you plant lovers). The name is a bit of misnomer because it derives only from the dark red, orange, and yellow flowers that cascade from its spike. Nothing evil about it. In fact, the butterflies and bees love it because it produces huge amounts of yummy nectar.

The origins of the 'scientific' Latin name *Kniphofia thomosonii* are more interesting. No—"Kniphofia" has nothing to do with sharp implements or the spear-like shape and size of the plant, but only with the name of the German botanist Dr. Johann Hieronymus Kniphof (1704-1763). He first formally defined and described the plant genus so it was named after him.

However, the "red hot poker" perhaps deserves its name because of the last name *thomosonii* in honor of the intrepid young Scottish explorer Joseph Thomson (1858-1895). He was one of the first Westerners to experience the "joy" of failing to reach Kili's summit by climbing too fast and by being unprepared to take on Mother Mountain.

To show you how he got to Kili, a bit of background: In 1878, at the very young age of 21 and a new graduate of the University of Edinburgh, he had to assume leadership of a Royal Geographical Society (RGS) expedition in what is today's Tanzania. The goal was to establish a trade route between Dar es Salaam on the coast and Lake Tanganyika in the deep interior, but the original leader died early in the journey. Thomson persevered and led the group more than 3,000 miles in only 14 months, set up the route, and returned with many "firsts" in the Western scientific study of Central Africa's plants and animals.

Now to his Kili adventure. After his first successful exploit, his second, an 1883 RGS expedition, sought a route from the East Coast to Lake Victoria that avoided German competitors and unfriendly Maasai tribes. If you check a map, you'll see that it's almost a straight shot from Dar es Salaam on the East Coast past Kilimanjaro to reach Lake Victoria. By the way, these explorers were NOT cutting new trails as they fought through impervious jungles, as so often portrayed in movies. First, they moved across well-traveled trails through tropical rain forests and open savanna grasslands. Second, Thomson sought to establish a British-controlled network across well-known routes used by Maasai, Chagga, and other historical tribes that had lived, traveled, and traded in the area for thousands of years.

Along these routes, you can see Kilimanjaro from dozens of miles away on a clear day because flat grasslands surround it in every direction.

After crossing the wide plain, Thomson tried to climb Kili in a day and failed. He turned back because of the daunting terrain and physical ailments. He might have fallen for the illusion that leads so many climbers astray. As I stressed before: Kili looks easy from a distance, but has dozens of subtle pitfalls when you start a real climb.

The intrepid, young Scots explorer Joseph Thomson tried to climb Kilimanjaro in one day and failed in 1883 during his expedition to establish a British trade route through what is now Tanzania to Lake Victoria. (Source: Unknown, Public Domain, Https://commons.wikimedia.org/w/index.php?curid=4824166)

But Thomson continued his journey and reached Lake Tanganyika successfully. However, his luck ran out on his way back because he was gored by a Cape buffalo and fell seriously ill with malaria and dysentery, according to Wikipedia. [https://en.wikipedia.org/wiki/Joseph_Thomson_(explorer)]

Adding insult to injury, a young writer, Henry Rider Haggard, "borrowed" liberally from Thomson's best-selling travel journal, *Through Maasai Land,* and wrote the world-famous novel *King Solomon's Mines.* Thomson was very annoyed because he had been the first Western explorer to accurately report snow-capped mountains in equatorial Africa, but Haggard reaped all the fortune and fame. Consider the many editions of his book and the large number of movies and television shows that have been based on it during the past 130 years.

Today, Thomson's meaningful contribution to the Western exploration of Central Africa is virtually unknown to non-scientists. By the way, he did receive scientific recognition. One of the most numerous gazelles in Africa is named after him—the Thomson's gazelle—as is one of its famous waterfalls, Thomson Falls. More on the Thomson's gazelle's unique role in the life cycle of the African savanna—and its humorous and apt nickname—eight days from now when I reach the Serengeti.

Unfortunately, due to the rigors of these and other years-long expeditions, Thomson died of the effects of several tropical diseases and pneumonia at only age 37 in 1895.

Recovery Lessons for the Day

I gleaned several lessons from this young explorer's story: First, one may be amazed at the stories of courage and sacrifice behind the names of many plants and animals. I need to study more deeply the stories behind the names to learn why explorers and scientists are rewarded with such an honor. I need to follow their example in my recovery—to persevere in living the 12 Steps no matter what challenges I face.

Second, even today, more than 130 years later in far more civilized conditions, climbing Kili, or any other high mountain in Africa, brings serious dangers with it: Tropical diseases too numerous to mention—I spent almost $1,000 just for shots to prevent the worst, such as yellow fever, and took malaria pills for three weeks to stay well. I also had to be wary of dengue fever carried by biting flies for which there is no vaccine. I already knew that while the wild predators may be acclimated to a human presence, they may still see me as a slow, easy—and tasty—meal. I wonder if we taste like gazelle or Cape buffalo to the lions, leopards, cheetahs, and hyenas? Too bad I can't ask them! We definitely don't taste like chicken!

Third, during this easy first trial hiking day, I saw a tree that reminded me of the deep roots and serious dangers of addiction. Let me explain. The rain forest near the Maio Falls consists in large part of very tall trees, many of which are being slowly killed by the tropical strangler fig—a parasitic vine, Samia explained. The thick vines begin as seeds that attach to the tree trunk. As the vines grow, they twist and curve up along tree trunks and onto their limbs like sinuous snakes.

"Snake" is an apt metaphor as Samia told us that the vines grow their roots through the thin bark and into the heartwood of the host fig tree. The parasitic vine roots suck the water and nutrients out of the fig wood and slowly kill the tree from dehydration. It takes years for the vines to kill the tree; it continues to grow taller, but always weaker as the vine grows thicker and tightens its grip like a boa constrictor crushing a hog.

Our Land Rover drives through a tunnel carved from an ancient, giant tree overwhelmed by the parasitic vines of the strangler fig.

Strangler Vines Like Addiction

The vines work a lot like addiction—a parasitic brain disorder that slowly worms its way into our lives and takes control so slowly and so insidiously that we ultimately find ourselves powerless over the parasite. That's how I became addicted first to food as a child. In a family of compulsive overeaters, my mother equated love with how much fattening food she could feed us. "Normal" was devouring second helpings of fried Southern foods, cleaning your plate, eating lots of dessert, and drinking thick milk shakes every night. Throw in the number of my aunts and uncles who were alcoholics and a father who often drank heavily—all of which was considered "normal" in my family.

By the time I reached college, I found it easy to both eat and drink too much of all the wrong things. In my freshman year at a prestigious Southern university, I quickly became a very confused, terrified, isolated lower middle class "grit" way in over his head among the much smarter and richer Yankees and Southern "preppies." Maybe the large soft drink and honey bun I ate as my only breakfast every morning and the beer I drank and marijuana I smoked at night had something to do with it, too!

I was undoubtedly born an addict with a scrambled body and brain chemistry, but the "nature-nurture" one-two punch of my family life ensured I had little defense against becoming a full-fledged addict by my late teens.

Addiction is cunning, baffling, powerful, insidious, silent, and deadly—just like the vines. The beautiful, majestic fig trees are defenseless against their parasites just as I was, and as so many of us are, in our ostensibly "normal," but truly insane "nature-nurture" families. The critical part of Step Two in my life was not "came to believe," but "restore me to sanity." By the time I joined my first 12 Step program in my mid-20s, I was nutty as a fruitcake, yet I thought everything in my career and my marriage was going just fine. Denial is *not* a river in Africa, and Denali *is* a treacherous mountain in Alaska!

The "ACOA" Group I Was With

When we returned to camp for lunch after our morning hike, I quietly declined a glass of wine commenting that I didn't drink. With my quiet decline, the truth about the members of my group suddenly poured out—pun intended. To protect my anonymity—and at the time, my government security clearance—I always explained that I stopped drinking when I was a freelance writer in the 1980s. I said drinking interfered with my work at the time, and since then, I found it too expensive and not worth the trouble. About my food addiction, I tell people I am allergic to wheat and that a history of diabetes runs through my family—which it does through several generations—so I don't eat refined sugars as well.

Usually, any group I am with will say things like, "Oh, how do you live without bread?" or "I wish I had your willpower," and I let the comments slide. I do feel awkward, but usually, the group gets used to my situation quickly and leaves me alone.

At the time, I worked in a sensitive government position, but years before I had taught professional writing to college students and adults. So, during my extensive travels with many tourist groups, I have had a ready-made cover story about which I can talk incessantly. When my fellow travelers (not in the conspiratorial sense, of course!) asked me what I did for a living, my "cover story" was that I taught writing to government workers. Talk about the world's most boring topic—I say that and people look at me with glazed eyes, and say something like, "Oh, how interesting," or "Boy, government workers really do need to know how to write better." I agree, and that ends any conversations about my occupation for the rest of the trip.

However, today, at lunch, Scott blurted out that his father was a recovering alcoholic, had gone to AA, and remained sober. Scott said about himself that he was a full-time banker and a part-time cop as well as "Mr. Mom." He said he loves the cop stuff, and as "Mr. Mom," always cooks breakfast and dinner and fixes lunch for his kids who live with him. Throughout the trip, he never said anything about his ex-wife and why he had custody of the kids.

I don't remember how, but we moved on to a discussion of medical use of marijuana, how crazy the laws were, and how the depictions of recreational drug use and alcohol in the movies and TV are so wrong. Our discussion took place several years before legalization began to sweep the United States, so it was interesting that it surfaced as a "hot topic" of conversation on a trek to climb Kili.

In the middle of this discussion, Etienne, who rarely spoke, said quietly and with pain in her voice, that she had been married to a drunk for 20 years. She said, "There is no fun in being with an alcoholic!"

Amen to that! Both being and living with any kind of active addict is no fun. But her comment brought silent agreement as we nodded our heads and changed topics.

It is very interesting that my FMG put me in the middle of this group of adult children (and grandchildren) and former spouses of alcoholics (ACOAs and potential Al-Anons). Neither Scott nor Etienne said they had ever been to Al-Anon meetings. I could have taken the situation as an opportunity to do anonymous service by being supportive and understanding; however, one of my shortcomings during my trek was that I chose to remain silent and anonymous. I must admit that I felt vulnerable, distant, and not very friendly most of the time. At some deep level, I felt unsafe and believed that I could not trust the group to protect my anonymity. I also needed to protect my security clearance, a reasonable need at the time. My isolation, however, cost me much physical and emotional pain later in the trip.

On the lighter side, at lunch we had a visit from four Coloebus monkeys who chattered at us from tree limbs right above our heads. They kept a keen eye on us for a while, probably hoping to swoop down and grab our leftovers. No such luck. Our team leaders and cooks quickly ate the leftovers as we went back to our tents.

The food was incredibly good—Chef Ely and his three assistants performed miracles of delicious food three times a day in a small—and very warm—tent with only a small, rectangular aluminum baking oven and two propane gas-fired burners.

I won't give every day's menu—although I wrote it all down every day as part of my OA abstinence plan. Today was typical of what they prepared, the non-wheat foods especially for me:

Breakfast - omelets, fresh fruit, bacon, non-wheat bread, and oatmeal.

Lunch - avocado salad, eggplant parmigiana without wheat, non-wheat zucchini bread, and non-wheat soup

Dinner - Lamb, pork, chicken, and beans in a casserole with steamed vegetables on the side and with more fruit for dessert.

Honestly, we ate like kings on safari, and I have no idea how Chef Ely and his crew managed it as we climbed higher and higher. Deservedly, they were the lucky ones who slept in their toasty warm cook tents during the extremely cold nights the higher we climbed. Samia and some of the crew would hunker down with them after dinner for a while as well.

Our Human HP's "Truths"

After lunch, our earthly HP Samia briefed us on our real climb that we would begin the next day. We learned we are going to take the Lemosho Trail up the southwest ridge until we reach the Shira Camp #1.

On the way, we will camp for two nights with lots of other hikers. Then we split off and do the Shira trail with our own camp away from other large groups of people who are doing the five- and six-day sprints up and down the mountain. We are going to take a total of eight days to reach the top and two days to get back to the bottom.

Tomorrow, we will begin with take a three-hour truck ride on bad roads to the Lemosho Trail Gate on the southwest corner of Kili. We will be awakened at 6:30 a.m., eat breakfast at 7 a.m., and be out of our tents and moving by 8 a.m. We will take a couple of breaks before lunch on the trail about 1 or 2 p.m. We will hike for only four hours from 6,500 feet to 9,000 feet and camp for the night. It will be even cooler than the chilly, damp forest we are in today, and we were warned to wear fleece as we go higher. Thank you, HP, that I brought lots of layers!!!!

By the way—and I'll continue to mention this—less than half of the 20,000-plus people a year who take the short routes, mostly college kids and millennials from Europe—ever make it to the top. They take 4-, 5-, or 6-day trips with little help, maybe one or two tough guys with small amounts of food and light tents. They try to climb Kili fast and cheap; to reach the summit before sunrise, they climb 4,000 feet in the middle of the night. Most of them end up miserable, sick, and disappointed when they give up and turn back.

But more than 90 percent of the very few people who take our long Lemosho Trail route make it. And that's how it worked out in our group: Of the eight who started, seven reached the peak. The primary difference, of course, is cost. Our 10-day trek was more than twice as expensive as the shorter treks, but the extra expense—and safety—were well worth it since I reached the peak and experienced the unforgettable sunrise over "Mother Mountain."

Climb—and Recover—Slowly and Surely

The difference between the fast treks up the mountain and our slow climb is a lot like recovery; most suffering addicts hit a bottom of pain and suffering and begin attending meetings. But they want the "5-day" recovery plan, that is, the easier, softer way the AA "Big Book" *Alcoholics Anonymous* warns us against. Many newcomers want to do the Steps One, Two, Three "dance," as we call it.

"One, Two, Three" is the perfect set of steps for the waltz, but a very poor way to stay clean, sober, or abstinent one day at a time for the rest of your life. Those who do this "waltz" tend to struggle mightily and relapse repeatedly, or drop out and never return. Those people who take the longer, seemingly harder path work the 12 Steps diligently, use the Tools of recovery daily, and dedicate their lives to living the 12 Step Way of Life one day at a time. They usually do very well in the long term. At least, that is what I have concluded from thousands of meetings, conversations, friendships, and service over more than 40 years. I have watched the vast majority of newcomers struggle and fail to recover because they are unwilling or incapable of following the suggestions of our simple, yet challenging 12 Step process.

Climbing Kilimanjaro was very similar: Climbing fast, taking shortcuts, drinking and eating badly, and not following their guides' directions made the perfect recipe for failure, if not disaster, on Kili.

Special Gift Welcomes Us to Samia's Tribe

After our briefing and a lazy afternoon, at 6:30 p.m. Samia gathered us, and we walked to the top of a small hill to watch the sun set over Mount Meru, the other mountain sacred to the local tribes. Mount Meru is a 15,500-feet tall dormant volcano like Kilimanjaro—about 40 miles away. Notice I stress "dormant." Both Meru and Kili still have active lava inside them and could erupt at any time.

Best view of Kilimanjaro's 15,000-feet-tall "cousin," Mt. Meru, a "dormant" volcano that last erupted in 1910, mere seconds in geologic time.

It was a cloudy, drizzly afternoon, so the sunset was more a pinkish-grey light through the clouds. On the way up the hill, we spooked several large Cape buffalo a few yards away from us; they scooted toward a herd of about 50-60 of these beasts that watched us from about 100 yards away.

At the top of the hill, Samia poured a small plastic cup of champagne for each of us and we toasted the sunset and our adventure—I pretended to sip. Then, Samia gave each of us a traditional Maasai tunic—bright red with dark blue, black, and purple threaded rectangular patterns. It was a very special gift as it meant Samia formally welcomed us into his tribal family; it is a gift and a tribute that I will always treasure.

A Bit about My Fellow Adventurers

Back at camp and after dinner, we introduced ourselves in more detail. Here's a thumbnail observation about each person—remember that the names have been changed to protect their and my anonymity:

- Etienne - A bit of a free spirit. A runner, lots of 10K races in the mountains of California. Lived in Hawaii on North Oahu, but now lives near North Beach and San Diego.
- Heinrich - Austrian born. Owns a sculpting business. Divorced for some years after 26 years of marriage with three grown kids. Made a happy life with his business, serious climbing, and long-distance bicycling. He met a woman who was a friend of Scott's and she got Heinrich interested in this trip. He had already climbed the 18,800 feet to the Mount Everest base camp in Nepal and wants to do the "Seven Summits," that is, the highest mountain on each continent. Good for him! Not me! Short, stocky with dark hair and a gray-fleck-ed beard. Had expensive and heavy camera equipment.

Heinrich inspired me at first because his experience showed me that I—recently divorced and alone for the first time in 19 years—could be okay and enjoy life. He has a long-term relationship, and both have no interest in getting married again. Nor do I, but I was interested in growing a healthy, happy, long-term re-lationship! It would take me a long time after this climb to recover and become healthy enough so that the right person could enter my life. God's time, not mine!

- Scott - As I noted, he's a banker and a part-time cop on weekends. Seems like a very good father to his daughter and his son.
- Felicia – His daughter is a cute, slender, tall blonde, recent graduate with a degree in psychology from a good California school. A swimmer in high school and college.
- Jason – Scott's 15-year-old teenage son plays in his high school band. His band marched and played in the Rose Bowl parade. Very tall, well above 6 feet. But from the first night, he felt nauseous and ill even at this low altitude and spent most of the next nine nights and rest times in his tent.

The last couple, Matt and Annie, had not yet caught up with us. Although arriving late, they would still have to get up early and leave without the extra day to acclimatize to the environment and bond with the group. We'd just have to welcome them to our merry band the next morning.

As Samia stressed—and the best of the lesson of the day, we're all here to help each other, so I guessed we better do so. The rest of this adventure will show whether I did or did not help the others, despite all of the gracious help I received.

Thank HP for Small Favors

One of the best things about this day was the "small favor" of my last real shower for 10 days. The shower contraption—very functional in fact—was a 5-gallon canvas bucket with a small sprinkler head attached at the bottom. It hung above an enclosed shower area behind the toilet with a regular seat and a "catch basin" beneath—no sewer pipes and no septic system. They had to dig holes and bury everyone's detritus and clean the basins every day. This "bathroom" area was at the rear (another intended pun) of my tent, separated from the living-bedroom area by a zippered canvas "door." The tent was all thick canvas and sewn tightly shut on all six sides like a water-tight box.

The thick canvas floor was stitched to the walls with heavy thread to prevent hyenas and jackals from digging under the tent and eating us while we slept in our beds. No joke, as you'll understand when you read about my face-to-face moments with mortality on the Serengeti 12 days from today.

The shower area was open to the skies and the monkeys in the trees, but thankfully, not to any people. At the top, the bucket was attached to a stout rope and pulley contraption.

At 4 p.m., two tough guys brought two buckets of hot water to the back of my tent and asked me if I wanted to take a shower. Absolutely! The men pulled up the large canvas bag over the opening, lowered it behind the tent, and filled it with the hot water. Then, they hauled it back over the top and tied it down.

The water bag with a small shower head had an old-style faucet tightly connected to the bag to prevent leaks. I was supposed to open the faucet so the water could spray out. Of course, being a "tourista doofus," I couldn't figure it out and had to "ask" the guys for help.

I must confess that I didn't ask. I stood naked and soaped up in this small area, chilled to the bone, and yelled for help. One of the men quietly—and with a little smile on his face like he had done this a thousand times before for dumb touristas—unzipped the rear of the tent, climbed in, and showed me how to turn the faucet in the right direction. We stood about six inches from each other—me a naked, soapy, shivering, pale, middle-aged white American guy and him a strong, experienced, slightly amused, young black guy in tattered clothes. He turned the faucet on and the water began to sprinkle out. He scampered out of the tent to avoid getting wet.

This "luxurious" 5-gallon bucket provided my last shower for the next 10 days!

I started rinsing off and realized I could control the flow, so I slowed the spray and enjoyed a delightful 5-minute warm rinse! Very luxurious considering the circumstances and considering it was the last shower I was going to have for 10 days! I toweled "dry" with a damp towel and felt clean, but I put my dirty clothes back on. No laundry for 10 days either.

Thank God for my long johns, another apparently small, but critical aspect of my journey! They were warm and I immediately felt better. In fact, not bad at all. This tent with the shower and the private toilet was as good as it got for the next nine days of this adventure.

During the next nine nights, I would learn that I could survive rough camping in below freezing cold weather. This feat was something I had last accomplished as a 10-year-old Boy Scout. Back then, I was in a large Boy Scout troop and my father was one of the scoutmasters. No lions, leopards, Cape buffalo, cheetahs, hyenas, jackals, or wild dogs roamed the mountains of North Georgia in the early 1960s. I had had 50 years of living the easy life and thinking a two-star hotel in Ireland was "roughing it." I was—and remain—just a slightly spoiled American.

Although some of my fellow trekkers didn't think so, another small HP favor is the invention of Diamox, originally a diuretic and now commonly recognized as the best drug to prevent altitude sickness. But it does have side effects that differ from person to person. By dinner time, several people were feeling some side effects—tingling in their fingers, but I felt fine and energized. That's how Diamox affected me—more energy, but that meant less sleep. I paid a heavy price for all this energy as we climbed higher and higher and I slept less and less. Since Diamox is a diuretic, I also had to drink lots of water, so I had to urinate far more often than normal, no fun at all on the trails when everyone can see and hear you.

Reflections on Step Two and End of the Day

This day was without a doubt a Step Two day—that only a power greater than myself could maintain my sanity during this climb. I reaffirmed Step One—that I was undeniably powerless over my situation—clueless, in fact, about how to protect myself from the monstrous Cape buffalo and all the wild things lurking around me. From the lessons Samia taught us during our hike and our briefing—and from my amusing experience in the shower—I knew that only earthly Higher Powers, like Samia and the experienced tough guys, could show me the way and keep me safe on this adventure.

Everything that had happened so far was wildly different from what I had expected. I had expected a slower start with a night in a nice hotel. I had expected to stay in the same kind of luxury tents I had stayed in during my previous African safari. And I thought hiking Kili would be a relatively easy hike. Even the earliest moments and first day's experiences had already dashed my expectations AND exceeded my wildest dreams. And we had not even begun to climb the mountain!

My last notes from my diary before I crawled into my sleeping bag on my cot:

"Thank you, FMG for all my many, many, many blessings. Thy will, not mine, be done!!

"Thank you, FMG, for a very good day.

"Now - quiet again, wind blowing steadily through the trees all around, bugs chirping, frogs croaking in the distance - Life is good!"

Recovery Lessons for the Day

- Take the long, "pole, pole"—slowly, slowly—route versus the short cuts. I don't recommend racing through the 12 Steps by yourself; dancing "the Three Step Waltz" to help you stay sober, clean, and abstinent; or working with uncaring or inexperienced guides/sponsors. Relapse is the analogy to the potentially deadly—certainly very painful—equivalent of severe altitude sickness. Remember that it can overcome anyone who ignores instructions and experienced advice, races up the mountain, and refuses to take one slow step at a time.
- Recognize your Higher Power when one is staring you in the face and is there to help you. In my case, Samia; on this day, I came to believe that he knew the mountain and the rigorous demands of the climb better than I ever would, and I came to trust that he would keep us safe during our adventure.
- Follow the experienced leaders—Samia and his crew.
- Follow their suggestions—Samia and his crew.

- Ask for what you need—forget about feeling embarrassed or ashamed. By the time I began this journey, my divorce and my grief had stripped me of all hope and flayed my emotions and spirit to their core. Yet, here I was in the African rain forest, asking weird strangers to haul my water and to help me learn how to work even the simplest process. Today, it was a simple faucet; in my life, it was my simple, but not easy, recovery program.

MONDAY, JUNE 21

Day Three, Step Three

Summer Solstice at Home/Winter Equinox on Kilimanjaro

"They want to be called 'tough guys'."
HUMPHREY'S COMMENT ABOUT OUR
61-MEMBER CREW OF TANZANIANS

Step Three: Made a decision to turn our will and our lives over to the care of God, *as we understood Him.*

Giant Step Closer to Humility

Whenever people talk with me about this journey, I ask them how many local people they think we needed to get us *eight* affluent, well-educated, allegedly in-shape Americans up and down the "Mother Mountain." The average guess is 10 or 12; the highest guess ever was 20. Not even close.

My most humbling realization of this entire adventure was that it took *61*—that's right, SIXTY-ONE—experienced Tanzanians—the team leader, three assistant leaders, four cooks, two servers, two latrine cleaner/carriers, and 49 other 'tough guys'—to make sure that we eight affluent Americans had any chance at all of reaching the top of Kili and getting back down in one piece. An almost 8 to 1 ratio. We were ridiculously spoiled; that number begins to put into humbling perspective the true nature of my recovery experience.

The first thing assistant leader Humphrey told us about our crew was: "They hate to be called 'porters.' They want to be called 'tough guys.'"

Every day for the next 10 days, these real tough guys carried up to 50 pounds each on their backs more than twice as fast as we could climb carrying only our daypacks with water, cameras, and snacks with walking sticks for balance and support. They were dressed in worn-out clothes and thin coats. On their feet, they wore either beat-up sneakers, plastic sandals, or sandals made of used tire treads; they wore them in sub-freezing temperatures by the time we reached 14,000 feet.

All I could see that they ate every day was two meals of what we know as polenta made from corn, but the Tanzanians call "Ugali" in Swahili or "Ngunda" in the local slang. Ugali is a popular staple because it is cheap food for the poor, and its grains are sturdy and grow well in the region's dry seasons and rich volcanic soils.

It consists of a thick roll of white corn, millet, or sorghum dough. According to Wikipedia and what I observed, the grain was cooked in either boiling water or milk until it turned into a thick porridge or dough. Then, the 'tough guys' used their right hands to shape the dough into a ball, a roll, or a small loaf. Sometimes, they ate the roll as it was; sometimes, they dipped it into a sauce or stew; sometimes they combined their rolls with our copious leftovers and enjoyed a bit of a feast. (https://en.wikipedia.org/Ugali).

As we drove through dozens of tiny villages of mud huts with thatched roofs, almost every family had planted a small patch of corn. The patches were usually surrounded by fences made of slim poles or thick reeds to keep out foraging herbivores (plant eaters). In the U.S., we would be worried about deer and rabbits; in Tanzania, they have to defend against threats that are just a bit more exotic: bushboks, springboks, impalas, gazelles, kudus, even elephants, to name just a few.

On the other hand, we eight affluent Americans feasted our fill on virtually gourmet meals three times a day. Every morning, we 'touristas' ate a leisurely breakfast while the tough guys prepared to take down the camp. When we strolled off "pole pole" to start our climb for that day, the tough guys broke camp, and loaded their heavy packs on their backs—and sometimes, eggs on their heads. They began hiking 30 minutes to an hour behind us, and caught up and passed us within the next hour. They raced ahead until they were out of sight. At the end of our day's hike when we reached the next camp site, they had our tents pitched, our gear and sleeping bags laid out, the latrines ready for business, the tins of warm water ready for us to wash up, and our gourmet dinner cooking on their tiny stoves.

"I am the Eggman!" Our "tough guys" carried layers of eggs on their heads every day until we ate them all. Never dropped them and never broke one.

Yet, they worked for only a few dollars a day and our tips. Most of the "tough guys" were regulars who had climbed the mountain many times. With their Kili climbs, they made a seasonal living while their wives and children stayed home, tending their small gardens and herding their small flocks. A very few of their wives had jobs in the city of Arusha; one tough guy's wife was a local teacher, so his family was considered upper middle class.

First Lesson of the Day

Perhaps I should have realized I was going to need a lot of help; after all, I certainly cannot stay abstinent, clean, and sober alone. For decades, I had tried going it alone to overcome each of my addictions before each in its turn brought me to my knees. Now, every day, I must rely on a multi-layer recovery community—from my sponsor to my recovery family to my therapist to my meetings to my Intergroup to the world service conferences to the general service offices—to make my continuing recovery possible. One day at a time, one step at a time, one moment at a time. As Samia had taught us, "Pole, Pole!" Slowly, slowly.

On this day and for the next two weeks, I learned over and over again that my survival, first on Kili and then in the Serengeti Plain, depended on my willingness to take Step Three: surrender my will each day to my human Higher Powers—Samia and his remarkable crew of "tough guys"—and trust that my spiritual HP had put me in their care.

First Day of Summer and Winter-First Day of Climb

My diary entry for this morning—the first day of our summer and the first day of their winter—began, "Off we go!" Kili is beneath the equator so their seasons are the opposite of ours.

As we drove away from Moira Camp about 8 a.m., we had a "goodbye" visit from a bushbok (also spelled 'bushbuck') standing by the side of the road. It very kindly "posed" long enough for us to slow down and take pictures.

Usually nocturnal and very shy, this beautiful bushbok "said 'Goodbye'" and "posed" for pictures within feet of our vehicle on the morning of our second day. A gift!

According to Wikipedia, the bushbok is a large, shy, mostly nocturnal antelope with curved horns that is the most common antelope in Sub-Saharan Africa. It lives in rain forests, savanna-forests, the bush savanna, and woodlands. All true as we saw only a few; almost all of them were out and about in early morning or late afternoon. Except for our "goodbye committee of one" on this day, the few others we saw scampered away as soon as we came near. That is what made its "posing" for us even more extraordinary—either that or it was afraid to move. Who knows which is correct or something else? Doesn't matter; it was a beautiful sight.

For the next three hours, we drove across a wide flat plain with glorious views of Kili in the distance. It was a clear day so we could see the snow pack and glaciers on the peak. The peak looked like a shock of smooth, white hair. A band of grayish-white clouds usually surrounds the mountain like a fur neck warmer at about 14,000 feet. The first time we turned a curve and saw the mountain, we stopped to take pictures. And I just stood there in awe, thinking "I'm really going to climb that. Oh my God!"

We in the group looked around at each other and made "ha ha" jokes about climbing the mountain with as much fake bravado as we could muster. We were daunted by the incredible sight of this enormous mountain literally covering the horizon with an almost perfect U-shaped curve.

After we took our obligatory pictures, we got back in our motor "beasts," lurching and bumping over very bad dirt and gravel roads through the poor tribal villages. As I mentioned, many of their homes were built of mud block, thin wooden poles, and thatch; others had sides made with adobe-like mud, red brick, and/or wood planks. Many had tin or metal roofs, but most had peaked thatch roofs made of long grasses woven into water-tight bundles and laid across thin poles. Each type of house signified that a different type of tribal family lived there.

Unlike in some other African countries torn by tribal strife, the Chagga, Meru, and Maasai tribes all live together in relative harmony in the vast plain beneath the mountain on the Tanzania side. At least, as far as I could tell and as Samia indicated, the tribes were civil with each other. They had learned how to live together and share the land rather than slaughter each other over tribal differences, religious conflicts, and resource disputes, as continues to happen in so much of Africa. In fact, our "tough guys" came from all three tribes and worked together without any obvious disagreement.

The colorfully dressed tribespeople, especially the Maasai in their red cloaks, herd small flocks of goats or small herds of cattle. A few, who apparently were "rich," had 50 or 60 head of cattle. In addition to maize, they also farmed small plots of potatoes, tomatoes, corn, and beans. Scrawny specimens by our Western standards, the plants produced very low yields per square foot. The people primarily walked, rode on scooters, or drove ox carts piled high with children and forage grasses to feed their cows. The carts were wooden and scrap metal structures; their base rested on the axle and two tires of a disassembled small truck.

We saw many babies and toddlers playing in the dirt yards outside their homes. But the "older" children—often as young as 5 years old—herded the goats and cows in small fields—sometimes private, sometimes communal fields, and sometimes by the side of the road. The best grass grows on the shoulders of the paved roads because the government takes care of them and seeds the shoulders. Although the shoulders are public rights of way, the local tribespeople believe they have a right to graze their cattle and goats on them. Whether it was "legal" or not misses the point—we were told it was neither legal nor safe, and often dangerous, for the animals and the herders to graze by the roads. But they were doing what they had to do to keep their livestock alive, and no local government official was going to upset the culturally accepted applecart—well, hay cart.

Kilimanjaro is ENTIRELY in Tanzania, NOT Kenya

After passing through a number of villages, we drove through a miles-wide reserve migration corridor. From late July through August, vast herds of animals—more than a million wildebeest, thousands of elephants, large herds of zebras, more than 500,000 gazelles, to name just a few, migrate from Ambesoli National Park in Kenya to Arusha National Park in Tanzania. By the way, this migration is **NOT** the better known Great Serengeti Migration. The animals move to find better grazing lands as their winter turns to spring, and the rains turn the grasslands a luxurious green and fill the watering holes and streams. Following closely behind or mingled among these millions of plant eaters are thousands of predators—lion prides, lonely leopards, solitary or small "coalitions" of cheetahs, and bands of hyenas, jackals, and wild dogs.

At this time of year, late June, however, all we saw were miles and miles of brown grasslands and scrawny acacia trees with long thorns. Somehow giraffes manage to eat around these long thorns and not rip their tongues and throats as they reach to the top of the trees to eat the most tender leaves.

By the way, the glorious posters of Kilimanjaro that the Kenyan government has published for years to attract tourists are a national irritation to the Tanzanians: Kilimanjaro rests entirely within Tanzania, but the Kenyans have "hijacked" the images and profited from those images to make hundreds of millions of dollars a year in tourism. The reality is that if you want to try to climb Kili from the Kenyan side, there is only one very steep, very difficult trail so that most people who try to follow it fail to reach the top. The five or six trails the vast majority takes are **ALL** in Tanzania.

The Rendezvous and the Tough Guys

After our "three-hour tour" of the grasslands, we drove an even worse road up the side of the mountain. Literally, there were swimming pool-sized dips with trenches two to three feet deep on the sides. As we slogged—from simply lurching and bumping to bouncing and gut-wrenching—up this road, we passed pine tree plantations and potato and carrot fields. The fields and pines often grew very close to the road. Some of the fields were open while others were enclosed with either short wooden or wire fences.

The pines were the same species of soft white pines they grow in my home state of Georgia to make paper; in Tanzania, they prefer these pines because they grow very fast, straight, and tall with few branches—often reaching 20 to 30 feet in a few years. Their shape makes them easy to cut down to make tent poles that make up the sides and roof beams of the thatch huts and small mud brick homes that so many of the farmers and herders live in.

The potatoes, carrots, and pines grew more and more densely as we drove closer to the edge of the Kilimanjaro National Park boundaries. The population spreading up the mountainside results from the pressure of Tanzania's rapidly growing population and the need to grow more food to feed more people. The Tanzanians push their fields right to the edge of—and sometimes encroach across—the park boundaries.

I can't say I blame them. It has been difficult for me to be an environmental purist since I saw the impoverished conditions of most of the farmers, herders, and their families. The farmers are under constant pressure to protect their crops. Unfortunately, as they plant more and more acreage up the sides of the mountain, they deplete the soil and create a downward spiral of needing to clear and cultivate more land because of their out-of-date methods. As you'll read in detail later, the deforestation also reduces the amount of rainfall, reducing crop yields, depleting the soil, and creating a downward spiral.

However, as important, Kilimanjaro is a unique mountain environment and national treasure, deserving of protection. The Tanzanian government also makes a huge profit from the fees it charges every person who crosses the park boundaries. It costs about $150 per adult, including an entry fee, a mandatory "rescue fee," a camp site fee, and shared costs for a vehicle.

Useless "Scare-Monkeys"

The only wildlife we saw as we drove closer to the main gate were Coloebus monkeys who have adapted to, actually love, living in the tops of the thick pines. Note that I use the human pronoun 'who' rather than the animal 'that' since they are our primate cousins. They delight in sweeping down to the fields to eat the beautiful blue flowers and leaves of the potato plants. Of course, they drive the farmers crazy—they are smarter and more wily than the dark black crows and huge black and white ravens that attack the corn fields, so the farmers put up "scare-monkeys;" that is my term for "scarecrows." Just as our farmers do, the local farmers stuff human clothing with straw and fasten the figures to sticks in the middle of the fields. However, the smart Coloebus monkeys have learned to ignore them.

Metaphoric Challenging Road Ahead – I Meet Rodrik, My Real "Tough Guy"

At about 6,500 feet, the road became impassable, far too rough to continue driving so we stopped about a mile short of the trailhead we would reach at 7,500 feet. Even the toughest vehicles in Africa—high-riding "Toyotabeasts," that is Toyota Land Cruisers—could not navigate the huge gulleys, trenches, and pool-sized pits.

So, we climbed out and were met by—believe it or not—our personal tough guys. Each of us "in shape" Americans had his or her own personal tough guy. My tough guy, who made it possible for me to climb the mountain, was Rodrik. He carried my 45- to 50-pound duffel bag on his back, put up and took down my tent every day, laid out my sleeping bag and gear every afternoon, and was on call to help me any way I needed or wanted for 10 days.

However, Rodrik was only about 5 feet 5 inches tall and weighed about 130-140 pounds, maybe less. He was extremely strong and very quiet and pleasant. During most of our climb, he wore ragged old shirts and sweaters, but had a good, heavy, warm coat for the higher altitudes where it was ferociously cold. He spoke little English and I spoke no Swahili, so we communicated with short phrases, sign language, and facial expressions. Rodrik seemed eager to please; as you'll read later, I lost my temper with him one embarrassing morning and had to make a huge Step Nine amends. But that's several days, many mistakes, and a lot of fatigue from this day. Rodrik is the tough guy shown in photos standing in front of the Furtwangler Glacier and with me at the edge of the Reusch Crater in the chapter for Sunday, June 27, Day Nine, Step Nine.

On this day after Rodrik said hello, he took my heavy duffel bag out of the back of the Land Cruiser, hefted it on his back, and started walking up the gutted road. Standing by the side of the road, I watched him in embarrassment, awe, and humility. Embarrassed because I felt utterly inadequate and powerless about the trek ahead, in awe because of his physical strength and personal willingness to serve, and humbled because I realized I had to trust this man and surrender my ability to survive into his hands. My HP puts angels—in many unexpected shapes, sizes, colors, be they human, animal, plant, or spiritual—in my path when I need them. I watched in awe as my personal angel for the rest of this journey walked quickly ahead.

After our tough guys took our duffels and moved ahead, the eight of us put our light packs on our backs, wrapped our cameras around our necks, and started walking up the side of the wretched road.

As we walked, I was amused by the metaphor of the challenging road ahead—and the fact that nothing so far had been as I expected—every minute had been full of wondrous surprises. I felt thrilled at anticipating, and trembled at, the far more challenging surprises to come.

A Plum Assignment

A mile later and 1,000 feet higher, we found two amazing sights at the end of the road: A large crowd of tough guys hoping to be chosen to carry all of our equipment and supplies and a table laid out with an enormous cold lunch of deli meats, bread, cheese, fruits, and vegetables!!! As I said, an embarrassment of culinary riches every meal—even by the side of an awful road at 7,500 feet elevation.

While we gorged ourselves on the delicious food, two crew chiefs picked the tough guys and assigned each one their load. No one was allowed to carry more than 50 pounds because that was the maximum amount the chiefs knew anyone could carry and climb fast enough to keep up. Some of the guys kept trying to take on more weight—I guess to show their eagerness—but the chiefs always rearranged who carried what.

Although we needed "only" 61 to carry us up Kili, unfortunately there were more tough guys in the group looking for work than we needed. Those not chosen had to walk back down the mountain and look for work with another tour group. I learned that the Wilderness Travel climb was a plum assignment because it guaranteed between six and 10 days of work whereas most of the group tours lasted at most five or six days. Many did not last even that long; many people gave up, turned around, and descended Kili before they reached the top, reducing their trips to just a few days.

After we reached 15,500 feet, as we climbed higher and used up our supplies, some of the tough guys were sent down the mountain. No reason to feed or pay them to do nothing but walk; fortunately Samia told me, all those who began the trip shared in the tips we gave at the end of our journey in proportion to the days they worked and the jobs they did.

After we ate, we were introduced to the tough guys we had not met yet. All of them were standing in a semi-circle around the open space. The crew chiefs, the cooks, especially Chef Ely, and the other assistant team leaders—Humphrey and Neal—were particularly important to my success. Next, with some encouragement from a crew chief—to make the 'touristas' happy, I assume—the men began to dance and sing what we were told was a welcome dance. Frankly, I felt a bit embarrassed because I felt like a "Bwana man" or English colonialist from the 19th century. It seemed to me some of the tough guys felt a little embarrassed and looked a bit sheepish, too. But we were told it was a traditional way to welcome visitors to the mountain, so when they stopped, we clapped and shook their hands to thank them.

My First Step on the "Easy" Route Up and Lesson Two Arrives

After lunch about noon, we threw our light packs on our backs, strapped on our cameras, and took our first step on our eight-day trek up the mountain. We walked single file following a lead guide who walked "pole, pole." Samia stressed that we must follow the guide, never get ahead of him, and basically step where he stepped. The guide knew the dangers on the trail—loose rocks, large roots, slippery spots. He set a 'pole, pole' pace so we would not be exhausted by the end of the day and could reserve our strength. We were going to need all of it we could save.

Lesson Two of the Day

The trail guide was like a good sponsor and another critical example of how a loving Higher Power leads me through my lifelong recovery journey. He knew the path to success because he had traveled it many times before. He knew the pitfalls to avoid, the subtle ways we could make mistakes, the steep ups and downs we would encounter along the way. He led us slowly and gently so we could enjoy the beautiful land while our bodies, our minds, and our emotions acclimatized to the altitude and weather. Yet he could not walk for me or carry me; I had to walk on my own two feet and take each step on my own.

I have had many sponsors—and continue to have two exceptional ones—during my 40 years in recovery. Everyone was like this trail guide. When I asked them to sponsor me, I had to take Step Three and acknowledge that their experience, strength, and hope were more substantial than mine. I had to be willing to follow their suggestions, work the Steps as they suggested, and use the Tools on my own if I were going to succeed in staying clean, sober, and abstinent. As the rest of this story unfolds, you will read how my actions reflected how often I fell short of the mark and how I did and did not apply the 12 Steps along the way—to my joy and to my pain.

The Route Upward

For those of you who want to follow on the map, our trek begins on the Lemosho route in the far southwest corner at the Lemosho gate. We follow the southwest crest of the mountain up the lightly trafficked trail to meet the expressway-busy Shira Plateau Trail. After several days on the crowded Shira

Plateau route, we turn north at about 14,000 feet to take the Machame Route to the Lava Tower at 15,500 feet where we camp for two days.

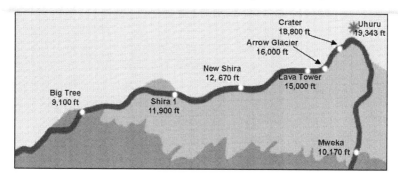

An elevation view of the Lemosho Trail, our camps, and the Uhuru Peak. The darker gray shows the approximate area of the montane forest. The lighter gray shows the zones that begin with heather and end with virtually bare rock.

Our rarely used variation on the Lemosho Route included the tough and exhilarating climb from Lava Tower to Arrow Glacier through the Great Breach Wall to the Furtwangler Glacier (3,800 steep feet-plus in 3 days).

Next, the real fun begins as most of the other climbers trek east while we take the road less traveled up to the Arrow Glacier camp at 16,000 feet—and with a nod to Robert Frost, it does make all the difference! Then, in one very challenging day, we take the most daunting and dangerous trail—the end of the Umbwe Route—up 2,800 very steep feet on very narrow trails over the Great Breach Wall to the plateau at the Furtwangler Glacier—what little is left of it, as we heard. After camping overnight at 18,800 feet, we get up at 3:30 a.m. to climb the final 543 feet to the peak in the dark so we can watch the sun rise over the "Mother Mountain."

Every journey begins with the first step and continues with the next step. And that's how we will do it. "Pole, pole," one step at a time.

In an amusing encounter during our lunch break, we ran into a 20-something couple with eight tough guys. It was a Dutch couple from Singapore climbing the mountain for their honeymoon! They were as cute as the dickens, but as my diary notes, "I don't 'thin' so," as Ricky Ricardo from the "I Love Lucy" show would say in his exaggerated Cuban accent. Not my idea of an ideal honeymoon, not even as much as I enjoy mountain climbing. More power to them, as they seemed very happy!

Surprise, Surprise, Surprise! (With Homage to Gomer Pyle)

My first surprise on the trail was that it was much steeper and far more slippery than I expected. My second surprise—which I should have known from my many other hikes up and down mountains—Duh!—was that the trail was filled with steep ups and downs. For some naïve reason, from the map, I expected a steady upward climb. Foolish me. My third surprise was to find that I was usually the last one to gear up after a break, and I almost always walked at the end of the line. Today was a tougher climb than I expected as I began to learn that I was not in the excellent physical shape I thought I was.

The good news is that because I followed instructions (today at least), I felt okay at the end of the first day with no signs of altitude sickness. I was also taking the only effective preventive medicine—Diamox, a diuretic. That meant I drank a lot of water and had to stop to urinate throughout the day in the bushes by the side of the trail. The trail guide kept walking so that meant I had to hurry to catch up rather than walk "pole, pole."

Although we only climbed a total elevation of 1,500 feet the first day—from 7,500 feet to 9,000 feet, we did thousands more feet of up and down "stair climbing" on slick, volcanic, clay-like soils through a damp and chilly montane rain forest. The other good news of the day was that although it was cloudy and cool, it did not rain.

In fact, one of the greatest blessings of this 10-day trek—and a critical reason that I would never do this adventure again—is that we had no rain at all in the forest for our six days below the cloud layer and four glorious clear blue-sky days and four full moon nights above the cloud layer. The chances of such perfect weather, Samia said, were slim; he said we were very lucky. I considered us incredibly blessed.

By the way, if you plan to climb Kili, don't expect to see a lot of wildlife. During the entire day in the rain forest, we saw only one Coloebus monkey and heard a few birds, but we did see two elephant trails.

Elephants DO Remember

During one break, Samia told us two elephant stories. First, elephant calves love to climb up the lush hillsides in the rainforest and slide down through the huge, leafy plants just as we love to slide down snowy hills on sleds or snow tubes. Some calves slide down on their rumps and stick their front legs out to slow their descent. Others slide down on their bellies with their back legs stretched out. They do it for the same thrill of going fast downhill that we feel sledding or rolling down grassy slopes: It's fun!

The second story is much less happy, but it does show the sharp intelligence of and the fierce depth of feelings elephants have for their herds. Samia stopped us and pointed out an elephant death pit. The villagers had dug a narrow, 10-feet deep trench on a path well-traveled by elephants. They drove sturdy, sharp wooden stakes into the bottom of the pit and covered it with fronds and thatch so the animals could not see it. Animals—the villagers hoped an elephant—would walk by, fall in, and be impaled on the stakes.

I know this hunting method is distasteful to our "civilized" Western sensibilities. Heavy sigh—the villagers have to eat, too. Note that we "homo sapiens" have used this method to kill large mammals for thousands of years. Consider that as recently as the mid-1800s, Native Americans chased buffalo herds over cliffs where by the hundreds, they plunged to their deaths and provided months of food, clothing, and accessories for those tribes. Of course, when we white folks migrated to the western United States, we managed to shoot more than 20 million buffaloes in less than 50 years and almost drive them to extinction.

"*Homo sapiens*" is Latin for "wise man"; We were named that by the great biologist Carl Linnaeus in the late 18th century. Today, our subspecies is known as "*homo sapiens sapiens*"—wise, wise man. However, considering our tens of thousands of years of conflict and wars, our innate "us versus them" fear-driven view of other people, and our predilection to despoil our environment, I often question the "wise" part.

Rather I would say we are highly intelligent, but much too smart, much too greedy, much too fearful, and much too oblivious to the consequences of our actions for our own good much of the time. I seriously doubt that as the only remaining race of the "homo" species left after millions of years of evolution, we have become as "sapiens," as "wise," as we should have become after all this time.

I know with my crazed brain chemistry and my "nature-nurture" addictive personality, I have often acted as my own worst enemy—much like the rest of humanity. During the next 10 days, I make many mistakes on my journey up and down Kili. My mistakes mean I'm perfectly imperfect and not really deserving of the title "sapiens sapiens."

Consider what happened to those "wise" villagers who dug the death pit. They wanted to kill an elephant so they would have literally thousands of pounds of easy meat, organs, fat, bones, skin, and tusks to use for their survival. However, they should have been careful what they wished for. Samia said a nearby village did kill an elephant in this pit some time ago. The entire herd became enraged (my diary says 'pissed'). Three weeks later, the herd attacked the village in broad daylight, killed two villagers, and trampled the entire village to the ground.

Moral of the Story

Don't mess with the herd. Elephants DO remember you and how you treated them, and they know how to wreak their vengeance. Many, including me, also believe that they express empathy and feel something very much like strong grief. The scientists do not yet agree whether elephants "grieve"—feel deep loss and pain at the death of a member of the herd as we do, according to an August 2016 *National Geographic* online article.

But the behavior of the entire herd, and even nearby herds, changes when one of them dies, either by natural causes, human poaching, or animal attacks. They interact with the dead bodies, often for weeks; the herd may stay near the body for days. Babies have been known to cling to their dead mothers for hours. Some appear to secrete liquids—tears?—from ducts behind their ears when they are near the deceased.

Huge elephant "momma" watching over her baby as its curiosity brings it close to us.

Even as scientists want to hem and haw and search for "evidence" of grief, sometimes folk wisdom and personal observation are enough. I have made two multi-week African safaris. Having seen hundreds of elephants in large herds, I have a huge respect for their intellect, their strong social bonds with their families, their fierce protective instincts, and their essentially peaceful nature. If you treat them respectfully and mean—or do—them no harm, they will leave you alone. Even if they feel threatened, they will make a big display by waving their ears and trumpeting to warn you off. Usually, they will just move away when they sense danger. You have to do something very annoying and directly harmful to arouse their rage.

I believe they feel intense emotions and communicate them with each other in their own way. Those emotions include a sense of loss at a different emotional and psychological level than we do. After all, they are a different species, but they are acknowledged as one of the smartest, if not the smartest, mammal species after good old "homo sapiens sapiens." Definitely something to ponder is that all over Africa, poaching and increasingly crowded habitats wipe out thousands of elephants a year. I wonder how all those herds that are losing so many members so quickly are adapting to these terrible and rapid changes. I suspect with great pain and sorrow.

Enough speculation about elephants—more to come during my "mortality" trek across the Serengeti. Just remember that they are smart, they do remember for a long time, they have strong social bonds, they feel strong emotions, and they can get very angry and act on it. Treat them with respect because they are magnificent examples of the wonders of God's creation.

The Crowded Campground on the First Night

After our first four-hour hike, we reached our first camp site and discovered just how crowded the other routes would be. Speaking of not-so-sapiens, crowded into a small area of bare ground—maybe an acre at most—with large tree roots lacing the dirt, were 40 to 50 tourist tents from 5 or 6 tour companies. These companies also had pitched 5 or 6 large cook tents, 15 to 20 crew tents, and 2 latrine tents for each group or about 10 total latrines.

The camp was crowded, noisy, dirty, and smelly. Tent stakes were driven in everywhere with ropes to pitch the tents upright. The tents were so close together that it was easy to trip over the stakes and ropes, even in daytime. They were treacherous at night when I needed to find our latrine.

Our men's toilet was a small 3 feet wide by 3 feet deep by 6 feet high tent with a peaked top. It had very little legroom. We ate so well, we burned so many calories, and we exerted ourselves so much that I stayed regular during the entire trip—a blessing and one of my serious personal goals. I was worried about constipation from the different foods, but the hard walking and large amount of liquids I drank prevented that problem. Literally and figuratively, a great relief!

Another "Vital" Lesson

I was very happy I brought my own U.S.-made toilet paper! The local TP was so thin and so badly made as to be useless. A simple, even silly reason, perhaps, to feel so deeply grateful to live in the United States, but I do feel like kissing the runway whenever I return home after an adventure to a less developed country.

Dinner that night was unbelievable! What Chef Ely and his cooks did with three burners and an aluminum bread baking oven was amazing—tomato and ginger soup, coconut rice and Thai peanut chicken with sauce, avocado and tomato salad, apple pie, and fruit for me. Yet the crew ate Ugali.

I had a two-person tent to myself, so it was comparatively spacious with lots of room to store my stuff. We were warned to keep everything inside because of the danger that the other crews and tourists might steal whatever we left outside. Fortunately, our crew was completely trustworthy; when we ended our trek, no one had lost, misplaced, or missed anything.

Reflections on the First Day—Humor and Humility

After dinner and I returned to my tent, I wrote in my diary—by my trusty headlamp—these observations and lessons of this first day.

Humor: It is definitely one step, one moment at a time. Yet, despite what you might think, my hike is rarely one of staring in awe at blue skies, natural grandeur, and gorgeous views. Mostly, I walked face down, eyes on the rough trail to avoid stumbling and falling. When I looked up, my view was usually only the butt of the person in front of me, often not a pretty sight. The hike is a lot like the nose-to-tail trail rides "greenhorns" take out

West on dude ranches in which the nose of each horse follows the tail of the horse ahead of it.

Humorously, the walking is like the saying on my favorite "Big Dog ®" tee shirt: *If you are not the lead dog, the view never changes!*

Next "Rash Robert Regret" and Next "Smart Robert Move" of the Day

My next—and ultimately most painful and costly—major mistake was that I did not bring any sneakers, sandals, or "Crocs®" with me. I did wisely bring very warm, soft, fleece-lined booties to wear in my tent when I slept, but I could not wear them in the dirt to walk around the camp or to the latrine. So, every time I had to get up in the night to pee—after all, I was turning 60 and that was my normal nighttime habit—I had to put on my heavy boots, slog to the latrine, slog back to the tent, and take them off again. I calculated that it took me 16 separate actions to get up, go to the bathroom, come back to my tent, and climb back into my sleeping bag. That process got old very quickly, but it worked.

My boot and shoe problem became critical as to how my adventure ended; the problem helped to shape the challenge when I had to confront my mortality—but that happens about eight days from now.

I did realize I had made one very "smart Robert" move for the trip—my adjustable aluminum walking sticks. They were strong, yet flexible. They never bent under extreme pressure, and I was able to adjust them to a very small size to strap to my backpack or extend them to an accurate length that took most of the strain off my legs when I was climbing.

Recovery Lesson: Choose strong friends on whom I can lean in times of trouble; those who will bend but not break, those like me who have suffered and recovered and who have been granted the kind of 12 Step life of joy that I want.

Group Roles Take Shape to My Chagrin

By dinner that night, the personalities and drives of my group were becoming apparent, and I felt very dissatisfied with my evolving role. I thought that I was being perceived as the slower, less capable, older know-it-all who points out what he knows too often to the others, but who also complains a lot.

As a result, I found myself falling into an old, negative pattern—distancing from others, playing the perpetual "outsider." I did not trust them to know the true me, and I feared their rejection. I felt unsafe and vulnerable and was not about to let anyone in the group come too close to my real life. I vowed to say less and be quieter and stronger the next day.

I didn't like the developing roles among the others as well. Heinrich had to be Number One with Samia and he wanted to go up the mountain faster. But he was not taking Diamox and was drinking a lot of wine with every lunch and dinner, so I expected him to run into trouble the higher we climbed.

Annie, an attorney, was the wife of the couple who had missed the plane from Amsterdam and caught up with us on the second day. She turned out to be an opinionated person who made biting comments in response to almost anything anyone said. At breakfast this morning, when we were introduced, she asked me what I did. Using my cover story, I told her I taught writing for the government. She said—laughingly, but bitingly, "You're not doing a very good job of it." I replied calmly that I agreed with her, and I thought we had good reason to think we were making progress. She also took on Felicia, but Felicia gave back as good as she got, so Annie left her alone. Good for Felicia!

Annie's husband Matt is a genuinely nice guy. He and I were usually the last two in line for "old guy" reasons—we both had terrible flatulence most of the time, so we sort of took turns holding back so we could break wind alone and not in someone's face. The group was usually that close to each other plodding along much of the time!

Matt also helped me with my pack whenever we broke camp or started hiking after a meal stop or break. He was quiet-spoken and listened to his wife tell him what to do and how to do it, and then generally ignored what she had to say. They had been married for more than 30 years, so I guess their repartee is part of their relationship, and all of it seems to roll off his back.

End of the First Day on the Mountain

As I ran out of steam the first night, I crawled into my incredibly uncomfortable Egyptian mummy-shaped sleeping bag. I expressed my profound gratitude for the day: safe hiking, cool day, good food, cooperative group, great crew, my third straight day with a bowel movement, clean water, and my high-quality, **WARM** gear.

My diary entry ends, "TY, FMG, FAMMMM Blessings. Wow! 9,000 feet - rough camp - in a tent for the first time in 50-plus years."

It was a totally unexpected day, and I joyfully anticipated that each day forward would be filled with even more surprises.

Step 3 Recovery Lessons on the Summer Solstice

This day, I repeatedly took Steps 1, 2, and 3—surrendering my will to Samia, Rodrik, the trail guide, the chefs, and the "Mother Mountain" herself. I was humbled by the tough guys and their spirit of service. Yes, they needed the work and they got paid, but it is part of the Tanzanian culture to serve and to be courteous, generous, and kind.

But taking Step 3 does not mean I get to skate—my recovery work was just beginning at this Step. I couldn't do the "Recovery Waltz"–Steps 1, 2, 3; 1,2 3; and go around in circles. On this mountain and in recovery, I still have to take first one step and then another. I literally have to do the legwork and leave the results up to my Higher Powers. I have to make a decision each day to turn my will and my life over. I have to follow the guidance, and trust the experience, strength, and skill of my personal angel Rodrik, the trail guides, my human HPs (Samia and the team leaders), and the dozens of other tough guys.

I knew I had to take the challenging road, not the soft road, but not the impossible and dangerous road. I had lived on metaphorical dangerous roads that could have led to ruin for decades; now, this journey was about choosing a challenging goal, preparing thoroughly to travel it, and knowing that it takes a recovery family to truly thrive and reach that goal. Then, to start all over again with the next one.

After 60-plus years, I have finally accepted I am a highly goal-oriented person; I need clear goals and paths to reach them, and I get "squirrely" when I don't have at least one or two. In my recovery, my primary goals—ODAT (One Day At A Time)—are 1) to remain abstinent, clean, and sober; and 2) to seek and do God's will for me.

A final word on the Summer Solstice and what it meant to me today. The first day of summer. The longest day of the year when we have more sunlight to enlighten us than any other day of the year. It was a day to appreciate the spiritual awareness, physical energy, and emotional release that our HP gives to us. It was a day to realize and cherish my unique skills, the unique service I have to offer the world. And it was a day to realize my humanity, the reality of who I am, and to begin to accept both my strengths and my shortcomings. It was especially a day to feel the deepest gratitude for the challenge that lay ahead and the dozens of angels—physical and spiritual—who were helping me achieve this goal. Today, I believe I began to understand what true humility means to me.

TUESDAY, JUNE 22

Day Four, Step Four

Sometimes, the deeper realities are revealed
by actual evidence and experience.
MY BELIEF ABOUT SPIRITUAL "TOTEMS" OR GUIDES

"THEN, we turned a corner…and there was KILI.
Enormous – filling the horizon – Glorious against blue
skies & puffy clouds all afternoon – 4-7 p.m. – Kili in
perfect blue skies & as sun set & cold set in quickly"
DIARY ENTRY ABOUT THE MOST
SPECTACULAR MOMENT OF THE DAY

Step Four – Made a searching and fearless moral inventory of ourselves.

Today, I made my fourth "rash Robert regret" (only one a day so far!) and almost caused an international incident. I was reminded once again to go "pole, pole" and take it one step at a time. Yet the day ended gloriously as we broke through the clouds onto the Shira Plateau and gained our first view of our challenging path to the summit.

I had a very difficult night with little sleep. I was in my tent alone in a crowded, noisy camp; the damp ground underneath was stony and criss-crossed with tree roots; the loudest snorer I have ever heard was about 15 feet away. He snored loudly and badly all night. I slept in fits and starts for maybe a total of 5 or 5 1/2 hours between about 10 p.m. and 6:15 a.m.

I had to get up twice to pee—once about 1:30 a.m. and again about 4 a.m., repeating my "creative" 16-step process to get up, out, and back into my sleeping bag. Once again, I gave thanks for the dorky headlamp that lighted my way to and from the latrines. It helped me avoid stumbling over tent stakes, ropes, tree roots, firepits, stones, and rough muddy paths in every direction.

Lesson of the Morning

The headlamp is such a simple, inexpensive, brilliant invention borrowed and downsized, I assume, from coal miners' lamps. It is so critical to everyone's ability to move around at night and not trip and fall. Similarly, as an addict, I must have a process to light my way and show me the obstacles in my path. When I am actively acting out any of my addictions, I live in deep denial—or steely stubbornness. I refuse to see the obstacles that I trip over so I keep repeating the same mistake.

My relapses always begin as a niggling thought in my amgydala—the tiny, almond-shaped, reptilian brain at the base of my skull where all my fears are hardwired. I wish with all my might that I could be "normal." Often, I feel a resentment that either I don't recognize because I am rationalizing that the other person is wrong when they are right. Or I want to cling to the resentment, enjoying my haughty feeling of self-righteous victim. Far too often, I have been unwilling to light the lamp of recovery in my darkness. Why not? Either I deny its existence, or I don't believe I deserve it even if it does exist, so I can hurt myself; self-sabotage is my greatest urge and my worst shortcoming.

To stretch my metaphor a bit, as I slowly stepped through the camp in darkness, the bright, but diffused lamp light did help to illuminate the dangers right in front of me, but I had to walk slowly and look very hard so I could make out the next obstacle just ahead. The diffused light in the camp shone like the rays of hope I saw only vaguely when I first joined OA more than 35 years ago. Then, as I worked the Steps and used the tools, the path became more clear and I began to avoid the pitfalls.

However, the headlamp has one flaw—small batteries that run out of energy, extinguishing the light. So, I had to know the batteries' likely lifespan in hours and replace the batteries whenever the light began to dim. The batteries are like the sources of energy and hope I get from working the program, using the tools, and following its suggestions. Just as I had so many years ago—to restore my energy so I can stay abstinent and sane, I must continue to work the steps, go to meetings, use the tools, and above all, give service. Through more relapses and more pain than I can remember—or care to—I have learned one basic fact: Only my commitment to and action toward living the 12 Step Way of Life ODAT keeps my batteries charged and the light of recovery illuminating my path forward.

My Next "Rash Robert Regret"

During the night, I finally concluded I had made a major mistake by buying a sleeping bag shaped like a mummy case—rounded at the top for my head, broad at the top for my shoulders, but very narrow at my feet. The outside was also made of nylon so it was always cold whenever my face or hands touched it. I am somewhat claustrophobic, and I hate having confined feet.

I have to be free to get out and move when I feel like it—and I have a lifetime of moving mistakes and joys to prove it. In my crazy first marriage, we moved a total of 23 times in 16 years. We were almost always in denial about our troubled marriage and blamed something or someone else for our problems. Much later, during my 13 years employed by a government agency, I sat in 19 different locations—from spacious offices with high windows to open cubicles surrounded by 10-12 other people. I also need peace and quiet to work effectively, so all the crammed cubicles and open spaces irritated me greatly.

But I had learned a lesson, either valuable or harmful depending on how I used it, in my dysfunctional family of origin: I learned to withdraw inside myself, shut down my hearing, and isolate myself in a group of people. When I was a kid, I would become so engrossed in reading a book—reading books was my salvation—that my mother literally could stand next to me and tell me dinner was ready, and I would not hear her. For most of my adult life, I have averaged driving about 25,000 miles a year, most of it highway miles just to get out and go—when I want and need to and on my own terms. That distance is twice as much as that of the average driver and costs a lot in gas, but my willingness to pay shows how important my freedom of movement is to me.

On the joyous side, I have visited 32 countries, six of seven continents, and all but eight U.S. states; I have climbed dozens of majestic mountains, hiked hundreds of beautiful trails, and visited many major U.S. and international cities.

So, you can understand my need to be able to move around. The first night on the mountain I felt uncomfortable, but this the second night, I found myself constantly shifting around inside the bag with my feet held tightly together at the bottom, feeling confined and claustrophobic. I tested new ways to stuff clothes and bags around me to stay warm. Finally, I zipped the bag open and spread it out across the bottom of the tent. I wrapped a fleece liner around my head and shoulders and slept in multiple layers, especially my heaviest fleece pants and my thick booties with wool socks. All that helped, but it was still cold. It got colder and colder every night as we climbed higher so I had to constantly try new ways to warm up. The constant turning and rearranging and getting up deprived me of sleep, and that deprivation caught up with me a few days later.

An "Easy Day"

Today, Samia told us, was an "easy day" as we climbed from 9,000 feet to 11,700 feet through more damp, cool rainforest. The highlight of my day was I saw from a great distance the incredible African crowned eagle, one of the most glorious raptors that live in Kili and Arusha national parks.

The African Crowned Eagle was my critical spiritual totem during my adventure. It appeared unexpectedly when I needed to see it most. [Photo: (c) Robert Flack]

Weird Alert

I have a deep spiritual connection to raptor birds; okay, think I'm crazy, but it's true. For many years, whenever I have been troubled, depressed, or confused about a decision, a raptor appears. They have appeared as I have driven along expressways, hiked a trail, sat outside on my balcony, sat at my dinner table and glanced out my window, and once as I walked through a ground-floor glass tunnel that connected two office buildings. The raptor, usually a hawk, either swoops across the front of my car, sits on a tree limb near me, soars above my head, or dives in front of me and captures its prey. It happens all the time. When I ask other people how often they see hawks, ospreys, falcons, or even eagles just appear out of nowhere, they look at me like I've lost my mind. Nope, it's just my totem bird—a spirit guide letting me know that everything is going to be okay.

Of course, as a semi-rational, somewhat intelligent person, I realize that part of my interpretation of what I see is what I want to believe. However, if it were only my mind finding something beautiful, powerful, and protective to believe in, I could find many other animals and images to do that. How often I see the raptors at exactly the moment I feel troubled—and that is always when I need it most—shows me that it is more than a coincidence. My spiritual and emotional connection to raptors is NOT only a mental construct.

Sometimes, the deeper realities are revealed by actual evidence and experience. Ask any person with long-term recovery in any 12 Step program and ask them about the miracles in their lives—inexplicable events that just happen without their direct action to cause it. I would venture that virtually all of them will agree that the facts and real changes in their lives directly result from their beliefs in their Higher Powers.

Although it may be hard to believe, considering my relationship with raptors, I am, in fact, a dyed-in-the-wool pragmatist: I "came to believe" based not on faith, but on one simple fact: When I work my programs each day, those days are much better than any day when I don't work my programs. Certainly not perfect; some days are lousy even when I am working the Steps and using the Tools. But they are always better than the days when I turn my back on the Steps and Tools.

They Don't Believe in Switchbacks

On the trail today, the eagle totem reminded me that all would be well, if I allowed it to be. The unexpected continued to pop up. I was so wrong about how easy the first few days were going to be! We began the morning climb in the glorious rain forest. The first 2 hours we climbed steep "ups." The Tanzanian trail cutters apparently don't believe in switchbacks to ease the pressure on the knees. Nope, "up" is straight up through the forest.

Then, literally in 10 feet, we entered a new climate zone. The fauna changed from rain forest to very large highland heather—6 to 15 feet tall. We stepped from the damp, cool shade into clear skies, hot sun, and bright light. I quickly became very warm because I had my heavy polyester long johns on beneath my light pants. I sweated all morning until we reached the lunch area at 10,500 feet when I almost created an international incident. Remember two things—we were still walking a trail shared by many other groups, and the small latrines, erected by the groups at each stop, all looked alike on the outside to me.

My Close Call with an International Incident

For the last hour and a half before the lunch break, my stomach had been in great pain, and I had been having very smelly gas. I couldn't stop by the side of the trail and go to the bathroom because though we could stop and urinate, we were asked (warned?) not to relieve ourselves along the trail. It would have been incredibly embarrassing anyway.

As soon as we stopped, I dropped my pack and cameras and ran into the nearest latrine tent. I knew it wasn't one of ours because it was a terrible squat toilet whereas our latrines had foldable toilets with real seats and a disinfectant pump. But I didn't care because I was about to have a very personal and very unfortunate accident.

As I came out of the tent, a "tough guy" with a yellow shirt from a different tour group stamped up to me with a scowl on his face. He said in broken English, "Pay me for toilet. It's not yours."

I thought he was "shaking me down" because I didn't understand that the groups were so possessive about their toilets. So, I scowled back and told him rudely, "Talk to Samia" and walked away. The guy walked after me. Fortunately, I found Samia and he talked to the guy, but the guy remained very upset. Finally, one of our dinner captains—I think he was a member of the same tribe or a relation—talked to him for a long time and smoothed it over. I did not see any money change hands. I have no idea how the captain calmed the guy down. But after the discussion, the dinner captain called me over, and I apologized for my mistakes.

My first mistake was that I didn't see the "XXX Tours Toilet" sign on the outside flap because I really had an emergency. My second mistake was scowling back at the guy and walking away rather than apologizing and asking him for more information or asking how much money he wanted and paying him. In hindsight (pun intended), I can see why each group would not want open access to their toilets in crowded areas—they have enough mess of their own to clean up and certainly don't need anyone else's.

Once again, my Kili Higher Powers—Samia, and this time the dinner captain, who understood the language, the culture, and the situation far better than I—saved me. It could have become a nasty incident if the guy and I had gone "all macho" and started a ruckus about a simple mistake. I did apologize to the captain. I asked him if I needed to apologize to, or pay the other "tough guy," but he assured me that I didn't. I did a quick Step Four—took my inventory and realized the nature of my mistake—and did Step Nine by making what amends I could. I was willing to take responsibility and correct the situation. Lesson learned. Steps practiced.

Breathing Less Air and Gorgeous Flowers at 11,000 Feet

After lunch, we climbed in the "hot" sun—probably 55 degrees—and it was even more difficult because the trail was steeper from 10,500 feet to 11,700 feet. We were now more than two miles high and almost as high as I had ever climbed. The climb was almost imperceptibly becoming more difficult, so subtle that we barely noticed it—at first.

The amount of air available to breathe was falling fast because the higher you climb, the thinner the air—literally, fewer molecules of air in the same amount of space from lower atmospheric pressure. In fact, at 10,000 feet or so, the barometric pressure is 29% lower than it is at sea level. By the time we reach the top of Kili, the pressure—and the amount of air we could breathe—will be less than half of the amount at sea level, according to the www.altitude.org web site.

Although the changes began slowly, and since most of us were in fairly decent shape, we were not yet huffing and puffing on this day.

During the day, we barely noticed that the average temperature was falling as well. The temperature dropped about 2 degrees Fahrenheit for every 500 feet we climbed. We definitely began to feel the change this night and the next morning; we had left behind the "warm quilt" of the thick trees in the rain forest and entered the wide-open space of the heather-moorland zone.

The higher we climbed, the shorter the pervasive highland heather became. From reaching far above our heads, with every step the heather seemed to shrink, and the sun grew larger and hotter. When we reached the top of the ridge at the edge of the Shira Plateau, the heather was no more than four or five feet tall. We began to see incredibly beautiful flowers—bright yellow marigold-like flowers, purple brushed cactus flowers, and subtle greyish-pink and white flowers called "Everlastings."

Technically, for you plant lovers, the first Everlastings I saw were Helichrysum meyeri-johanis (pale pink and named after Johannis Meyer, the first white man known to actually reach the summit) and Helichrysum citrispinum (pale greyish-white flowers that felt like thick paper). I felt like I had transformed from a dwarf in a huge brown forest of long stemmed bushes into a giant in a rock garden of tiny exotic plants growing in tight clumps across the landscape.

By the way, the "Everlastings" are the most prevalent plant above 11,000 feet. According to Wikipedia, six or eight major subspecies populate the Shira Plain and the entire area around the mountain between 11,000 and 17,000 feet elevation. One very hardy subspecies even grows near the summit at 19,000 feet in the nooks and crannies where the rocks hold the warmth of the sun, and the rare rain and snow trickle down to water the roots.

Turning the Corner and WOW!

As we were admiring the flowers, we climbed past the edge of the ridge and walked around the corner of a hill—and there was the "Mother Mountain" soaring above the plain. Bathed in glorious reds, golds, rusts, oranges, and ochres, she was an enormous peak filling the horizon framed against a crystal clear, deep blue sky and puffy white clouds. Patches of snow draped over the ridges leading to the summit and stretched down narrow valleys called barrancos.

When Kili burst into view, I just stopped in my tracks and said, "Oh my God..." in sheer amazement. The site was beyond belief as the sun glistened behind us. A crystal blue sky with wispy clouds framed the mountain, and an almost full moon hung over the top of the Great Breach Wall.

Humphrey J., assistant team leader and one of my human
Higher Powers, with Kilimanjaro in all its glory!

"She" looked daunting because the sky and air were so clear that we could make out every trail, every step of the way ahead to the top. We were standing at the edge of the Shira Plain—an enormous volcanic caldera we would take two days to cross. We could see all the way to Lava Tower at 15,500 feet and to the 2,800-feet-high Great Breach Wall that we would have to ascend in a single day. The Breach Wall, between 16,000 and 18,800 feet, looked like a very, very long "black diamond" ski slope made of rock slides and scree slopes at very steep angles. We would have less and less air to breathe with every step we took up that obviously dangerous path.

The sight was so startlingly stunning that all in my group stopped in their tracks and stared. We all exclaimed our awe and shock at the reality of how difficult the rest of the trip was going to be. I thought, "One day at a time—one step, one moment—is how we will all do this."

Samia then told us that the snow and the glaciers had been disappearing very quickly during the 14 years he had spent leading climbers. The prospect for the snow to disappear completely within the next decade was high, he mourned. (Note: Since my climb, I have heard much more of the snow and glaciers has melted.)

Whether caused by man-made global warming or a broad combination of factors, including local deforestation up the sides of the mountain, one thing was clear: Without the rain in the forest and the thick snows during the winter, much less water will flow down the mountain every spring and summer. The local farmers and their families, who raise the sweet potatoes, corn, and pumpkins we had seen driving up the mountain, will suffer. But patience—I will share much more about the fate of the glaciers and snow cap when we reach 18,800 feet in several days.

After our stop to wonder at the beauty and the challenge, we hiked across the Shira plain through the stunted heather and gorgeous flowers for three more hours from 4 to 7 p.m. When we arrived at our camp site—yes, everything was already set up and dinner was cooking thanks to our tough guys— we enjoyed a glorious sunset. Its multi-hued glow of pinks, blues, yellows, and purples radiated like the trails of fireworks from behind the peak. Even more stunning, the radiance shone all around the setting moon as it seemed to touch the peak of the Breach Wall.

The moon was about nine-tenths, or about three days from, full, so it seemed I might enjoy a full moon on my birthday, too!

After the sun set, the temperature plunged as the warmth of the day flew off the land into the sky. In the dinner tent, Samia told us it was going to be well below freezing before the morning. He took our pulse rates and blood flows as he did every morning and evening. Mine remained in the healthy range, although they were creeping up. In the dinner tent, all of us were thoroughly bundled up, we ate quickly, and we scurried into our tents to sleep.

As I wrote my notes in my journal at 9:10 p.m., I wore wool mittens with the fingers cut off so I could write as I sat on my uncomfortable sleeping bag with all my clothes on. I was so tired that in the bright white light of the headlamp, my eyes began to hurt and my head began to ache. I switched the light to an infrared color that filled the tent with a burgundy glow.

My notes said about my status, "Well, so far – doing OK. Legs OK, arms/ shoulders OK. Quick recovery times after steep climbs." My condition was a pleasant surprise because this day, we had climbed 8 miles straight up and down after we had climbed 7 1/2 miles the day before and gained a total of 4,000 feet in altitude.

Despite the attention my embarrassing incident this morning caused, I had not disturbed the bonhomie of the group; all of us remained focused on the goal and getting along well.

My food was excellent, but I ate too much during the day. For breakfast, I had eggs, bacon, oatmeal, non-wheat bread, and fruit. For lunch, a vegetable cream soup, cold cuts, more non-wheat bread, and cold vegetables. For snacks on the trail, I had two 1-ounce packages of toasted almonds. We had a huge dinner—potato-leek soup, a delicious green banana and beef stew, cucumber and onion salad, carrots, and grilled fish and potato chips.

The stew is a Chagga tribal staple because as farmers, they grow a lot of bananas. They developed this stew generations ago to lend variety to eating plain bananas all the time. The stew was made of green bananas that when boiled, turned into the consistency of slightly boiled potatoes with a similar, though slightly sweeter, taste. They were added to beef with many spices to give the stew a tangy flavor.

Today, I decided I had to stop eating the soup and non-wheat breads. I skipped them and even my favorite fruit—sliced fresh pineapple. I remained abstinent from the "3 Bs"—wheat bread, booze, and bon-bons, but I was eating large quantities of healthy food. Unfortunately, the good stuff, including the delicious cream soups and breads, was giving me gas and frequent bowel movements. (I promise I am about to stop talking about them!)

Between the heat and sweat during the day and the intense cold at night, we were burning thousands of calories a day—at least 4,000 to 5,000 on a day like today—and I was losing weight. I was drinking two to three liters of water a day plus at least one bowl of soup and three or four large cups of decaffeinated tea a day. Every meal included at least one or two soups or stews with lots of liquid because they knew we would suffer if we didn't stay hydrated.

Lessons from the Day and Step Four

Today I had a serious lesson in Step Four—taking a searching and fearless moral inventory of myself. I did do Step 9—apologized to both the other company's "tough guy" and to our dinner captain. I also made an amends with the captain about the tent incident. But, I had to come face to face with several shortcomings—my arrogance toward, and dismissal of, the other group's guide; my stubbornness about the latrine tent incident; and my increasing sense of isolation from, and paranoia about, our group.

However, I felt really angry and resentful today toward the others in my group because they did not seem to trust what I said. Annie and others seemed to be very focused on whether I told the truth or not about my earlier adventures, such as visiting Antarctica and Machu Picchu, among others, while they seemed to accept everyone else's versions of their stories. Maybe I was afraid because I felt so vulnerable and didn't trust them. I do have a long history of feeling, as we say in OA, **BINGE**--"because I'm not good enough" in groups of people whom I don't know, or who seem to be smarter, more capable, and more accomplished than I.

I reminded myself of an important program saying: *Their opinion of me is none of my business.* I was feeling tired, lonely, afraid, and overwhelmed, and probably overthinking the situation. It could even have been how I was showing a touch of altitude sickness.

On the positive side of my Fourth Step ledger today, I did ask for help when I needed it. One of the little "godsends" for our sleep was a hot water bottle that the stewards brought us every night. If I kept mine next to my body, even under my fleece, the bottle would stay warm, never going below my body temperature during the night. Somehow, I broke the neck seal of my hot water bottle and it began leaking. Fortunately, I asked for help, and one of the tough guys either let me have his or he had a spare. Bless his generosity and kindness!

In some ways, too, I was more considerate and helpful to others today than I had been so far despite my emerging paranoia. Even if my feelings were correct and the group was not friendly, it was No Big Deal. I was climbing the mountain for myself and my recovery, not for them or theirs.

My final journey entry for the day—and its major lessons—as the time passed 10 p.m., and my hands became too cold to write:

"Oh well—TW, NM, BD (Thy Will, Not Mine, Be Done.). Thank you, FMG, for this day and its many blessings…I release all to FMG and bless them and pray for their H, H, P, A, & J!" (health, happiness, prosperity, abundance, and joy).

I also was willing to check myself and my paranoia, but I was concerned that the negative signs were beginning as my addict brain was kicking in more often as I became more tired and got less sleep. As these little problems began to emerge, I came to learn—with perfect 20-20 hindsight—that I needed more rest and more balance. But at that moment, at 10 p.m., alone in my tent, with numb fingers, a dull mind, and the shock of sub-freezing temperatures, I blithely thought I was just rolling along doing very well. Not quite.

Tomorrow we climb from 11,500 to 13,800 across the Shira Plateau. Yahoo! Only 2,300 feet up a slow, steady incline!

Best of all this night, the "front porch view" from my tent is the vast expanse of Kilimanjaro glowing in the brilliant moonlight. What a huge blessing!

WEDNESDAY, JUNE 23

Day Five, Step Five

*"Taking the next step slowly and rightly takes care
of you…Perseverance in completing this journey
gives you 10 years of confidence and patience."*
TEAM LEADER SAMIA

*Step Five – Admitted to God, ourselves, and another human being the exact
nature of our wrongs.*

We had a tough, short climb today from 11,800 feet up to 13,400 feet, then down hundreds of feet and back up to camp at 13,800 feet in a chilly, stiff wind. Samia continued to be consistent with his theme—take one step, one moment at a time and pay close attention to the trail. We enjoyed a delightful break to see two of the rare plants found only on Kili—the giant senechio trees and the lovely lobelia plants. I'll share more on the fascinating ways these plants have evolved to protect themselves from the harsh climate and rapid weather changes later in this step. Both are just two more small examples of how Mother Nature can teach us key recovery lessons, if we are willing to open our eyes to see them and then act on them.

Finally, late in the day, I also learned an interesting little secret about the mountain that many of the guidebooks don't tell you. That secret meant much to the lessons I learned today.

Kili and its Feisty Volcanic Neighbors and Their Future

Over night, a glorious, nearly full moon rose over what I would later learn is the false summit. This apparent peak is the upward-turned lip of the collapsed former peak of "Mawenzi," one of Kili's three ancient cones—mouths through which volcanoes erupt. The other two are "Kibo" and "Shira," according to Wikipedia. Kibo is the most famous, as it is the largest, most accessible, and only cone that still has fumaroles emitting sulfur fumes. Its rim begins only 100 feet below the highest peak next to the Furtwangler Glacier—what little, if any of it is left by now. You can climb to the top of the rim—which I did four days later—with a 400-feet slog up a steep slope to 19,200 feet; you also can stumble—I mean, "walk"—down a scree slope to the mouth of the cone itself about 600 feet down. I didn't go down to the cone rim because I was exhausted. More on that very difficult day and my extraordinary experience at the Kibo Rim on Day 9. That was our worst climbing day—2,800 very steep feet in only seven hours.

The second of the cones, the Shira, is barely visible because it has eroded into the enormous collapsed caldera many miles wide that makes up the Shira Plateau; it took us two days to walk across it. In fact, on this day, we are in the middle of the Shira Cone.

The Mawenzi cone on the northeast side faced away from our climbing direction. It is hard to see the circular rim pattern as it has severely eroded. It creates a horseshoe shaped ridge with steep peaks and razor-like ridges that face the northeast. Remember we were walking from the southwest toward the northeast. Its peaks and ridges were caused by both erosion and ancient lava flows. From the Shira Plateau, I could see the Mawenzi area easily, but not the cone shape, because at 15,500 feet, the 200-foot tall Lava Tower sticks up in its middle like a solid iron fist. The view of Mawenzi is also distorted by a few large cirques, depressions caused by collapsed crater walls, that slice into the otherwise ring-shaped cone.

The largest cirque is at the head of the Great Barranco gorge. The gorge is a long, deep ravine that cuts down and through the northwest side of the Mawenzi crater; it is also home to some of the most exotic and beautiful plant life on Kili. Its depth and narrow sides protect these plants from the wind and cold and channel water from rainfall and glacial melt down its deepest point.

Dormant, NOT Extinct

As the tallest peak in Africa, Kili is the largest in a string of ***dormant, not extinct volcanoes.*** The good news is that both the Shira and Mawenzi cones are extinct—no eruptions in about 500,000 years. But Kibo, while dormant, still has sulfur fumes spewing from the aptly named fumaroles (vapor holes in the surface) around the crater rim. When the wind blows in your face, the fumes smell like rotten eggs.

Kili's "children" are the many other volcanoes that stretch north to south along the well-known Eastern Rift Valley that extends from Sudan and Ethiopia in the north through western Kenya past Kili to the southern end of Tanzania.

Like the multiple active and dangerous faults that threaten California, the Eastern Rift Valley is only one branch of a chain of many rifts known as the Great Rift Valley. This valley extends about 3,700 miles from as far north as Lebanon through Jordan in the Middle East to as far south as Mozambique in southeast Africa. Fault branches extend as far west as the Congo and Lake Victoria and as far east as Kili in eastern Tanzania and western Kenya, according to Wikipedia. (https://en.wikipedia.org/wiki/Great_Rift_Valley).

The critical area is called the Great Rift Valley. It has two branches, the Western Rift Valley and the Eastern Rift Valley. The Western Rift, also called the Albertine Rift, is bordered by some of the highest mountains in Africa and includes some of the deepest lakes in the world, including Lake Tanganyika on the western border of Tanzania; it is more than 4,800 feet deep. The Western Rift covers significant portions of the eastern Congo, eastern Uganda, and eastern Rwanda. The famous Lake Victoria is between the two rifts.

The Eastern or Gregory Rift stretches from Ethiopia in the north, through Kenya, Tanzania (along a line past where Kilimanjaro rises), and Malawi and ends in the Zambesi Valley in Northern Mozambique. The southern part of the Rift Valley, where the two rifts rejoin, includes Lake Malawi; it is the third deepest freshwater body in the world, more than 2,300 feet deep. (https://en.wikipedia.org/wiki/Great_Rift_Valley)

The rifts are caused by the plates sliding against each other and pulling apart, causing the rifts. This grinding slide many thousands of feet deep opens fissures in the earth's "thin skin" or crust; the fissures allow magma just a few thousand feet or less beneath the surface to surge upward and erupt into a volcano.

The bad news is that geologists say the rate of separation is accelerating, but the good news is that the separation totals only a few millimeters a year.

Sometime in as few as several million years to as many as 50 million years, East Africa from Somalia to northern Mozambique will completely separate from the rest of Africa and form either a huge island or a new continent.

I have discussed the Rift Valleys in detail because Kilimanjaro and the entire string of extinct, dormant, and active volcanoes that stretches from Ethiopia to Mozambique resulted from this separation.

On this day, however, just the seemingly "dormant" state of Kibo at the top of Kili was enough to make one think. It has active magma bubbling at about 1,700 feet deep below its active caldera, that is, about 17,800 feet above sea level and only 1,000 feet below where we camped beneath the summit next to the Furtwangler Glacier.   Fumaroles emit sulfur dioxide fumes and deposit sulfur on the edge daily. The ground inside the cone is constantly, consistently very warm all the time as well.

Fortunately, the geologic record shows that Kili has not erupted in at least 150,000 years, **BUT** its "baby" 15,000-feet-high Mount Meru, merely 43 miles west, is considered an active volcano; it last erupted in 1910, a mere blimp in geologic time. Right now, Mt. Meru is literally overshadowed by Kili, but who knows what the long geologic future will bring if Kili continues to erode rapidly and Meru remains active.

The Mountain of God

A "very young" volcano 103 miles north of Kili has erupted and deposited almost 1,000 feet of lava during just the past 15,000 years as the two tectonic plates continue to slide in opposite directions. Named Ol Doinyo Lengai, it is the only currently active volcano in the Eastern Rift Valley; remember the scientists think Meru is "dormant." We'll see! Ol Doinyo Lengai is "only" 9,650 feet tall; it has two active cones that last erupted in 2013 with frequent eruptions between 2006 and 2013. Mere seconds in geologic time.

The Maasai tribe calls it the 'Mountain of God.' Consider this idea: That name could mean that while Kili and nearby volcanoes were extinct or dormant for thousands, even tens of thousands, of years, Ol Doinyo erupted for the first time when the early ancestors of the Maasai tribe—and ours too most likely—lived in the area.

If I were a hunter-gatherer living on a flat plain filled with animals to hunt and plants to gather, I would freak out if suddenly, the earth erupted and spewed lava hundreds of feet in the air. Perhaps it continued for days, weeks, or months, and perhaps off and on for generations. As its toxic clouds rose tens of thousands of feet in the air, it would have rapidly polluted the skies and the earth. It would have killed or frightened away all the animals and killed the plants with piles of ash and toxic fumes. I hope the Maasai ancestors fled the area and most survived, but if any remained, they would have suffered for many years from a "temporary" winter with little to no sun and precious little breathable air.

It could be that the groups or tribes migrated far away to survive. Perhaps other small groups or tribes migrated to the land hundreds or thousands of years later after the "Mountain of God" calmed its "wrath," the land cooled, and plants and animals returned to the area.

It may be that the Maasai ancestors either had a concept of a Higher Power, or the Maasai later named it the Mountain of God because its power literally controlled their lives. It definitely brings to mind interesting ideas about how we *homo sapiens sapiens* developed our idea of an all-powerful "god." If the "god" idea was connected to a volcanic eruption, I can easily understand why those people thought their "God" would be a vengeful one. Thank goodness for more enlightened views of "God" in Western civilization during the past couple of thousand years; especially, I am deeply grateful that the founders of AA had the courage, after years of debate, to add to Step 3 that any member can have his/her own concept of a Higher Power, or no HP at all.

I hope that many hundreds, thousands, and tens of thousands of years from now our descendants will enjoy the same right of enlightened choice. I hope that future *homo sapiens sapiens*—if we deserve the title by then—will get to enjoy how the Eastern Rift Valley, its magnificent volcanoes, and unique ecosystem continue to evolve. For those of you who believe in reincarnation, maybe you'll be able to come back in a million years to see what happens!

Watching Asses and Enjoying Astounding Plant Life

Today began as one of those days when the rocky "stairs" were so steep that practically all I saw for most of the day was the butt of the person in front of me. Since I was always last or next to last, I saw a lot of butt—"unfortunately," most of the time it was Matt's 62-year-old one since he was usually second to last! Matt and I often changed places when one of us would have to stop for "old guy" reasons. Matt also had begun to develop a nasty cough; as a physician, he diagnosed himself with an upper respiratory ailment. Unfortunately, it was not "physician, heal thyself;" he ignored it, and by the seventh day, he was very uncomfortable.

We continued to hike onward and upward and follow the 'tough guy' leader of the day "pole, pole." We took breaks to drink more water and rest and to enjoy the gorgeous view and the incredible flora and fauna, especially the giant senechio and a unique species of lobelia, technically the *lobelia deckenii*, that is the only alpine desert lobelia species that grows on Kili. It is nothing at all like the lobelia you can buy at the plant nursery for your garden. (Source: http://www.onlineplantguide.com)

The erosion of the volcanic rocks around Kili and throughout East Africa has created rich soil. It is very rich in many kinds of minerals, especially iron, manganese, and magnesium. Combined with eons of decomposed plants, the soil is packed with nutrients and can grow abundant crops. As I noted, the soil's fertility attracts more and more farmers to push their croplands to the very edge of the national park boundary and beyond when they can get away with it. It would be better for the "Mother Mountain" and for them in the long term if they find more productive ways to increase their yields rather than grow too many crops too fast, drain the soil of its nutrients, and then move farther up the mountainside.

The Self-Defense of the "Gin-and-Tonic" Lobelia

Remember that plants and animals evolve with, if you are a Darwinist, or develop, if you believe in Intelligent Design, uniquely wise ways to protect themselves from harm—whether it is a zebra being chased by a lion or a lobelia plant using natural "insulation" to stay warm through the ferociously cold nights.

Let me use an animal analogy that might help explain the lobelia's defensive measures. Later in my trip as we toured the Serengeti, I saw how herd animals protect themselves and their young. For example, grazing zebra stand in zig-zag lines, each one facing a slightly different direction so that the herd as a whole has a 360-degree view of the plain all around them.

If any zebra spots a predator like a lion or a cheetah, it brays a warning to the rest of the herd, and they turn and watch the predator. If the predator moves too close, they form a protective circle with their foals in the middle. The mature zebras face outward and essentially dare the predator to attack. A healthy, adult zebra can kick a lion to death with its hooves; a zebra herd is a formidable foe that most big cats avoid. The cats try to lurk around the edges of a herd until they spot an old, injured, or young zebra that has wandered just a bit too far away from the herd.

I'll explain more about some other animals' fascinating defensive measures—herds of elephants, pods of hippos, troops of baboons, and the like—when we get to the Serengeti Plains part of this adventure. That is where I observed one of the most amazing examples of instinctive self-sacrifice I can imagine, perhaps showing us that our "noble" idea of service and self-sacrifice does not make us as special as we think we are.

I cite the zebras because like them, the alpine lobelia on Kili reinforced my amazement at the evolved wisdom or protective instinct of plants and animals. Personally, I believe *homo sapiens sapiens* has a very egocentric definition of its own superiority and intelligence; I believe plants and animals have something like an innate "intelligence" that helps guarantee their survival beyond genetic-based instinct. I have no idea if I am even close to correct, but paying close attention to the plants and animals in Africa has made me think far more deeply about this question than ever before.

The flowering alpine lobelia uses a technique very similar to that of the zebras to protect itself from freezing cold weather. It has created an interdependent relationship with the large bees that flock to them. The purplish-blue lobelia flowers actually grow inside the plant leaves.

On the left, Samia shows the hidden, blue flowers of the "gin-and-tonic" Lobelia plant that are protected from freezing by its thick green leaves and an alcohol-like mucus. On the right, you can see how the lobelia has evolved an extraordinary drapery of leaves to prevent its flowers and stalks from freezing at the high altitude. (Source: http://www.theplantencyclopedia.org/wiki/Lobelia_deckenii)

The leaves develop a sugary, thick, almost alcohol-like mucus and store it among the inner leaves. The mucus feeds the plant and attracts the bees that eat the pollen off the flowers, but the pollen also falls into the mucus and sticks to the bees' feet. The bees then carry the pollen from one plant to another and pollinate other lobelias.

Most importantly, the mucus is an insulator that prevents the leaves and stalks from freezing at night. Humorously for you recovering alcoholics reading this, the mucus can freeze into crescent-shaped ice cubes because of the shape of the leaf where the leaf joins the stalk, so this lobelia is also called the *gin-and-tonic lobelia*!!

Layers of Self-Protection for the Giant Senechio

Perhaps the most well-known rare plant on Kili technically has a new scientific name--"dendrosenechio" or "tree groundsel," but everyone still calls it "senechio." This huge—often 15 to 20 feet tall or more—plant includes two subspecies that grow only on Kili, one at altitudes between 8,300 feet and 10,500 feet in the heather zone, and a heartier cousin that grows only above 11,000 feet in the much colder alpine desert.

These slow-growing trees resemble palm trees, but the "fronds" are actually large rosettes or "cabbages" that take up to 25 years to grow. You can tell the senechio's age by counting the layers of brown wilted rosettes that seem to cascade down the sides of the tree trunk in waves.

These layers of wilted rosettes are the secret to the senechio's self-defense. Like the lobelia's leaves, they insulate the trunk so that the water in the upper trunk and closest to the growing green rosettes stays liquid in freezing temperatures. By evolution or design, this plant has found a unique home for itself in the barrancos out of the wind near or in seasonal stream beds. When the winter ice and snow melt and the rain falls, the water flows down and through the barrancos and nourishes the plant year round.

The variety that grows in the heather zone rarely flowers, but when it does, the petals are yellow and bud from a three-foot-long spike at the top of the plant. The alpine cousin has only dull yellow flowers.

The giant "dendrosenechio," or tree groundsel, protects its trunk from freezing with wilted "cabbages" that droop layer by layer for years to form a warm "coat."
(Source: Stedman, Henry, *Kilimanjaro, The Trekking Guide to Africa's Highest Mountain*, 2010, Trailblazer Publications)

We saw both the lobelia and the senechios when we hiked a small segment of the Machame route (one of the "killer" routes that go straight up the mountain) on the way to the crowded Barranco Camp. The good news is that this camp is the intersection for two major routes, the Machame and the one we have been on for two days, the Shira Plateau Route, and we will soon leave the crowds behind.

The More Challenging Road Analogy

Next, we'll follow the Machame Route for one more day to Lava Tower at 15,000 feet and then take the road less traveled, the challenging Umbwe Route up and over the Great Breach Wall. As we follow it, most of the other "touristas" take a different route southeast around the Summit Circuit to take the "easier, softer" Mweke Route up the more gradual South East Valley. However, what these climbers may not realize—or understand the implications of—is that the "easier, softer" way entails climbing 4,000 feet in the middle of the night to reach the summit by sunrise—which about half ever accomplish.

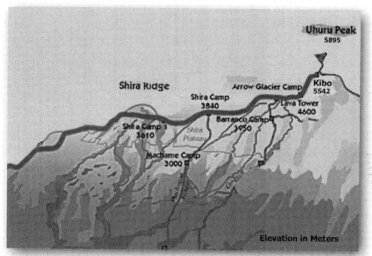

We took the more challenging "road less traveled" from Lava Tower to Arrow Glacier, over the Great Breach Wall to the Furtwangler Glacier campsite, a staggeringly steep climb in two days! (Note: The numbers on this map are in meters; to estimate the number of feet, multiply by 3.3 feet/meter.)

Because we take the more challenging "route less traveled," we get a good's night sleep at 18,800 feet (5,895 meters on map) and have only 553 feet to climb before dawn so we have a very good chance to see a perfect sunrise.

The analogy to the basic philosophy of 12 Step recovery is obvious. As the AA "Big Book" and most other 12 Step programs make clear, the easy road of addiction that leads only to despair, ruin, and often suicide or painful, un-timely death. The more challenging road—our 10 days of "pole, pole" over the Great Breach Wall instead of 5 days of "quickly, quickly"—leads to sobriety and success in recovery and in life as well as on the mountain.

This day was our last day on the Shira Plateau, and what a magnificent hike it was, when we stopped stair-climbing, staring at asses, and looked at the view. We had incredible views all the way across the caldera that appeared to be flat, but actually increased more than 4,000 feet in elevation. Tens of thousands of mountain marigolds, clusters of the papery white "everlastings," huge dandelion-like plants, and many other colorful, flowering plants dotted the rocky plain for miles in every direction. One of many breath-taking moments on my journey.

The Biggest Wins—Most of the Time

Along the same trail, I kept noticing little bits of fur and occasionally small bones here and there. When I hike in the Shenandoahs or the Rockies, it is often difficult to see live animals because they hear you coming and they hide. But I have learned to look for scat—animal droppings—and learn which animal leaves behind what kind of scat. I have often seen bones, fur, feathers, and partial carcasses in scat piles of carnivores like bobcats and coyotes. So, my curiosity spiked when I saw a fairly large pile of fur and a partial skeleton of an animal about the size of a cat or dog. I asked Noel, one of the assistant team leaders, what it was.

He said the small bones and fur were the remains of mice or small rodents that the jackals stalk, capture, kill, eat, and digest. They pass the fur and bones through their digestive tract and leave them in their scat.

But the larger skeleton was a duiker—a small, common antelope, also called the great or bush duiker. It has short, curved, black horns and a black stripe from its skull between its horns down between its eyes to its mouth. It is about the size of a medium-sized dog (25 to 55 pounds). Very quick on its hooves, it bounds along a trail and leaps like a small deer across the moorland heather. It lives all over sub-Saharan Africa in the savanna and moorlands like those on Kili. (Source: Noel and https://en.wikipedia.org/wiki/Common_duiker)

Noel explained that hyenas chase a duiker in packs, wear it down, and then pounce on it. Hyenas truly scare me more than the big cats because they are more aggressive and have no fear of people. Since they attack any size antelope in packs, they think people are just slow, dim-witted, two-legged antelopes. This "slow, dim-witted, two-legged antelope" had his own frightening encounters with the hyenas on this adventure. But they happen a few days from today, first on the edge of the Ngorongoro Crater, and again in the Serengeti, so my dislike is well earned.

Noel added that both the jackals and the hyenas leave the fur and bones as scat to mark their territory and keep others away, or least let any interlopers know they are in for a fight if they want to intrude.

He also claimed that in the natural, necessary competition for survival, the bigger animal generally wins. I think he is mostly correct, but my adventures in Africa and mountains across the U.S. have taught me that it is not only the biggest and strongest that survive, but the healthiest, the fastest, and the smartest.

For example, hyenas are much smaller than a Cape buffalo, but they often hunt in packs. They find and chase an older, sick buffalo or small calf, nipping at its legs to try to cut the tendons that connect its hoof to its leg and cripple it. As the buffalo tires, they may jump on its neck, smart enough to stay away from its huge horns and strong skull. If the buffalo is strong enough, it will kick the hyenas away, or turn and butt them with its horns and scatter the pack. If outmatched, the hyenas will slink away. If not, they bring the buffalo down and have a feast. That feast, though, just might be interrupted by "lazy" lions who are known to chase the hyenas away from their kills and eat the "yummy" parts—the stomach and intestines and the prime meat—first and leave the remains for the hyenas.

The Wretched Truth about "Dry" Bathing and Positive Change in Diet

After this day's interesting, but steadily uphill hike, I felt more tired than the day before—the altitude was beginning to tell. But my pulse rate and oxygen rate were still good, and I figured out that I had to stop eating the delicious soups because they used a base of instant milk that did not agree with my digestive system.

Before dinner, while I was still warm, I had my first "dry bath" in three days. God, did I smell when I peeled off my fleece and long johns! I thoroughly cleaned my crotch with dozens of "handiwipes," toilet paper, and cold water from my quart-sized water bottles. I filled three bottles three times a day so I could stay hydrated and have more available water than the small pan-full of lukewarm water we were given each morning and evening.

I also discovered two more seemingly minor mistakes that caused unfortunate consequences. I had left both my gas relief pills and my lip balm behind in my other luggage. These mistakes contributed to my upset stomach and left me with dry, chapped lips.

Fortunately, I received a gift of a tube of lip balm from Annie after I complained about my lips. Both Annie and Matt were very nice to me, yet I am sure I did not repay their kindness as I was as rude to them as I was to everyone else for much of the trek.

I also have skin problems, so thanks to all the sweat and inability to bathe, I had severe inflammation of my "private parts." I put a prescription healing cream on these areas and used a moisturizer on my face. Surprisingly, the rest of my skin was holding up fairly well—so far, much better than I anticipated. I had feared my skin, especially my back and face (since I wasn't shaving) would become inflamed with welts or hives, but the sweat of climbing every day cleaned the toxins out of those pores, and the cold, clean air kept the external inflammation at bay. Unfortunately, the clean air did not reach the areas where the sun doesn't shine!

By the time I finished cleaning myself up, the sun had set. One corner of my tent was covered in handiwipes and toilet paper, and I was freezing. The setting sun seemed to suck all the warmth with it as it fell beneath the horizon, leaving a glorious, clear, but very cold night.

Admitted to Myself at Least

As the sunset seemed to suck the warmth out of the world, my own spirits drooped, despite the beauty of the night sky. I realized a few unfortunate things about myself. I did a Fifth Step—at least to myself and to HP. I realized: So far throughout this adventure, I have been cranky, judgmental, harsh on myself and others, perfectionistic, and highly irritable about the slightest difficulty, such as getting in and out of my tent. I have fallen into my old pattern of isolation and "terminal uniqueness," that is, thinking I am different from everyone else. I withdraw and act unfriendly and distant. I brought with me to the mountain all my "ass-like" qualities—the impossible expectations of myself and others I have always carried on my shoulders and in my mind. As the wise philosopher, the late, great baseball player Yogi Berra said, "Wherever you go, there *you* are."

That statement is especially true for me as a recovering addict who, either by obsession or by choice, has carried decades of unreasonable expectations on my back. Those expectations, embedded by my father, fueled by my own anger, and fed by my self-loathing, have done me great harm and great good.

The harm, of course, is that I act out my addictions when I make a mistake because of fear of punishment, or I sabotage my success because I don't believe I deserve it. Either way, I feel like a failure because I have not lived up to the impossible expectations to be a perfect son, a great baseball player, a brilliant student, and the savior of my family. *Like I was ever responsible for those roles and goals in the first place!*

Only my years of recovery, the support of my 12 Step recovery family, and years of therapy have gradually chipped away at my self-loathing, feelings of worthlessness, the "never good enough," and my frequent acts of self-destruction.

On the good side, deep inside, I always knew that my father was wrong, that I had to be my own person. My anger and my embrace of my real self—whatever it was I did not know, but deeply felt—fueled a tremendous energy and determination to learn who I was, become the person I wanted to be, and live the life I wanted. Despite my "best" efforts to undermine it all, I have achieved a wonderful life with successful stints as a writer, teacher, consultant, and trusted public servant. Compared to everyone else in my dysfunctional, addicted family, I live happily, healthily, and prosperously. After two failed marriages and various romances, I have learned how to love unconditionally and now for the first time, share unconditional love with the best woman I have ever loved. And I have the love or respect of many dear friends who have walked with me step by step through the past 20 years of my best and my worst.

Another Costly "Rash Robert Regret" That Turned Out OK

Before dinner, I put on some—relatively—clean layers. And lo and behold, I made my first successful satellite phone call! Overall, paying more than $800 to rent a satellite phone for a month turned out to be a huge waste of money for a very ironic reason. Preparing for the trip, I had thought the cellphone service would at best be spotty and at worst, impossible. I had a humorous surprise when we started climbing the mountains; in the late afternoons, I watched the "tough guys" climb the nearest high point, whip out their cellphones, and call their families many miles away down the mountain or across Tanzania. All I really needed to do was get an international SIM card and take my cellphone with me, and I would have saved hundreds of dollars.

Another humorous contrast of modern communication was the radio transceiver Samia had to use to contact his headquarters every afternoon. It was an old hand-cranked radio. Each afternoon when they pitched camp, Samia and four men would walk to an open area away from the tents. Two of the men had to walk with an antenna wire in opposite directions and stretch out the wire about 50 feet while the third man held the wire over his head, the fourth cranked the radio power, and Samia made the calls. Sometimes it worked and sometimes it didn't!

A tough guy holds up the middle of the long antenna wire as Samia tries to use the team's radio to contact Wilderness Travel headquarters with "modern communications."

So, in camp we had three generations of "modern" communications— inexpensive cellphones, an expensive satellite phone, and an old radio set. The cheap cellphones worked best of all.

My sat phone worked sporadically because the signal was transferred across a large array of satellites that circle the earth in stationary orbit so that the entire planet is covered, supposedly. However, each satellite was in range of my phone for only 15-20 minutes as it whirled around the earth at 17,000 miles per hour. Each satellite was supposed to seamlessly transfer my call from one to the next one. But it seldom worked that way, and I had more missed and dropped calls than complete ones.

Less humorously, the satellite phone was heavy and clunky compared to a cell phone, so it added unnecessary weight to the duffel bag that Rodrik had to carry every day.

But this night, it worked! Sitting in my tent in my "sexy" black long johns and white silk insulated socks, I actually reached a good friend and talked for a few minutes. My diary notes said, "Worked perfectly. Awesome!" But that was the only time it did until I reached the summit.

Food for the Day

About dinner and my food plan this day, I noted in my diary, "Too good! and too much.

- Breakfast - non-wheat toast & pancakes, peanut butter, fresh papaya, oatmeal. What? No eggs! Ha!"

The "egg man" had carried seven layers of eggs—about three dozen in each layer—on his head for the first four days. By today, we had run out of eggs and "had to make do" with the delicious food I just described.

- Lunch - carrot soup, finger veggies, tuna salad, guacamole salad—both excellent—bananas, and non-wheat bread.
- Dinner - Two pieces of non-wheat bread with a little peanut butter, *NO SOUP!*

"Drink more water," I admonished myself in my diary. 'Modest' servings of cooked veggies, rice, and beef, two small pieces of bananas fried in lentil flour. I put 'modest' in quotation marks because I am a compulsive overeater, and I was burning so many calories every day, 'modest' on the mountain is not the same as 'modest' at home. And I was still losing weight as my clothes became visibly looser by the day.

Indisputable Glory of Creation

After dinner, it was a glorious, clear, crisp—well, freezing cold—night with tens of thousands of stars, constellations, and 15/16ths of a full moon! This mystical, breath-taking sight more than made up for the cold. My notes said, "TY—FMG!!! Your glory and your entire creation are beyond belief - I feel blessed and at one, <u>and</u> I wish I had lots of fur on my skin and more heavy clothes so I could stay outside at night longer!"

I have seen the Milky Way and the Southern Cross twice: the first time on a clear, hot night from a small boat in the middle of a lake in the Amazon and this night from a freezing cold plain at 13,800 feet on Kilimanjaro. I cannot imagine anyone who sees these magnificent sights in all their glory who is not compelled to look up in stunned awe and understand in their souls that a Higher Power is responsible for it all.

I have no other explanation for this Universe, and perhaps many other universes. I have studied the astronomy of the universe and the physics and metaphysics of why we exist. No study has ever answered the only questions that count: How and why did it start? Not the **when**—that the Big Bang happened about 14 billion years ago is an accepted theory, but no one can account for how and why the Big Bang happened. It didn't just happen, just as the principles of recovery—honesty, humility, and service, to name my favorite three—do not just help me recover from my addictions by accident. I, too, must continue to take action every day just as the Universe continues to expand and evolve each day.

There may not be a "grand plan" for each person's life—I was raised a Southern Presbyterian and "predestination" is a bit much for me. I do believe that whatever Higher Power/Creator there is constantly rearranges everything through the trillions and trillions of daily changes in the universe and in people and their interactions. If I consciously make a decision each day to live according to the 12 Step principles as well as I can—though certainly far from perfectly—then my interactions best align with the positive physical and metaphysical principles that guide the Universe. When I live a 12 Step "Way of Life" each day, my life always turns out for the best, regardless of what happens around and to me. So far, my 40 years of ups and downs and slips and slides have shown that belief to be both painfully and gloriously true.

After the glorious heavens inspired these thoughts—and the cold seeped into my bones, I went into my tent to reflect on the lessons of the day. It was too cold for anyone to sit in the dining tent and socialize after dinner. I felt good that I was keeping up my prayers and working to maintain conscious contact with my spiritual HP when I was alone. During the day, I was always in constant contact with Samia and my earthly HPs!

I said five or six prayers at least every morning and often through the restless nights—the Lord's Prayer; the Third Step, Seventh Step, and Eleventh Step prayers; a gratitude/acceptance prayer; and of course, the Serenity Prayer. Except for the Lord's Prayer and the Serenity Prayer, these prayers were first written by the founders of AA. Almost all 12 Step groups have adopted them or variations as meaningful expressions of humility, gratitude, and willingness to each member's Higher Power. I pray a personal variation of the Lord's Prayer—although ostensibly a Christian prayer, the prayer is not to Jesus, but *by* Jesus to his God. So, I figure I can use it to pray to my FMG.

I also brought with me copies of the daily meditations (June 18-July 6) from three meditation books. I read them every night before I slept or during the night when I could not sleep and needed words of wisdom. When my insomnia got the best of me, I talked with my HP for hours on end—usually my monologue to Him/Her. I don't think I listened very well most of the time. Note that I read them *at the end of the day*; I wanted to contrast what they said to my actual experience of that day. I did not want reading them in the morning to shape my day or "warn" me what would happen; reading horoscopes and the like in the morning, I have found, influences how I act during the day. The truly amusing result was that almost every day, what I did for good or ill was predicted by the meditations. I have summarized the relevant passages for each day—more Higher Power humor!

More Good Health and More Awe for Tough Guys

More good health news was that the clean, cold, dry air had cleared my pollen allergies. My sinuses were as clear as they had been in years. I was not stiff and sore in the morning because I was taking ibuprofen twice a day, and I was diligently taking my medications and my vitamins. I was staying very consistent with my self-care, something I often found hard to do in my more hectic life at home.

Mentally, I felt a bit ashamed and annoyed at my constant flatulence and having to hang back on the trail so I didn't break wind in people's faces. Other members of the group do the same thing because we eat so much and expend so much effort. At lunch and dinner, I even sit next to the tent flap, where it is coldest, so I can slip out of the tent if I need to. I hope that avoiding soup and bread and eating less in general will cause less gas in the coming days.

As I sit on my cold sleeping bag in my tent, bundled in all the heavy clothes I could wear, I can hear the cooks, their helpers, and other tough guys laughing and joking and banging pots as they clean up after dinner. The number of cooks, cook's helpers, and stewards (eight altogether!) was another major "perk" of being on this trip! However, I had observed after lunch that the cooks and stewards had their own well-deserved perk: We the "touristas" left a lot of food behind, but it did not go to waste. After each meal, the stewards, cook's helpers, and tough guys who carry our duffel bags discreetly wandered into the dining tent after we left the mess tent and chowed down on our leftovers before they broke camp. This perk of their jobs means they eat more and better food than the other "tough guys." And **ALL** of them still beat us to the next camp site by at least an hour!

The Need for Close Attention
Otherwise, today I learned to continue one step, one moment at a time, and always pay close attention to the trail to avoid tripping and falling—very rocky and stumpy so to trip and fall would have been very painful, even dangerous. In fact, I did slip stepping on a large loose rock that looked solidly set in the ground before I stepped on it, but I maintained my balance.

Obvious Recovery Lesson
Someone or something that seems solid and reliable may not turn out to be. That is why I have to proceed slowly and cautiously, testing the next rock in the stream or on the path. That is why I learned the hard way in my early recovery to give up my will **only** to my HP and follow the programs' and my sponsors' suggestions, but **not** surrender my personality to others, especially not sponsors, as they are perfectly imperfect as well.

I had often done that in my life—feeling so worthless and "lesser than" that I surrendered my will and my identity to stronger, more charismatic personalities. Many people whom I thought had strong recovery, and had trusted at first, turned out to be hypocrites, "13th Steppers" preying on women, or on the verge of or in active relapse. (In 12 Step programs, the facetious "13th Step" refers to men who hit on the vulnerable women to get dates and have sex with them.) I have never been a "13th Stepper," but I have been an unreliable sponsor and selfish SOB, interested only in what I could gain from the program, not what I could give. I have learned that we are all human and we all make many mistakes each day. I have to observe people's behavior and test them over time to develop deep trust and friendships.

Samia's Wisdom of the Day

At dinner, Samia knew that all of us were beginning to tire and the two-day trek up the so-called "flat" Shira Plain had begun to wear on us. We were asking ourselves, "Geez, we see the peak just ahead; why aren't we getting closer to it faster?" Knowing this mental slump would happen from lessons he learned during his 197 other trips, Samia talked with us about another critical recovery principle—though he had no idea he was: perseverance. He said:

> *Perseverance in completing this journey will give you*
> *10 years of confidence and patience.*

His comment echoed what I always say to newcomers: Any minute of service you give to the program—attending a meeting, setting up chairs, calling a newcomer to welcome them to the program, listening to a stranger who just needs to talk, anything—will return 10 minutes of recovery. Any hour, 10 hours of recovery. Simply put, the Universal "Law of 10" works; that is, one kind act will return 10 acts in kind. Period.

I also would add *perspective* to Samia's confidence and patience—perspective about what's truly important. Just compare the squabbles of petty office politics or family spats with the inner strength that I both showed and gained as I completed this incredible journey on my own two feet—of course, humbly with the help of 61 tough guys *and* my HP *and* everyone at home praying for my safe trip.

From Samia, I learned that doing the next step "pole, pole"—slowly and rightly—takes care of me. It takes huge faith, whether conscious or not, to do this. It takes real faith to keep my head down almost all day, taking the next step on the trail, trusting that the "leader of the pack" will get me safely to the next camp or where I need to be when I am supposed to be there.

It is also very important to stop occasionally and enjoy the view as I did to enjoy the thousands of flowers across the plain and the soul-touching night sky. One day many years ago, when I was a brash young man (yes, me! Ha!) and very angry at my parents, my mother told me "to stop and smell the roses." At the time, I thought it was one of the most asinine things I had ever heard. I pooh-poohed her comment, but I began to learn on these glorious nights and brilliant days how right she was. Now that I am almost as old as she was when she died of lung cancer, I try each day to find some little piece of beauty to enjoy and to thank my HP for even the smallest blessing.

Recovery Lesson: *Trust the 'pros' who truly know the way and care for your safety!*

In recovery, that means I stop trying to do it my way and follow the simple, though more challenging, road laid out for us in the 12 Steps and 12 Traditions by the founders of AA more than 80 years ago. Those Steps and Traditions have been, and are being, practiced by hundreds of thousands of truly healthy, happy, prosperous, generous recovered addicts who have closely followed this path.

Higher Power Humor! Although I am not a Christian, at this stage in the history of 12 Step programs, I feel like the second generation of Christians who know people who knew Jesus, but who did not know him themselves! I was in my early twenties when Bill W. died in 1971, five years before I joined OA, and I was a newborn when Doctor Bob died in 1951. I have met real AA old-timers--the first generation of recovering "apostles" carrying the message—who knew Bill W. or heard Bill W. speak at AA conventions in the 1950s and 1960s, and I have listened to both Bill's and Doctor Bob's old tape recordings.

I have thoroughly studied the literature of five 12 Step programs, (AA, Al-Anon, OA, DA, and CODA). The core tools, the core principles are exactly the same for each and work exactly the same—if I work them the way the programs and experienced members suggest I work them.

The same principle will play out during the rest of my Kili climb in painful, humiliating, yet ultimately marvelous ways.

The Little-Known Secret of Kilimanjaro and My Hubris

Okay—I promised to tell you a secret that we learned today: There is a rescue road capable of handling ambulances and trucks up the far southwest side of the mountain to about 13,000 feet. We crossed this road about half way through our hike today, and we saw a young guy walking quickly down the road with a guide and two tough guys. Samia said the man was about 20 years old. In a hurry to climb the mountain, he had hired a truck and been driven up the road to 12,500 feet with **NO** acclimatization. With his small team, he began to climb very quickly and just as quickly became very ill. His guide had to turn him around and take him down the mountain, carrying his pack while the young man held onto the guide's shoulder as he walked. Later, from a distance, we saw a white medical van rushing up the road to pick him up and take him down the mountain. Altitude sickness is a scary bastard, able to strike anyone at any time at any altitude, regardless of your age or physical condition.

My diary for this evening concludes with this arrogant and contradictory quote: "Dumb Ass!! Youth will learn the hard way!...I do pray that he is alright and be well at a lower altitude."

My hubris and its karma will catch up with me very soon...

Summary of Daily Lessons

As I noted, in another example of HP humor, almost every daily meditation I read from the three meditation books ends up being a perfect thought for the day. Today, for example, the first reading stressed how no chain is stronger than its weakest link, how the best way to grow stronger is communion with God. Another one advised me to rest when weary until my cares, worries, and fears leave me. It said that every thought is a prayer—positive or negative. It called on me to wish people well and imagine them happy, and I had not been doing any of that very well so far. The third one stressed that the only time to abstain and practice recovery is this moment. Only my efforts today to recover grant me sanity and freedom from addiction.

What did I learn today:

- **Perseverance** - Samia's comment: I gain 10 years of confidence and patience from this one-day-at-a-time climb rather than living this day impatiently and becoming ill.
- **Learning** – It is reinforced slowly, one step, one moment, one action at a time. And I have to stop occasionally to smell the roses (Thank you, Momma!) and enjoy the view.

- **Trust the *pros who truly care!*** Follow the path of those who have gone, and still go before, and achieved strong recovery. Stick with those with long-term success and who truly care.
- **Put your progress into *perspective* and celebrate your victories.**
- ***Sleep!***

THURSDAY, JUNE 24

Day Six, Step Six

"There are no happy faces above 15,000 feet."
SAYING I CREATED IN HONOR OF THE MISERY
WE ALL FELT BY THE END OF THIS DAY.

"It's still better to bump my head on the lava rock
than fall and hurt myself and others badly."
MY JOURNAL NOTE AFTER I HIT MY HEAD DESCENDING LAVA
TOWER WHEN I WAS TOO AFRAID TO FOLLOW DIRECTIONS

Step 6 - Became entirely ready for God to remove all these defects of character.

This day included six critical events and I created a meaningful new motto:

- First, a spiritual revelation led me to take Steps 4, 5, 6, and 7 on a major issue in my life.
- Second, I proved beyond any doubt that iron-based lava rock is much harder than my thick skull. Once again, I repeated the lesson that I should follow Step One: Follow my human HP's—Samia's—direction;
- Third, I embarrassed myself and the others and the crew by letting loose a stream of curses that would have made my late father and four late uncles—all sailors—proud. Well, probably not.

- Next, I got to practice a favorite program motto: "Progress, not perfection" far more than I liked.
- Fifth, it was the day before my 60th birthday—almost there!
- Finally, I created an apt new motto for Kili climbers: **There are no happy faces above 15,000 feet**; the difficulty breathing as we climbed, the respiratory distress and nausea several of my group had developed, and the biting wind and subfreezing cold made it hard to smile, even when I felt so grateful for another brilliant, clear day and equally brilliant moonlit night.

Every night, when I reviewed the daily meditations, I had to laugh at myself for my HP's attitude: He/She was hoping I would make the right choices during the day. Every evening, I could hear Him/Her saying: "Well, it's your choice to pay attention and do the right thing or suffer the consequences. You can always improve tomorrow."

To paraphrase, the first reading asked the critical question of whether I harm myself by deliberately shutting people—and all kinds of good things—out of my life. Well-duh! I had spent most of my life doing that outside of my trusted friends in 12 Step programs. The second reading had a prayer that encouraged me to avoid becoming too upset and go calmly along my path. The final reading quoted a famous 12th century nun, Hildegard of Bingen, who stressed the connection between light—both physical and spiritual—and life. As you'll read soon, I did a wonderful job of ignoring the first two, but I was literally blinded by the third in an unusual position.

Glory, Awe, and Revelation

I spent a very fitful night with little real rest, though I was "warm" enough to unzip the sleeping bag and take off a layer of fleece pants and gloves. I got up twice to go to the bathroom—each time going through my elaborate 16-step process.

During my first trip about 4 a.m., I had one of my most amazing experiences that led to a spiritual revelation. When I got out of my tent, I walked groggily and gingerly **east**, looking down to dodge rocks and low bushes so I did not notice anything around me. When I backed out of the small latrine tent and turned **west**, the moonlight was so awesomely bright and the full moon so huge

TAKING THE 12 STEPS UP-AND DOWN-KILIMANJARO

that it literally blinded me. I stood still, stunned at the magnificence of the thousands of planets and stars that shone bright, framing the full moon. The glaciers and snow on the hillside shone iridescent white. It was a unique moment, far brighter than the night before because we had climbed about 2,000 higher. The full moon looked like a huge white ball hanging right over me. I felt deeply the awesome power of Nature that our so-called primitive ancestors, not "blessed" with electricity, experienced every clear, full-moon night. The moon and the stars exuded a power that we, in our artificial cocoons of electric light and mechanical noise, can no longer comprehend or appreciate. The sight touched the core of my soul as it must have touched the souls of all of my hundreds of millions of ancestors who might have first felt in awe of a Creator by this light.

Taking Steps 4 and 5 on My Divorces at 6:10 a.m.

After I sort of napped for about two hours, I woke up for good at 6:10 a.m. For some reason, I immediately remembered that the day before—June 23— would have been the 37th anniversary of my first marriage and this day—June 24—was the first anniversary of my second divorce. Happy Anniversary???! Yes and no. I had not thought about either occasion during the entire trip until I woke up this morning and began my prayers as I lay there in the cold.

I thought deeply and asked my HP for guidance: Why had both of my ex-wives remained so mad at me for so long? I had been so perplexed that neither one wanted any contact with me—22 years (and counting) without contact with my first wife. After my second divorce the year before this adventure, my second wife made it very clear she did not want to anything to do with me. In that freezing tent with the brilliance of the heavens filtering down through the tent canvas, I knew that it was time to do Steps 4, 5, 6, and 7 on this quandary to figure out what I had done wrong so I could finally clean up my side of the street.

Several reasons for their resentment and distancing became clear. First, I had kept playing our dysfunctional games for so long and acquiescing to whatever they wanted, rather than facing our problems, that they did not believe I would leave. They were shocked when I did so, maybe because we had had too many fights and I had "cried wolf" about separating or getting divorced too often. Maybe they thought my actual final breaking point was only another idle threat. If true, I was responsible for sending unclear signals about my misery in the marriages so they had ignored my warnings.

I now know for a fact that I stayed in each marriage long after I knew in my heart it was time to leave. Staying when I wanted to leave had been dishonest and unfair to them.

I want to avoid blaming them and focus on my side of the street; however, it does take two to make a marriage work, and each person is responsible for his or her part in a successful relationship. A bicycle with one working wheel is not going to get very far, even if it is a tandem bike and both people are pedaling in the same direction. If the two people are trying to peddle in different directions, or one partner wants to pedal and the other takes her foot off the pedals, it will be very difficult, if not impossible, to move forward. In fact, both of you are likely to keel over into the street, crash the bikes into a wall, or fall into a ditch.

This analogy pretty much explains why both marriages ultimately came to the same sad end. First, neither wife appeared to have a strong desire to or to be capable of changing; both were quite happy with the status quo, even when I felt miserable.

The primary difference that has mattered—in my failed marriages and in my years of recovery—has been my willingness, however reluctantly and imperfectly, to do the work that might have helped save our relationships. These actions included asking to do marital counseling, doing individual therapy every two weeks for years, and working on my own recovery, however imperfectly, in my 12 Step programs.

Sadly, they never attended any 12 Step meetings to see what my programs were about and why the 12 Steps helped me. Each of them stopped going to marital counseling after only two sessions. Neither ever attended Al-Anon or individual therapy to help themselves. I can't say much about their not attending Al-Anon because I had been in recovery for 32 years before I attended my first Al-Anon meeting. Considering my family history, that was only 32 years after I should have begun to attend!

Furthermore, I had not been a good role model much of the time when I "skated" through my recovery for years and experienced my sometimes minor, but occasionally major, relapses. I claim only progress, not perfection. Often that "progress" has meant that I went backward for a while before I took another leap forward.

I also often ignored my therapist's advice and did not use the methods he suggested to improve our communication.

Most distressing to me, I must admit that I was often incredibly selfish, wanting what I wanted when I wanted it and feeling resentful and angry when I did not get my way. As I said, it takes two to tango; As much as I love to dance, I don't do the real tango very well, much less the marriage one.

The rest of my thoughts this morning in my freezing cold tent—and in the time since—have been "If Onlys" and "What Ifs"—coulda, woulda, shoulda—and they are irrelevant. Deep in my heart, I know I loved them both very much. I feel deeply grateful to them for all of our positive experiences. In both marriages, we did have great times in very different ways. Most notably, in my first marriage, we became very successful freelance writers and enjoyed many trips to Ireland, Paris, and Key West. In my second, I experienced financial stability for the first time and more important, the incredible joy of fathering my two stepchildren to adulthood and marriage. Together, my second wife and I visited five more continents and more than two dozen other countries. I am deeply grateful for all the good.

My journal puts it this way: *I love them and myself, I release them to their Higher Power, and I surrender the future to my Father-Mother God.*

With this consideration and prayer—and now in this writing, I believe I have taken Steps 4, 5, and 6, and 7 about my marriages: I became as willing as I had ever been to have God remove my character defects in my relationships, I forgave them and myself, and I prayed for God to remove my shortcomings in my relationships. Even so, it has taken a long while since that cold morning and several other relationships "practicing" this lesson badly. I hope, and I believe, I have made great strides in understanding how to create and nurture loving, supportive, open and honest relationships. One day at a time with my beloved significant other and with my dearest friends and family. Better late than never!

Lava Tower Misadventure

My Higher Power also "reinforced" the primary lessons of Steps 1 through 3—my powerlessness and need to surrender my will during this very challenging day. After breakfast, we left the Shira Plain and hiked from 13,800 feet to the famous Lava Tower at 15,000 feet; the hike was cold and windy but delightful, with another brilliant blue sky and a steady "pole, pole" pace upward.

Lava Tower is a 200-feet-tall extrusion of volcanic rock that is much harder than all the rocks around it; it's mostly iron ore. Over the millions of years since Kilimanjaro first erupted, all of the softer lava rock and soil around this pile of lava has eroded away. The Tower stands like a palace guard protecting the final passage to Mother Mountain's "throne."

Lava Tower, a 200-feet-tall lump of iron rock at 15,000 feet, "guards" the spot where several trails to the top of Kili divide. Note that while our tents were out in the open, the crew tents were hidden between huge boulders next to the Tower—out of the wind. Smart crew!

We stopped at about mid-day to camp beneath the Tower because we were going to take another full day to acclimatize at this altitude. It also was the dividing point where the allegedly "easier, softer way" on the Summit Circuit separated from our "more challenging road less taken" up the Umbwe route. We spent two nights here—this day and the next day—my 60th birthday!!—with short, "easy" 800 feet hike straight up to Arrow Glacier at 16,000 feet and back down to the Tower.

Of course, instead of resting, Samia asked us at lunch who wanted to climb the Tower—by the way, a technical and challenging climb straight up. None of us wanted to act like a wimp, so we all said we wanted to climb it. During the climb, there were four places where it was difficult and dangerous.

To reach from one rock to another, I had to swing from one rock and hand-hold to another while holding on with one hand and then swinging several feet out and around the rock and grabbing the next hand hold.

Samia shows one of my fellow climbers where to put her hands and feet to cross the most dangerous gap on the way up the Lava Tower.

Climbing up was actually fairly easy. The views from the top were magnificent. I could see across the entire Shira Plain, dozens of square miles of caldera covered by the many tens of thousands of flowering plants. I could even see all the way down the trails we had walked for the past three days to the edge of the montane forest.

Most stunning of all were the clouds and their constant clash with the high stone rim of the Plain. Where the Shira Plain caldera begins at about 12,000 feet is a huge overhanging "lip" or rim, 200 to 300 feet high. At the edge, a thin layer of clouds that constantly wrapped Kili in a grayish white embrace seemed alive. The clouds seemed to fight to climb up and over the rim to spill onto the Plain. But some interesting atmospheric condition acted like an invisible wall; the clouds rolled up to the top of the lip, banged into the "wall," and then turned back over on themselves. It looked like a huge ocean wave falling in reverse where the wave fell backward onto the sea rather than forward onto a beach.

In my joy at the scene, I forgot an obvious lesson about climbing—and gravity: what goes up must come down. We had gone straight up, so we had to go straight down. Going down is almost always much worse than going up.

At the most challenging gap on the way down, I let my fear of falling and lack of faith in the 'tough guys' take control; I felt terrified, virtually frozen in my tracks. In my fear and confusion, I misunderstood their directions. I tried to push through when I should have asked for help. As I tried to hide my fear, my 'machismo' kicked in, and I ignored Sami's instructions—to my pain and chagrin.

Near the bottom was a six-feet-wide gap between two large lava boulders. The critical action to crossing this gap was to bend down, stick out your butt and swing your body and your left leg wide around the edge of a large lava rock. Everyone else crossed the gap fine, even the 62-year-old couple because they said they did this kind of rock climbing in New Hampshire all the time. So, they crossed the gap cautiously and well. I went last across this gap.

Frankly, it wasn't that dangerous because only six feet below me were three 'tough guys' waiting to put their hands on my butt and catch me if I fell.

But I have a severe fear of heights and falling. This was the first time I had had to cross so large a gap going downhill during all of my years of hiking. I panicked and swung too close to the rock with my head down, watching the "catchers" below rather than where my head was going. So, I banged my head on the edge of the rock—hard.

I let out a stream of curses that could have turned the air purple, and everyone looked at me like I had lost my mind. I kept cursing after I did close the gap and got down to the base, angry at myself and embarrassed, knowing it was my own fault for not following Samia's instructions—again!

First Lesson of the Day

Steps One, Two, and Three: Follow my HP's instructions; heed his warnings; and surrender my will—and above all my fears—to my HP. Trust those who support you—three strong men were only a few feet beneath me; it was their job and their mission to support me, help prevent me from falling, and catch me if I fell. I wondered at the time why I chose to ignore their help. Did I not want to cause them trouble? Did I insist on doing it my way? Did I simply not trust them? Did I feel some strange combination of all the above and more? My machismo's "going to show them?" Co-dependence, stubbornness, fear, lack of faith, belief I didn't deserve the support—who knows? All jumbled up.

The "why" is largely irrelevant because my personal themes for this adventure were becoming more clear by the day: Responding to challenges to my faith—or lack of it—by placing trust in others, practicing perseverance, and gaining experience. Any similar experience would have taught me to be cautious and slow and trust the catchers. But my isolation and fundamental distrust of others got in the way.

The results? A small knot on my head; a mild headache; scraped, red skin on my forehead; and more distrust and questioning by Samia and my group. I could cure the scrape and knot with time and my headache with ibuprofen, but my relationships were going to get much worse before they got better.

Ah, Youth!

As I noted, Lava Tower is the convergence and divergence of three major trails—Shira Plain, Machame, and Barranco. We saw or passed hundreds of climbers and their "tough guys" all day today. Dozens of people camped at the Tower overnight. Most of the climbers were "kids"—the 20-30 somethings mostly from Europe—hurrying along the trails in their wonderful overconfidence and youthful immortality. These small groups of 5 or so had few "tough guys" with them, small tents, and what appeared to be little food compared to our cornucopia of abundant food and dozens of experienced "tough guys."

As in facing the challenges of recovery, it is not wise to either try it alone—which would have been suicidal on Kili and would have been suicidal for me in my addictions—or with the scant support these kids were using to try to conquer Kili. For my recovery to continue, I must have a large recovery family of sponsors, meetings, friends, and networks that extend across both the physical world and the virtual world of the Internet.

In one example of how denial and obliviousness will get you into trouble on Kili, one cute blond young woman from Houston, Texas—Southern accent and all—was practically running the trail. She was laughing and talking as she sped by us; blond hair streaming behind her in the wind. She wore no headgear or hat despite the bright sunlight and no jacket despite the stiff wind and cold. The sun was brilliant enough, and we were high enough, for me to get a sunburn even with my layer of 30 SPF suntan lotion. I thought at that moment that either she must have an angel watching over her, or she was in deep trouble. She had two 'tough guys' straggling behind her; one of them looked over at Samia as she sailed by, shook his head sadly, shrugged his shoulders, and kept plodding along behind her.

I asked Samia what he thought about how she was acting. He said that if she did not slow down, she would become very sick. In fact, her fast pace and laughing were signs that she was already coming down with altitude sickness, but didn't know it, he stressed.

We "old folks" had just kept plodding along all morning, yet we still climbed 1,800 feet and 5 miles in just 4 hours. So far each of us was either healthy or seemed to be showing only mild symptoms; Jason had had a headache most of the time and Matt had begun to medicate his respiratory illness, but the rest of us were still good. My morning pulse rate had been 63; my afternoon rate was 82. My oxygen rate was hanging stable at 92-93.

My diary said, "God bless my strong heart and my strong, clear lungs!" Amen! Never smoking, being sober for 25 years at the time, eating healthily, and staying thin for most of 35 years had paid off on this adventure—and taking Diamox every day!

But I was beginning to feel the altitude more each day. My diary notes were becoming a bit over the top—"Food fantastic—The Chef is a God!!!... Continues an embarrassment of riches!!!" With less hyperbole, my food choices continued to be healthy. I stayed abstinent today with oatmeal, three pieces of non-wheat bread, peanut butter, and fruit salad for breakfast; veggies, salami, and "the best guacamole ever" for lunch; and ratatouille, rice, cheddar cheese, 3 slices of non-wheat bread with butter, and Caprese—mozzarella cheese and tomatoes with pesto sauce that our "god-like Chef" cooked himself. I skipped the soup again, and that was helping my digestive process a lot as I continued to drink a lot of water and take my medications and vitamins.

Colder, Windier Night—Smart Tough Guys

That night, the wind began to howl up the valley. We were camped in an open space between the Lava Tower and the beginning of the next major hill for our "comfort" on relatively flat ground. But I saw that the "tough guys" had pitched their tents among the huge boulders at the base of the Tower—blocking the howling wind.

After we finished our descent down from the Tower, I took a walk around the campsite in the afternoon to calm down and extricate myself from the stares and disapproving frowns of my companions. At this altitude, there were very few plants except for hardy grasses and a few flowers. The flowers "hid" in the cracks and crevices of the boulders and rock slides and near the narrow beds of the springs that occasionally popped out between the rocks and flowed downhill.

Although I did not see any animals, I did see some Cape buffalo tracks and "cow pies" in the grasses near the southern base of the Tower. Samia told me that the buffalos often climb the slopes at night to lick the rich minerals on the far side of the Tower, eat the grass, and drink the water in the little valleys with fresh springs.

A Different View of Hemingway's Frozen Leopard

To take nothing away from Ernest Hemingway, the buffalo tracks and scat spurred a compelling thought about a real explanation for one of the most famous and most bizarre—and as far as I know, fictional—situations ever written in 20th century fiction. I suggest in sheer speculation an alternative explanation about what happened to the frozen leopard that was found on Kili in Hemingway's *Snows of Kilimanjaro*. After all, that story had stayed in my head and my heart since I was a young teenager; it had helped inspire me to climb this mountain 50 years later.

Based on my two experiences in Africa, I want to relate to the story in a different way. Let's assume the story is true: So how did the leopard die or freeze to death at the higher altitudes? Consider these possibilities that Hemingway does not address. Maybe the leopard had been following a herd of buffalos up the valley in the middle of the night; perhaps it had tried to attack the buffalos in the early morning and they had fought it off, perhaps injuring it. Perhaps the leopard could not walk and when it lay down, it was hit by a sudden blizzard or subfreezing cold snap and died of exposure and hypothermia.

Who knows? But these ideas certainly provide a better explanation than a leopard wandering up a mountain and freezing to death for no reason at all. Since buffalos are a major food source for the leopards, it just makes sense for a hungry, maybe old and slightly confused, leopard to follow the buffalos higher than it had ever been so that it paid the ultimate price.

One of the common interpretations of Hemingway's story is that it is an analogy for the dire consequences of overreaching, going beyond your real abilities. I prefer a simpler, more natural explanation—extreme hunger driving the leopard to extreme actions to try to survive—with the same dire consequences.

Perhaps much like the addict's blind beliefs and powerless obsessions: Take another drink or another shot of heroin, eat another box of cookies, buy more stuff you don't need on your maxxed-out credit cards, make that next trifecta bet on the long shots at the Off-Track Betting parlor, find another sex partner. These acts of self-will and irresistible compulsion will solve your problem. **Not!**

Freeze-Dried Socks and Freezing Batteries

As I had these fanciful thoughts, it was still mid-afternoon, so I completed a second complete wash-up because the sun felt warm (relatively) and the tent was warm inside. I had seen Matt and Annie wash out their socks and hang them on the side of their tents to dry, so I did the same thing—but just a little too late in the afternoon.

The temperature fell from about 45-50 degrees F. to well below freezing in an hour after the sun went down. As the sun went down, we had a glorious sunset with mixed purples, pinks, reds, yellows, oranges and pale blues. I tried to take pictures, but after two or three shots, the batteries in my cameras became too cold and stopped working. Each time, I ran inside my tent to hold the cold camera under my several layers of clothes for several minutes until they warmed up. Then I ran back outside and took more photos of the dark Tower in the sunset and the dark terrain of our campsite as the cold set in.

When we were called to the dining tent for dinner, I took my still-wet socks off the outside of my tent, knowing they would freeze if I left them outside. I hung them from the metal ribs that formed the roof of my tent. I thought the warmth in the tent would dry them overnight. Another bit of Higher Power humor.

After I returned from dinner less than an hour later, I found the socks were frozen solid! I have never figured out how low the temperature had to be to freeze thick wet wool socks in an hour, but it had become very cold with a howling wind. The next morning, the socks were even more like fuzzy icicles, so I had to strap them to my backpack so they could dry during our short hike.

In less than one hour, my newly washed socks froze solid after sundown, even in my tent!

Lesson Learned: Never wash your socks or underwear in the late afternoon in a subfreezing cold environment!

The evening ended very well because on the eve of my 60th birthday, I was gifted with another unimaginably bright full moon with the Milky Way like a precious pearl ring with a stunning setting—a billion tiny diamonds in a galaxy-size setting for an enormous priceless pearl. I felt blessed beyond any blessing I had ever felt before.

Step 6 for the Day and HP's Choice about Character Defects

As I explained, after banging my head on Lava Tower and ignoring Samia's instructions, I thought deeply and prayed about my shortcomings in my marriages. I faced my old, bad habits of lashing out, embarrassment, and isolation. I became as willing as I could be to have my HP remove my defects of character. Or so I thought, but my HP had more—and more severe—tests in store.

A favorite lesson I have learned is that just because I believe I am willing to have my HP remove my defects does NOT mean He/She is ready to remove them. Nor does it mean I am truly ready to release them at a deep, spiritual, subconscious level. As the AA Big Book and other "12 and 12" books stress, I can never really know for sure when I will be "entirely" ready to surrender my defects; all I can do is take two actions: First, work my Programs steadily. Second, pray for the willingness 1) to release them and 2) for my HP to first make best use of them and then remove them when my HP no longer needs them. That's right, "make use of them."

Too often, my shortcomings have stayed with me for years after I thought I was entirely ready for HP to remove them. It dawned on me some years into my recovery that either my HP had some positive use for my character defects—after all, stubbornness properly channeled could be perseverance toward great goals. Or my HP was far more aware than I that I had many lessons to learn that only acting out a defect could teach me. To my chagrin, during this adventure, either I chose to practice, or my HP set me up to practice, the defects that I thought I wanted so badly to be removed.

Key Lessons of the Day

Obviously, the critical lesson of this day was: ***Stay sharply focused on where you are stretching or leaping.*** It is as important to pay close attention to the actions you are taking to get to your goal as it is to keep your eye on the goal. I mean that in a serious moral and ethical sense as well as a business or personal one. This adage holds true in climbing rocks, beginning new habits, forming new friendships, starting new relationships, and taking the next Step in your recovery. Not only look ahead, but study the terrain and have a support network in place to help you.

Other Lessons of the Day:

- It's better to make a small mistake—bump my head—rather than a big one—fall off the ledge onto the people and large rocks below. A scrape, a bump, and a headache are better than broken bones and injuries to others.

- It is OK not to insist on being first; it is OK to make the journey healthy, happy, and safe. I was not praying to be first; I was praying to get to the top of the mountain and back down in one piece.
- Don't overdo anything from machismo, arrogance, false self-confidence, or denial.
- Listen to the instructor, follow directions, ignore the crap in your head, and trust those with experience.
- Ask for help and gratefully and graciously receive it—none of which I did.

In addition to these brief lessons, as I sat up in my cold tent, I wrote down more of my "rash Robert regrets" and "smart Robert moves." You can find the complete list of these "regrets" and "moves" on my blog at our website at www.recoveryfca.com. I certainly need to keep reading and reminding myself about them!

After I jotted down these long lists, it was time to try to make another satellite call to my friend at home—it failed. The chill was setting in, despite my multiple layers. With open finger mittens for writing, my notes end like this:

"Tomorrow is our 'rest day.' Only 800 steep feet to Arrow Glacier and back down in 3 hours with the afternoon off to clean, relax, and prepare for the optimal hike. TY, FM-G, for another H, H, S day!!! TYFAMMMM blessings!!!"

Amen and I tried to sleep. Tomorrow is my 60th birthday, and I will celebrate it on the Mother Mountain at the highest altitude I have ever climbed!

FRIDAY, JUNE 25

Day Seven, Step Seven

Happy 60th Birthday! The Best Birthday of My Life!

"Truly, truly the most wonderful, the very best birthday ever.
An enormously, beyond-belief God—FMG—day of blessings.
FMG—I will do whatever you want me to do because it will
all (be) alright throughout—despite any difficulty—I am truly
blessed beyond measure. I feel AND am wrapped in God's love."
DIARY ENTRY AFTER BIRTHDAY BLESSINGS

Step Seven – Humbly asked Him to remove our shortcomings.

This day was the best birthday of my life. I learned that angels come in all shapes, sizes, and species; that most surprises are usually very good ones; and that people are as generous as you allow them to be. I woke up this morning, suddenly 60 years old at 15,000 feet—I had felt confident that I would make it this far. I felt astonished with gratitude at the beautiful weather, my good health, the incomparable physical and spiritual experience, the strength and compassion of all our "tough guys," and the much-more-difficult-than-expected climb.

At first, it did not seem that my birthday was going to be very good, much less the best ever. I had another tough night, getting less than 3 hours of fretful sleep. The "mummy" sleeping bag continued to feel very uncomfortable and I was freezing when I was not inside it. (By the way, I did return that bag when I got home, and I did get a full refund from Eastern Mountain Sports, so good on them.)

At first, it seemed like Samia and my fellow climbers had forgotten it was my birthday. No one mentioned it at breakfast, and I didn't bring it up because I was feeling a little neglected and disappointed. After breakfast, I took Samia aside and asked him if the tour company had told him it was my 60th birthday today. He just kind of glanced at me and said nonchalantly, "Oh, I know. Happy Birthday," and walked away.

I felt even more confused and dejected, so I just went back to my tent to suit up for our acclimatization hike up to Arrow Glacier. Frankly, I started feeling sorry for myself, but I told myself, "Well, heck with them. It's a great day. It's my day, and I'm going to enjoy it." A bit defiant, a bit isolating, but I did shift my thinking to a positive frame of mind for myself.

Angels All Around

The 4-hour hike was very windy and cold, and the remarkable experiences of this hike quickly changed my attitude as I experienced the first of the day's many loving actions from the angels in our crew and my group. After we began the hike about 8:30 a.m., I found to my chagrin that I had left my windbreaker in my tent because the sun felt warm and the sky was bright. But I quickly became very cold from the biting wind. I asked Samia for help. He asked the assistant leaders if any of them had an extra jacket. Neal did not have a spare, but he gave me his own to wear for this hike. He is Angel Number One of this day.

I had left my lip balm at our lodge, and Matt and Annie gave me one of theirs when the wind began to chap my lips. Angels 2 and 3 for the day.

My journal said about the gift of the jacket, "Live and learn." Yep, but the hard part is the learning.

About the gift of the lip balm, I wrote, "Ask and ye shall receive."

Every step of this trip, I had what I needed when I needed it, either because of Samia's vast insight or someone's generosity and compassion.

Blessing Delivered by A Very Rare Bird

We reached the base of Arrow Glacier in about 90 minutes. I was standing in the middle of the campsite when Angel Number 4 literally flew directly over my head. I thought it was either a very large hawk or an eagle. Both are rarely seen at this altitude because there are so few small mammals or birds to eat.

But I learned later that I was wrong—and gladly so. In fact, it was a "fairly rare and very awesome vulture called a Lammergeier or Lammergeyer," according to the experts at Wilderness Travel. "This bird is rare worldwide but seen with some regularity on Kili. It is special as it picks up bones, soars high with them and drops them in the rocks to break them open. It then goes and eats the marrow. This is a 'life lister' for bird lovers because it is so rare. Whole travel groups are set up just to give people [avid birdwatchers] the chance to see this bird and tick it off [their list]."

Yet, there it was on my 60th birthday, flying less than 10 feet over my head as I photographed Arrow Glacier and the daunting Great Breach Wall rising 2,800 feet straight above us. I saw its shadow and got a brief glimpse as I turned quickly; after swooping over me, it soared and flew away toward a nearby ridge.

Maybe, just maybe, I smelled so bad by that time (7 days without a shower) that the Lammergeyer swooped down to see if I was dead since I had been standing still for a while. Sorry, Charlie! I was still alive and kicking!

Seriously, what an amazing blessing to be honored with a visit by such a rare and—for a vulture—attractive bird. Thank you, HP!

A reminder about "weird Robert" and my spiritual totem raptors (hawks, eagles, falcons, ospreys, and now, Lammergeyer vultures). I know it's my own choice to believe that raptors are the physical manifestations of my guardian angel. However, it is uncanny how whenever I need one, one appears very close to me. I cannot call them to me. I cannot predict when, where, or how they will appear. I cannot look for them—in fact, it seems the more actively I try to find them, the less often I see them. When I let go and least expect it—and most need my HP's reassurance—a raptor appears. The Lammergeyer flew as close to me as any bird had ever flown before or since. I did shoot a very brief video of it flying far away, but the video is unsuitable for posting because I was moving the camera too fast and the video is too jittery.

So, on my 60th birthday at 16,000 feet where it rarely flew, the Lammergeyer flew close to me, I believe, to deliver another one of my HP's many blessings for this day. I felt overwhelmed with gratitude for the gift and so amused at my HP's timing that I laughed out loud and jumped for joy.

This awesome view from Arrow Glacier at 16,000 feet shows Lava Tower (left), our camp (right), the trails' crossing, and the entire Shira plateau in the distance.

After we completed our "easy" 4-hour roundtrip hike and we ate lunch, my journal begins at 2:40 p.m. The journal entry begins with "Happy Birthday to me? Incredible! Crystal clear blue skies, cool to warm temps—800 feet tuff (sic) hike to Arrow Glacier and back to learn how to walk on scree with V-shaped short steps." Sort of walking like a duck.

Word to the Wise for Hiking

Learning to walk up steep scree slopes with V-shaped steps was one of the most important things I learned on this trip. I have used it many times on every steep climb I've made since then. Just more clear, simple direction from my human Higher Power, Samia, that protected me—when I followed direction.

After I wrote in my journal and warmed up in my tent, I was still feeling dejected about no one mentioning my birthday. I had seen Samia sneaking around tent to tent during the day. I had wondered what he was up to. Frankly, to see if I could pry any information out of someone, I wandered over to the mess tent about 6 p.m.

I met Angel Number 5 there. He was a short "tough guy" and member of the Maasai tribe. The crew called him the "Pastor" because he was a born-again Christian and liked to proselytize the crew. He had a mouthful of the most terrible teeth I have ever seen, and he was wearing very poor quality clothing, almost rags by our standards. But sitting on an upturned plastic pail by the tent flap, he had a beatific smile looking up at me when I walked in.

After I said hello, somehow we very quickly got into a serious conversation about carrying God's word. I think he asked me if I was a Christian or had been saved or something like that. I thought at first our talk was going to be a shallow bit of his trying to "save" me, but we delved deeper into the message than I had expected. Looks were deceiving because he was very smart and observant. His wife was a primary school teacher for the villages at the base of the mountain. He knew much more than the average 'tough guy' about the United States although he had never traveled there.

In a quiet way, I felt blessed by his presence, and our conversation kept me focused on God's presence and reminded me of my own true mission—to carry through all my actions the message of recovery to those who still suffer from their multiple addictions.

I felt that he saw in me something that either the other crew members did not recognize, or something about me that he did not recognize in the other members of our group.

By the way, there are no coincidences—just the Creator rearranging the flow of events to suit His/Her purposes of the moment. At that moment, the "Pastor"" was just the person I needed in my life to remind me of what is truly important—recovery and service. It was a delightful experience.

As we waited for dinner, the next blessing of the day slowly appeared—another glorious sunset. You cannot imagine the sharp clarity of the edges of the clouds and the brilliance of the sky's "palette" at 15,000 feet high in clear, cold air.

Surprise!!!

After everyone had piled into the tent, including Humphrey and Neal, we ate another amazing dinner. As soon as we finished, suddenly Chef Ely and his three cooks—Angels Numbers 6-9—came through the tent flap carrying—not a cake, but an enormous fruit salad because they remembered my allergy to wheat. Surprise!

The crew and my fellow climbers all sang "Happy Birthday" to me. Samia gave me a huge birthday card with everyone's signature, including all of the remaining crew and all of our group. My fellow group members were Angels 11—17 of the day this wonderful night!

Nicest of all, Samia and the crew gave me a gorgeous royal blue dashiki jacket with all of the colors of Africa sewn along the trim and hem. That jacket became the centerpiece of a queen-sized quilt I had made as soon as I returned to the U.S. The quilt was made from the dashiki, a dozen Kili and Tanzania tee shirts, and numerous small pieces of artwork on cloth or fabric with African motifs. My quilter, Kathleen Rice of www.summersisterdesigns.com, said herself that this quilt was a masterpiece. A black and white photo cannot do this magnificent quilt justice, so go to our website at www.recoveryfca.com to view the beautiful color photo.

We had a bit of a party—the crew did bring everyone else a small cake to share. We took some pictures—in which I show the widest, happiest smile I had had in years.

The Joke Was On Me!

Of course, since I had told the Wilderness Travel office about my special reason for climbing Kili, they had told Samia. Of course, he had set up the whole thing and asked everyone to keep quiet about the surprise. The crew truly honored me with their sincere kindness, close attention, and generosity of spirit. I cried—and as I wrote in my journal later that night, I continued to cry—tears of joy at the awesome power of God's love.

The Last Angel—and Another Miracle of the Day

Back in my tent after our surprise party, I was feeling overwhelmed and needed to share the enormity of all these gifts—the Lammergeyer "non-eagle," the party, the crew's generosity, the brilliant sunshine—with someone close to me, and I received another miracle. Lo and behold, my sat phone worked after it had been "on the fritz" all day, and I reached my best friend Alan the first time I dialed his number.

What made it even stranger, although Alan lives in Maryland, he was working that afternoon in New Bern, North Carolina on a special faux finish job. (His time was seven hours earlier than my time on Kili. Alan is a home remodeler and decorative artist.)

He just happened to hear his phone ring. I have no idea how or why my sat phone reached his cell phone except God's grace; cell coverage in that area of North Carolina often is not very good and my usually worthless sat phone worked. A major blessing of the day and a message that my HP gives me exactly what I need when I need it.

In the same way Alan has always been one of my human "angels" for more than 20 years, through my tears and gasps for breath, he listened quietly to my story as a great friend does.

His last word was meant seriously and it could not have been appropriate; he literally said: "Breathtaking!"

'Beyond the Beyond' Full Moon

After our call, I stepped out of my tent filled with joy. Just then the moon rose directly over the peak as full and as large as I had ever seen it before or have since. Beyond the beyond!

My journal notes written at 8:30 p.m.:

"Truly, truly the most wonderful, the very best birthday ever.

"An enormously, beyond-belief God—FMG—day of blessings.

"FMG—I will do whatever you want me to do because it will all (be) alright throughout—despite any difficulty—I am truly blessed beyond measure.

"I feel AND am wrapped in God's love.

"End of the Perfect Day: Time to take ibuprofen and pepto and lie down and rest before my first bathroom trip. COLD—but I am warmed by this truly blessed day. TY—FMG—TW, NM, BD!!" (Thank you—Father-Mother God—Thy Will, Not Mine, Be Done!!)"

Daily Meditations–More Higher Power Humor

Of course, the three meditations for June 25 that I read at about 4 a.m. were again snippets of my HP's perfect love and perfect timing.

The first one said that recovery promises a life beyond my wildest dreams, and my main job each day is to do the legwork to strengthen my recovery.

The second one encouraged me to experience the awe of my blessings so that I can worship my HP in deep wonder. It also stressed that I can turn my greatest weaknesses—my addictions—into my greatest strengths, if I am willing to overcome the crags and pitfalls of the metaphorical mountain of recovery. Ha! I was living numerous opportunities every day on a very real, and very high, mountain and exposing my greatest weaknesses.

The last one advised me to practice listening to what my guardian angel has to say and learn to feel its nearness to me. Again, ha! Only one guardian angel?! This day, I had almost 20 guardian angels and my HP, all blessing me in ways that I could not have ever imagined!

Step Seven for the Day

With the joy I felt most of the day today, I took Steps 1-3 and 11 easily because I received so many kind acts throughout the day from my "angels," and my HP gave me the great gifts of the vulture visit and the gorgeous weather. My Step 7 was to be as grateful as I could be for everything, including my character defects, and ask FMG to remove them, when He/She was ready to remove them. Not what, when, where, how, or why I wanted a specific defect removed, but according to my FMG's time, occasion, location, and reason.

I was going to find out early the next morning—just a few hours away when I finally slept—that either I was not ready to take the Sixth and Seventh Steps, or my FMG wanted me to keep a few of my worst shortcomings for a while longer. It turns out I got to keep them—whoopee!—for the moment so that my FMG could bring me a far better situation in a few days.

SATURDAY, JUNE 26

Day Eight, Step Eight

"I had to do something to fuck up the best birthday ever."
MY JOURNAL NOTE AFTER AN EMBARRASSING
LOSS OF MY TEMPER

"Lesson: Accept the help from experts when 'offered'—
take direction when your health and safety are at risk
and lose your ego. It's not about you/me—it's about letting
people who want to help, and know how, to do so."
MY JOURNAL NOTE ABOUT SAMIA'S "SUGGESTION" THAT I
GIVE UP MY DAYPACK AND LET HUMPHREY CARRY IT FOR ME.

Step Eight: Made a list of all persons we had harmed and became willing to make amends to them all.

This day demonstrated one of the simplest, but most overwhelming facts about my addiction, and I believe, those of all addicts: True joy terrifies the addict. My addict brain cannot stand it and will do its best—something cunning, baffling, powerful, subtle, and insidious—to sabotage happiness. I had had the best birthday ever just a few hours before. I had watched the most incredible moonset I have ever seen as the moon slowly rested behind Lava Tower just before dawn this morning.

Yet, within two hours, I had completely lost my temper and my composure. I had grossly insulted Rodrik. I had embarrassed myself in front of the entire crew and my fellow climbers. I had severely harmed all the good will and camaraderie among the group that my celebration had created.

Worst of all, at dinner this night, Samia called me out for my behavior and my deteriorating condition in front of the group. He gave me a choice: Give my backpack to Humphrey because I was no longer capable of making the summit if I carried that much weight, or be sent down the mountain.

By the end of this day, my Step Eight list was a very long one; I was feeling humiliated, embarrassed, ashamed, extremely sad, very sorry for my actions, and as willing as I could be to make amends to everyone I had insulted.

That's how my addict brain works. For my entire life and this morning, I had always done something—completely and utterly subconsciously—to sabotage my success. I had never allowed myself to reach my full potential as a writer and author. For 25 years, I had settled for low-paying work on little-known publications because I was always way behind on my bills and I needed the fast money they paid. Despite the 22 books I wrote that were published by small publishers, I screwed up or failed to deliver to major publishers several book manuscripts that promised to be strong-selling, breakthrough works. I never tried to write for serious, respected, high-paying magazines because I never believed I was good enough. I lied to publishers for whom I edited small newsletters about the quality and quantity of work I was doing for them. Lastly, I often cut corners and delivered inferior work to my best-paying customer.

Through all those years and so many mistakes, my HP constantly saved me from myself. Both because of and despite the actions of my first wife—also a freelance writer—we were able to be perceived as very successful. We made more than $850,000 in 11 years or about $80,000 a year during the 1980s when the average freelancer earned about $17,000 a year. Yet, we ended up more than $100,000 in debt when the marriage ended. It takes real "talent" and a serious addiction to compulsive debting and spending to do that.

This morning on Kilimanjaro, my addict brain exploded into rage over what appeared to others to be a trivial embarrassment. The incident triggered something so deep in my addict brain that to this day I still do not fully understand it. I have prayed, thought long and hard, talked with my closest friends, and had numerous therapy sessions about what I did this day.

The only reasonable explanation I can offer is the simple one: The lack of air at this altitude, my denial of my exhaustion, my lack of sleep and oxygen, and my unusual meals—and especially, my huge joy—pulled all of my subconscious triggers so that my addict brain could not stand how wonderful my birthday had been. It was kicking and screaming that I did not deserve it. All the joy and good will were not right, they were not "allowed." It overwhelmed my rational mind with the thought that I had to wreck it as soon as possible. In psych terms, it is called "homeostasis": My addict mind will drive me to do whatever it has to do to re-establish what it believes—falsely—is "right and normal." In my case, that is exactly what my addict brain did in spades this morning.

My Distasteful Behavior

Here's the distasteful story of what happened, how I reacted, why my Eighth Step list was so long, what Samia did at dinner, and how the day ended:

The situation began when I had another very fitful night with little sleep because I was still "flying high" from my birthday. It was very cold again, but at least it was calm with no wind. I woke up—for the last time—before sunrise, and I'm very grateful that I did. When I stepped out of my tent, I saw by Lava Tower the most incredible moonset I have ever seen. It was so beautiful that I should commission a painting of the scene by a fine artist. In an inky blue-black sky splattered with huge, twinkling stars, the full moon fit perfectly into the gap on the right side at the top of the Tower. The moon shone with a brilliant glow around it. Light blue-grey vapor trails of wispy clouds streamed upward from behind the Tower. They shone like negatives of the bright rays of an early morning sun that shoot over the horizon just before the sun rises.

As I just stood there transfixed in awe, I heard jackals barking far down the valley. One jackal was yipping and barking from far down the left side of the Tower; another replied with yips and barks from far down the right side. Samia told me later that either they were mates or pack members trying to find each other, or one was telling the other that it had made a kill and the other should join it to "have breakfast." At that moment, though, their calls were magical as I thought about their and my infinitesimal, but vital, role in the universe and in the Creator's grand scheme. I accepted with profound gratitude the blessing to be right there at that moment to hear their calls and see this once-in-a-lifetime sight.

Addiction Strikes Back

That was the best moment of this day. This day we were going to hike back up the 800 feet to Arrow Glacier and camp there for the night before we made the daunting 2,800-feet climb over the Great Breach Wall the next day. Only two more nights and we would be at the summit!

After the usual delicious breakfast in which I enjoyed the company and thanked everyone again for the party, I had to have a major bowel movement, to be polite. Others had to go to the latrine before me, so I had to wait for a while. I felt more and more uncomfortable like I was going to go in my pants. When my turn came, everyone else was beginning to get ready for the day's hike. My bathroom break took about 20 minutes. I felt embarrassed and annoyed with myself because I was taking so long and I was making noises I thought the others could hear.

When I emerged from the tiny 3 feet x 3 feet latrine tent carrying my toilet paper in my hand, it seemed like everyone—the crew and my group— turned and looked straight at me. I looked around quickly and saw that the crew was taking down all the tents. My group was all suited up, ready to go, and waiting for me. My 'tough guy' Rodrik was throwing all my stuff out of my tent onto the frozen ground. And I lost it—utterly.

I ran across the camp to my tent, yelling at Rodrik, "Don't do that! Please don't do that! Don't ever touch my stuff without my permission!" And I furiously began to pack my stuff "my way"—obsessive about the most trivial things to the end!

As I ran and screamed, Samia, the crew, and my group watched me with such incredulous looks on their faces that I will never forget them.

When I reached my tent, Rodrik jumped back and away from me. He looked at me with real fear because he knew that he could be fired if I was unhappy with him. I stormed around acting like a wild man and cursing under my breath for about 5 to 10 minutes. As I did this, the crew resumed taking the camp down, but watched me out of the corner of their eyes. My group turned away in embarrassment. Rodrik just stood there about 15-20 feet away, bewildered by my attack.

When I began to calm down, Samia came to me and told me that we were behind schedule so the rest of the group was going to start hiking. As he turned away, I realized the enormity of my mistake, so I stopped him and apologized to Rodrik and him and took full responsibility for my actions.

Samia didn't say much, but he told me Rodrik would stay and hike with me so that I could catch up with the group.

By the time I was ready to go, the group was about 15 minutes ahead of us. The crew was just about ready to start their hike as well.

My Well-Deserved Comeuppance

I got my well-deserved comeuppance as Rodrik, carrying my 50-pound duffel bag on his back, started walking at his regular pace—four to five times faster than I had been walking for days. Going up the steep trail was very strenuous; we were moving fast and the weather was much colder, cloudier, and windier than during our "test hike" the day before. But I kept my mouth shut, I took my medicine, and I kept up with him until we caught up with the group.

Before Rodrik left to join the rest of the crew, I apologized again and thanked him for helping me catch up. He graciously accepted my apology, a kind act that at the time I did not believe I deserved.

At least I had learned something from the hike the day before; I put my windbreaker underneath my vest and heavy coat, I tied my hat tightly. My journal notes from this day said: "I'm educable—eventually."

This morning, my HP had created an opportunity for me to continue to feel my joy, laugh off the situation, cooperate with others, practice patience with myself, and avoid my character defects. But from my deep shame about my toilet habits, my overly sensitive triggers, my physical exhaustion, and a heightened sense of embarrassment, my addict brain sprang out like a crazed lion, and my rational brain took too long to reassert control of my emotions.

It may seem like I am trying to "blame" my addict brain and let my "real self" off the hook. Far from it. My addict brain, my triggers, my rational brain, my emotions, my responses are all part of who I am. The total "I," the complete Robert P., am all of these and more.

Mess at Arrow Glacier Camp

After I joined the others, I followed last in line with the group up to Arrow Glacier. Even on this short hike, the crew had run by us and were pitching the tents and preparing lunch when we arrived. I am sorry to say that at that time, Arrow Glacier Camp was in terrible condition. In one of the most beautiful spots in the world, trash was strewn everywhere, and other climbers had damaged or destroyed many of the on-site latrines. Four-feet- to eight-feet-long boards with four- to six-inch nails sticking out of them were scattered about and made it dangerous to walk around.

I felt sad and angry because all of the other camp sites were well maintained. I asked Samia about these sad conditions. He told me that the national park would occasionally hire local crews to clean the camps, but the tour groups were primarily responsible for keeping the campsites clean. Clearly, no one had cleaned this camp in quite a while.

It was sad because from that location, I could see the entire vista of the last four days of our climb: all of the Shira Ridge 4,000 to 5,000 feet below, westward past Lava Tower across the entire Shira Plateau, and down the Barranco Valley in front of us. When we arrived, the cloud bank at the edge of the Ridge covered the view from the west to the northeast down the mountain.

Another Higher Power Gift

As I again watched the clouds roll up the Shira Ridge and turn back like the reverse ocean waves, the wind picked up just enough. The clouds parted for just a moment. Suddenly, I had a "God's eye" view all the way to the base of the mountain—16,000 feet—more than 3 miles straight down—to the plains below. I felt like a soaring eagle or an angel—not exactly one with "white wings" today. The glimpse lasted just a moment, and then the clouds closed in and many kinds of wave-shaped clouds rolled across the horizon. To this day, I remember that moment as clearly as if I were still standing there.

Sticking out of the clouds to the west was the peak of Mt. Meru, Kili's overshadowed companion at 15,000 feet. Meru, the active volcano 43 miles west of Kilimanjaro, was always visible through the clouds after we reached Lava Tower. But we never had a clear day where we could see all of it from Kili. Meru is a lot like Mt. St. Helens in Washington State in that its eastern face was blown off in a violent blast about 8,000 years ago. Mt. Meru had a minor eruption in 1910, and numerous small cones and craters show relatively recent volcanic action. It forms the heart of Arusha National Park (remember Kili is in its own National Park). Its slopes rise above the savanna, and the bare peak juts above a lush montane forest from about 6,000 feet to 12,000 feet. The forest is home to many species of flora and fauna, including 400 species of birds as well as monkeys and leopards. Maybe that's where Hemingway saw his frozen one!

I give these details because for the rest of our hike, the peak of Mt. Meru and its location west of Kili constantly offered an incredible sight, especially on the morning we reached the summit two days from now.

Crash Helmets and Glare Goggles–Great Breach Wall Prep

After this "angelic/eagle-eyed" experience, I was quickly brought crashing down to earth after lunch. My long Step Eight list included everyone on the crew and everyone in my group. At lunch, I had apologized to everyone in my group for my behavior. They all assured me in what seemed like understanding tones that it was okay. However, I could tell that my second (or third or fourth?) major transgression had destroyed their confidence in me. I knew my simple Ninth Step apology was not going to be enough. I knew I had to make a living amends for the rest of the trip and change my behavior, act politely, be a positive contributor, and hold my temper no matter how exhausted or irritated or triggered I felt. As to how it turned out, I claim only progress and willingness to correct my mistakes, not perfection.

After lunch, Samia had us bring out all the clothing and equipment we planned to wear or carry to the summit. He gave us a major "prep" session for ascending the Great Breach Wall. He warned us that climbing the Wall was going to be the most physically demanding 7 to 9 hours of our lives. It will be very strenuous—a 2,800 feet elevation gain with less and less air with every step.

I agreed with Samia. This climb will be the most difficult feat I have ever attempted. For the past 40 years, my most strenuous activity had been a short hike–3 or 4 hours–from about 9,000 feet to about 12,500 feet on a beautiful, sunny, cool July day in the Rocky Mountains outside Durango, Colorado. I had never had any serious altitude sickness. I had had plenty of rest and healthy food before I made any other climb anywhere. Better still, on all my other hikes, I knew I could turn around at any moment and wander back down to my car easily and safely. At the end of each of these hikes, I always had a warm, cozy home or timeshare condo, a hot shower, a good meal, and a warm bed waiting for me.

Here on Kili, unless I became very ill or fell, I had no chance to turn back. At best, I had at least two more days of tough descent and rough camping to reach real safety.

My journal notes summed up my feelings quite well: "? Scared – Oh Shit! Yes & No. Daunted at the prospect. Reasonably apprehensive. Concerned [because] not as well prepared as I thought I was. Confident FMG will carry—or the crew will help me–push, pull, lead, and follow me up to the rim."

Samia's Plan to Breach the Wall

Here's Samia's plan: We will start climbing at 5 a.m. in the dark after a quick breakfast of hot carbohydrates and tea at 4:30 a.m. We will climb 1,300 feet of dangerous scree slope in the dark and early morning from about 5 a.m. to 7:30 am, that is, from 16,000 feet to 17,300 feet. We will take water and rest breaks every hour.

The scree slope trail is very narrow. I am not kidding: It is often no more than half a boot wide–six inches narrow at most–along the side of a very long slope of loose gravel, small rocks, and large boulders. If I slip and fall, I could roll for hundreds of feet practically straight down before I hit bottom—unless I get "lucky" and slam into a huge volcanic rock boulder on the way down.

After we cross the scree slope, we will turn up a virtually vertical trail and climb from 17,300 feet to 18,800 feet—1,500 feet of scrambling over rocks and "stair climbing," sometimes on hands and knees. Each stair step will be a different height and width; many stones will be loose, although they will look solid. Each step will put serious stress on our calves, our knees, and our quadriceps.

When he asked us if we had anything to ask or say, I told Samia that if I had to crawl and hug the mountain, then I would do it. I will do what it takes to make it safely and healthily. I had a strong willingness despite all of my missteps and fears.

When we reach the edge of the Wall, we will climb a mercifully short expanse of rock through a gap and find ourselves on a small glacial plain at 18,800 feet where we will camp for the night. In the middle of this plain is the fast-disappearing Furtwangler Glacier. Toward the northeast, the 400-feet high active caldera called the Reusch Crater at the Kibo cone has smelly, smoking fumaroles, and sulfur deposits around its edge.

If you aren't yet convinced this climb was going to be strenuous and dangerous, the clincher is this: At the end of the briefing, Samia outfitted each of us with a hard, plastic crash helmet. I would need to wear my thinner balaclava (ski mask) under it rather than the thicker, warmer one I had been wearing for the past several days. When we start in the dark, we also have to wear our headlamps over our crash helmets so we can see the person's feet in front of us and follow the "trail," such as it will be. It is more like a thin line of worn rock along the side of a half-mile-long rock slide!

After the briefing, Samia instructed us to put on all of the clothes we planned to wear to scale the Wall. We did so and he did a "gear check" of the other seven climbers. He pulled on backpack straps, checked layers of clothes, and made sure we had the sun goggles they had given us. If something was not to his liking, he told the person to change it.

Samia Calls Me Out and I Surrender to My HPs

Then, it was my turn. In front of everyone, Samia told me that I was the least capable because I have vertigo and balance issues. He could tell I had become exhausted because I was not getting much sleep. He knew because he had asked me every morning how much sleep I had the night before; I was honest with him that I was sleeping fitfully and getting only 2 or 3 hours sleep most nights. Of course, my outburst that morning had "sealed the deal" that I was not capable of making it on my own.

Samia politely explained that I had a choice: Humphrey would carry my daypack with my three bottles of water and backup clothes, or I was going down the mountain. I had a relatively mild ego and shame attack, but I kept my mouth shut while I considered my choices for a moment.

I looked him in the eye and said, "The goal is to get to the top happy, healthy, and safe." I gratefully, if somewhat less than graciously, accepted his offer to help. I did not like it at all; I felt like a weakling and very frustrated that I was not good enough to make it on my own. I resented that I had spent thousands of dollars for two trainers for more than a year to get me into shape. I also blamed myself because I had had two minor accidents that hurt my left foot and right leg, separately, so I had missed several months of serious training during that year, especially the last six weeks before the trip.

Both of those "accidents," I believe, again show the insidiousness of my self-sabotage disorder—or whatever you want to call the self-destruct button. Let me preface by saying I virtually never have accidents where I hurt myself physically. My last serious accident happened in the early 1990s; I cracked my right ankle playing adult volleyball and I was on crutches for a month. So, nothing serious had happened for many, many years before I began training for Kili.

But before my Kili trek, I had two accidents in less than a year, either of which would have killed my chance to climb the mountain if it had been just a little bit worse than it was. I believe deep in my soul that my HP wanted me to succeed, so He/She ensured that the accidents were relatively minor. They certainly got my attention about doing stupid things, a lesson I wish I had remembered more often while I was climbing Kili.

In the first accident, I was walking around the corner of my kitchen in slick socks on a Friday night as I was getting dressed to go swing dancing. As I turned the corner, I slipped and somehow my left foot slid *under* the sharp edge of the refrigerator and sliced a deep gash between my left big toe and the second toe. I started bleeding like crazy, but since I was in the kitchen, I was able to crawl to the pantry and get a plastic bag. I wrapped my foot in a dish towel and put the plastic bag around it. I crawled on the floor into the living room where I found my cell phone and called 911.

Fortunately, the ambulance was literally less than a minute away in a fire-house two blocks down the street. They arrived quickly, and I crawled over to the front door to let them in. They looked at my foot, did their EMT thing, put me on a stretcher and into in the ambulance, and got me to my local hospital in less than 15 minutes.

The emergency room was not crowded so they brought me in and checked out my foot. They took X-rays and found nothing was broken. A doctor sewed about half a dozen stitches to close the wound.

Most importantly, he said that I was very lucky: If the cut had been just one quarter of an inch deeper, it would have severed the ligament connecting the toes to the rest of my foot. I would have had to have had an operation to fix it. I would have been out of training for months after that.

I don't believe in luck, but I do believe in blessings and messages. That gift of a one-quarter of an inch was a blessing. The message: Don't run around the house in slick socks on slick floors without paying attention! I still have the minor scar between my toes that reminds me of this lesson every day.

Even with my good fortune, I was off my feet and on crutches for a week, and I could not run or dance for about a month. The enforced idleness severely curbed my effort to get into shape during the early stage of my prep for my climb. I could sit and do floor exercises and lift weights, so I did what I could, but my leg strength and stamina suffered.

The second accident happened six weeks before my odyssey began. I was in the gym on a cross-training machine, warming up to work out with my trainer. The machines were very close to each other in a small space, and the ones to each side of me were being used. When I finished my warm-up, rather than step off to the side as I had done dozens of times, I stepped off toward the back into a narrow space between the machine and a metal railing. As I put my right leg down, the end of the large right pedal swung back and down, scrapping a large chunk of skin (maybe 4 inches by 3 inches) from my right shin.

I looked down and saw that it was only a large scrape that did not reach the shin bone. It did not even bleed much. But I was literally less than an eighth of an inch away from having either the skin ripped down to the bone or a broken shin bone. I immediately limped over to my trainer who put a temporary bandage on it. The next day, I saw my doctor who told me I had to let it heal and could not run or dance on it for at least several weeks. I could walk, gingerly for about a week, and then slowly, but normally. So, for the last six weeks before my trip, just when I had started jogging several miles every two days and was focused on boosting my stamina, I hurt myself again.

Again, I was blessed that I had not injured myself so badly that I had to cancel my trip. If I had broken my shin bone, I wasn't getting close to Kilimanjaro for my 60th birthday. Again, I have a minor scar that will always remind me to look before I step and then step in the right direction.

Deciding What Is Truly Important

With these setbacks flashing through my memory—and Samia's polite, but firm ultimatum—I decided that I did not care that I felt somewhat humiliated and "lesser than." What was important was that I was going to finish this trek and reach the summit as long as I did not have severe altitude sickness. As long as I could put one foot in front of the other "pole, pole," I was going to reach the top. Remember that my favorite Chinese fortune cookie says, "Fall down seven times, get up eighth time." So I did, and I made the right choice by surrendering to the greater wisdom and will of my human Higher Powers.

My Gear List for Breaching the Wall

After our preparation, we ate a quick dinner at 5 p.m. and everyone else went to their tents and tried to go to sleep at 6 p.m. while the sun was still up. Instead, I first wandered around the camp wearing the goggles and helmet to get a feel for them. I learned I must use them, but I will have to wear my regular eyeglasses under the goggles so I can see anything at all. I am very nearsighted.

In my tent, feeling bad about giving my daypack to Humphrey, I repacked everything and put as much as I could into my duffel for Rodrik or in the pockets of my "Bwana man" vest to help lighten Humphrey's load. All I had to carry was my two cameras strapped across my chest like bandoliers and my walking sticks.

To give you an idea of what it was going to take to master the Great Breach Wall, here is my gear list for the ascent. It includes about twice as many clothes as I had been wearing plus the crash gear:

- Crash helmet
- Headlamp
- Eye-covering goggles
- Heavy wool socks and nylon liners
- High-top boots
- Gaiters to cover my shoe tops and keep sand and gravel out of my shoes
- Long john pants
- Heavy rainproof pants
- Long john top
- Thin, but incredibly warm LL Bean jacket
- "Bwana man" multi-pocket vest
- Goretex outer shell jacket
- Heavy waterproof gloves and glove liners
- Spares that Humphrey carried in my daypack

- Hiking pants
- Fleece jacket
- Rainproof windbreaker
- Bandanna
- Extra glove liners

Unpleasant Portents

Two unpleasant portents clouded this already difficult day. First, I am not a fan of ravens; I think they are sly, cunning birds that steal from other birds, eat their eggs, and do their best to bully everything that flies near them. In fact, their flocks are called either "an unkindness" or "a conspiracy," according to www.audubonbirdbanding.org. In my opinion, those names are very appropriate as a group of crows, the ravens' thieving cousins, is called a "murder."

On Kili and throughout the area, "unkindnesses" of huge, black-and-white winged ravens boldly scavenged climbers' camp sites. At our sites, during and after every meal, they zoomed in and stalked around our food containers and trash sites. Especially evil sounding was the noise their wings made in flight: This unique, harsh sound was a deep, syncopated "wuff, wuff, wuff" that was like the sound of a fast-moving freight train as it nears, passes by, and rushes away. The ravens and their wing noises felt evil and creepy. Yuck!

An "unkindness" of ravens scavenges our camp site as two tough guys clean our breakfast dishes and cooking utensils.

Furthermore, it was windy all day, the windiest it had been the entire trek. As soon as I climbed into my tent after dinner, the wind began to howl and buffet (no pun intended) my tent. After the wind almost flipped it—and me!—over, I had to scramble and stuff all of my gear, except what I was sleeping in, around the edges of the tent to weigh down the sides. My evening journal notes described the howling winds; then, after I wrote my "loooonnnggggg" gear list, I wrote hopefully, but very prematurely: "OH—wind has died down a bit – TY, FMG – Oh well, spoke too soon – a wee respite – now blowing but not quite as ferociously or so I pray."

In fact, the wind howled off and on all night, and I could hear all of the tents flapping and shaking. I was very nervous about my tent either being blown down on top of me or being blown away, so of course, I did not get much sleep on the night I needed it most.

Little Sleep, Lots of Insight

As the wind howled outside, my thoughts swirled inside my head as I found it very difficult to sleep, despite my open sleeping bag, three layers of heavy fleece, and three heavy layers on my feet. The temperature plunged into the single digits with below-zero wind chills. I probably thought too much and wrote notes in my journal for too long. I had my headlamp turned on red because my eyes were tired and dry.

This night was the first time I thought about writing this book, though almost all of my thinking was offhand: "Oh yeah, it might be a good idea to write a book about all this. We're going through some amazing experiences, and every one of them seems to relate to my recovery and 12 Step work."

I prayed and thought a lot about mostly random ideas. I asked my HP for direction, and I gave thanks for my relatively good health and for the compassion Samia showed me this day.

Whether it was my exhaustion, the howling wind, or true spiritual insight from my guardian angel, I heard this message from over my right shoulder—where my guardian angel always sits: The 12 Step mission to carry the message is my mission. Recovering addicts are servants, stewards, and fellow sufferers, not priests, preachers, popes, imams, or other religious "authority figures" who believe that only they know the right path. I decided that when I come down the mountain, I need to write about my experiences and share them with others. Not because I am so "special," but because this adventure captures the essence of the challenges and triumphs of living the 12 Step Way of Life that everyone who chooses recovery must face one day at a time.

More Meditation "Humor"

There must be a mischievous spirit that aligns the daily meditations with my actions. Here is how very apt each one was again: The first advised me to stop lurching around in the dark and allow the light to come. It also asked what I needed to put down on paper, assuring me that I could look in my heart without fear and write down what I found. Direct inspiration to tell this story, though I didn't recognize it at the time.

The second told me not to take action at the wrong time, to face my shortcomings, and accept my addiction as the incurable disease it is. It also advised me to not charge into any situation on my own. The third advised me to have a special place to write, meditate, pray, and get to know my guardian angel better. Well, by the end of this day, I had a new human 'guardian angel,' Humphrey who carried my daypack. For days, the "gift" of a freezing cold, uncomfortable tent had been evoking my middle-of-the-night written ramblings that shaped this book. More Higher Power humor.

Samia said the next morning that the wind had often gusted at least 40 miles per hour, but he "reassured" us by saying how fortunate we were: He had experienced winds of 50 to 60 miles an hour or higher, tents had been blown down on many occasions, and one time, they had awakened to find two feet of snow covering this campsite. I can't imagine how they climbed the Great Breach Wall that day!

Although my physical health was good, and I was eating well, obviously my lack of sleep and the altitude had taken a toll on my emotional health and my stamina. My pulse in the morning was 72 and 69 in the evening. My oxygen rate was 93 in the morning and 89 in the afternoon. But I was exhausted, emotionally and mentally.

In fact, I was in fairly good physical shape compared to most of the rest of the group. Dr. Matt had a bad cough and diarrhea; Jason continued to feel miserable with nausea and barely ate anything; Scott was taking multiple pills for respiratory trouble; Heinrich, who had refused to take Diamox, had begun to suffer from climbing too much altitude without it and had severe headaches and nausea; he wisely started taking the pills at this camp. Annie and Felicia were tired, but seemed to be doing okay. Although I didn't know it then, Etienne was a different matter. As I said, there are no happy faces above 15,000 feet.

Recovery Lessons from This Day

As you can tell, I learned far more about myself this day than I either expected or particularly cared to learn; I learned how much shame I felt about normal bodily processes, how I truly hate to be embarrassed in front of others, and how fragile my sanity and serenity remain even after all these years in recovery.

I also learned that by taking Steps 8 and 9, I am willing to take responsibility for my mistakes quickly, apologize, and determine the most appropriate amends I can make to everyone I have harmed. I also prayed more earnestly than ever before, taking Step 7 and asking my HP to remove my shortcomings. Most importantly, when I admitted my weakness and powerlessness to Samia and before the entire group, I gained the emotional support and physical strength I needed to reach the summit.

A brief summary of my lessons learned this day—with many more to come:

- Accept help from the experts when "offered"—admit I am powerless.
- Take direction when my health and safety are at risk.
- Lose my ego—it's not about you or me; it's about letting people who want to help, and know how, to do so.
- I never know from what source or what direction my FMG will send good advice and angelic help.
  - In my recovery, the help I have received when I most needed it has come from both expected and unlikely angels—ranging from sponsors, respected elders, close friends, and credible speakers to even the mouths of children, newcomers, and many people I honestly do not like. I need to listen to everyone because I never know when I am going to hear exactly the message I need.
- To conquer the toughest challenges, obtain and use the best tools, equipment, and support.
- Going "pole, pole"—slowly, slowly—multiples my power.
- Humility is good. And so it would prove to be.

SUNDAY, JUNE 27

Day Nine, Step Nine

"Horrifically Difficult Day"
MY FIRST JOURNAL ENTRY AFTER I CLIMBED 2,800 FEET
UP AND OVER THE GREAT BREACH WALL AND 400 MORE
FEET TO THE RIM OF REUSCH CRATER AND THE ASH PIT

Step Nine: Made direct amends to such people wherever possible, except when to do so would injure them or others.

Altitude Sickness Is an Equal Opportunity Destroyer

The day began with very bad news about Etienne. During the middle of the night, her tent mate Felicia had gotten up and awakened Samia. She told him that Etienne was getting up and going outside and coming back throughout the night. She said she was afraid Etienne had been getting more and more ill for the past two days.

Felicia was right: Etienne had reached second stage altitude sickness—diarrhea, vomiting, severe nausea, serious headaches, and loss of appetite. Yet, she was trying to hide it from Samia because we were so close to the top and she wanted to reach the summit so badly. A serious mistake. Here's why:

Altitude (or mountain) sickness (AMS) does not care who you are, how old you are, what kind of physical shape you are in, or much of anything else. It can strike anyone at any time. It has three stages: First, you get headaches and nausea and feel miserable. Like me, you may not sleep well. Most people do experience these symptoms for a day or two during any climb to an altitude past 6,000 feet, but their bodies adjust and they feel well enough to keep going.

That is why we have stopped for two full days to acclimatize to the increasing altitude—19,343 feet is quite different from 10,000 feet. Recall that this day at 16,000 feet, we were breathing about 60 percent of the air we had at sea level. At the peak, we will be breathing less than half the air we could breathe at sea level.

Etienne was a thin, fit, long distance runner who lived at 8,500 feet and regularly ran at 11,000 feet. The perfect candidate to do Kilimanjaro, one would think. But she hid her first stage symptoms that became progressively worse. She began to develop the classic second stage symptoms at 15,000 feet and got worse as she climbed to 16,000 feet. The second stage is the beginning of a deadly illness because in the third stage, you can develop edema of the lungs and/or brain—that is, your lungs and/or your brain begin to swell and bleed. Unless you move very quickly to go down the mountain to a lower altitude—even from 16,000 feet to 10,000 feet was enough—you can die a very painful death.

As they always do for these emergencies, Samia and the crew had brought with them what is called a **Gamow bag** (pronounced Gam-Off). Named for its inventor, Dr. Igor Gamow, it is an inflatable pressure bag large enough to accommodate a person inside. You put a sick climber inside the bag: you seal it, pressurize it with valves set to a target pressure, and inflate it with a foot pump attached to an oxygen tank. In just a few minutes, the "altitude" the person inside experiences can be reduced between 3,000 and 9,700 feet; the reduction varies with your elevation when you put the person in the bag. High-altitude trekking companies use the bag to treat severe cases of altitude sickness, high-altitude cerebral edema, and high-altitude pulmonary edema, according to www.altitude.org.

On Kilimanjaro, if you became ill above 12,500 feet where the rescue road ended, or like us, were on the other side of the mountain, you would be put in the bag and the crew would put you on a one-wheeled "gurney." Then, two of them would roll you down the mountain as fast as they could to the end of the road where an ambulance or truck could carry you to the nearest clinic.

The "gurney" was, believe it or not, an old World War II-era flat bedspring with metal railings on all four sides. The "gurney" was attached to a motorcycle wheel. The wheel was fixed to the middle of the gurney so two tough guys could easily balance the person in the bag.

This gurney—an old hospital flat spring bed attached to a motorcycle tire—is how a victim of severe altitude sickness is rolled down the mountain in a Gamow bag.

Fortunately, Samia determined that Etienne was still able to walk. At breakfast—at 4:30 a.m. in the dark—he made her eat a small amount and drink hot tea. He told us that at sunrise, assistant team leader Neal, who was feeling fairly badly himself, would walk her down the mountain. We would meet them in two days at Mweka camp at 10,170 feet.

Of course, we all felt sad and disappointed for her, but also glad because she could have gotten very ill and died; if she had come down with third stage AMS and survived, she could have had permanent brain and/or lung damage.

As selfish as it may seem, when I heard she was very ill and going down the mountain, I was glad I was willing to let Humphrey carry my daypack for me. I prayed for Etienne and her safety for the next two days until we found her safe and well at Mweka Camp at 10,170 feet.

Lesson Learned: AMS is an equal opportunity destroyer of dreams. I won't name any names in this book, but if you research AMS and Kilimanjaro on the Internet, you'll find world-famous athletes who did not make it to the top. Remember, too, that fewer than half of the 20,000 "normal" people a year who begin the climb reach the summit. Not many fail from serious AMS, but most suffer from enough symptoms, such as fatigue, stress, nausea, severe headaches, diarrhea, and faltering courage, that they turn back. Etienne had the courage, but her body just would not cooperate.

A Dangerous Day Measured in Boot Widths

The 2,800-foot climb over the Great Breach Wall today onto the Furtwangler Glacier plateau at 18,800 feet was exactly as Samia had described it; it was measured in boot widths. The "trail" up—at angles as sharp as 75 degrees—was often only half a boot wide. I literally climbed step by step on the edge of my boot for hundreds of feet. We had to put one boot at a time into a space wide enough only for half the boot to fit. We stepped "pole, pole" along the very narrow trail with drops of hundreds of feet down steep slopes on at least one side, sometimes on both sides. None of the trail was ever more than 3 boots wide, and we had to do serious rock scrambling. Several times, I had to walk on all fours like a crab, fumbling ahead as my "beloved" walking sticks flailed behind my arms.

We began at 5 a.m. after a light breakfast of half a bowl of oatmeal and hot tea. We climbed with three hours of the magnificent shine of a full moon. The glorious moon set in the west just as a glorious sunrise began in the east. We watched Kili's shadow pass over Mt. Meru 43 miles away.

Two More Mistakes from Fear

The day was, as Samia promised, the most strenuous of my adult life. We actually completed the climb in 7 hours, 400 feet of elevation an hour. We moved quickly, considering the treacherous terrain. Eight to nine hours is the average, Samia said. All of us made it safely, but two times my fear got the best of me and I lost my temper with Humphrey.

After Etienne's troubles, I had gladly let Humphrey take my daypack after breakfast. My first frightening, unfortunate moment with Humphrey happened when we were doing serious "stair" climbing up a very steep part of the trail. Without warning me, he tried to grab my arm when he thought I was losing my balance. I wasn't; I was just turning my body to look at the scene in the morning sunlight.

I was taken by surprise: Rather than simply accept his grip, I yelled at Humphrey. I was frightened by his sudden movement and a strong fear of falling—a fall he thought he was helping me to avoid.

The second time, at about 17,500 feet or more, I was crab crawling over a large, long, slick, bare boulder with no handholds or foot holds. Just plain rock at a steep angle. I was crawling slowly, dragging my climbing sticks behind me when Humphrey stood over me and told me to stand up and walk. Although he appeared to be trying to encourage me, I felt frightened and my vertigo felt severe, so I refused to stand. I told him that if I had to crawl to make it, I would, so I did. Samia heard the commotion, walked back down the trail to us, checked me out, and told Humphrey to let me do it my way.

My vertigo had kicked in because there were sheer drops on both sides. I could see all the way down to Lava Tower some 2,500 feet below. I felt that if I had tried to stand up, I would have fallen backward off that rock and rolled all the way back down to the Tower. Fear of death was a strong motivator for me to crawl up that rock on my hands and knees, although everyone else was able to walk.

By the way, as the seven of us struggled up this steep climb, the tough guys, including my 5-feet 5-inch tall Rodrik, raced past us. We had to step gingerly a foot or two off the trail to let them pass. I have photos and video of them with their 50-pound packs, tent poles, tent bundles, food and water containers, and latrines on their backs. They climbed past us at an angle that was virtually vertical to me. They climbed without complaint and with a strength and nimbleness I watched with gratitude and awe.

Our "tough guys," carrying 50 pounds each, run past me on the steepest part of the difficult trail to the Great Breach Wall, a few hundred feet farther up.

Practiced Step Nine with Humphrey

After the second incident, the rest of this horrific climb passed quickly. In mid-afternoon, I eased through a gap at the top of the Breach Wall ridge and saw in front of me the 70-feet-tall Furtwangler Glacier and the real summit, called Uhuru, for the first time. To my left, I saw the 400-foot-high, wide-open Reusch Crater where the dormant volcano still boils with "live" lava 1,700 feet below the surface. Of course, on the plateau below, the tough guys were setting up our campsite, and the smoke was rising from the cook tent as the chefs began to prepare our dinner. Bless them because I was starved by that time!

After we climbed down the short ridge to the plain, I did the 9th Step with Humphrey in front of the team leaders and our group. I apologized for my outbursts and thanked him for carrying my pack. I acknowledged that without his help, I could not have made it this far. He graciously accepted my apology. I made a commitment to him to understand that he only wanted to help me, and I would listen to and watch what he was trying to do for me before I reacted. I also asked for his forgiveness, which he seemed reluctant to give at that moment as he didn't say he forgave me.

I also felt badly because the repercussions of my losing my temper were weighing heavily on me. What I perceived as my character defects seemed to be popping out all too often. I was certainly tired of them. It appeared everyone else was distancing themselves from me, so I felt more and more isolated. My apologies clearly were not going to be taken seriously as I continued to lose my temper so soon after my previous outburst, apologies, and amends. I was having trouble keeping the promises I had made in my previous Ninth Step amends.

Rapidly Shrinking Glaciers

After my apology and amends before the group, I walked around the plateau and the Furtwangler Glacier. This glacier and all of the glaciers and ice fields on Kilimanjaro have been shrinking rapidly for the past 160 years or more, at least since the first Western observations in the 1850s.

I observed this rapid melting for myself. As I prepared for this trek, I bought and viewed a documentary video made in 1996, more than 14 years before I made my climb.

By the way, although they were not given credit during the video, Wilderness Travel was the organizer and Samia was the team leader for the

12 climbers featured in the video. I would not have known had I not remembered that the tents in the video were exactly like the ones we were using. I confirmed this fact with Samia.

In any case, during just these 14 years, a blink of an eye in geological terms, the Furtwangler had shrunk in half. In the video, it was a huge, solid mass that covered most of the plateau. This day, only two large pieces remained and I easily walked between them. Very little ice was left on the plain; this day it was almost all rocks and lava ash and dirt. Although Furtwangler was still 50 to 70 feet high, Samia said the ice was melting quickly on the entire north side and without a profound change, it would be gone in 5 to 10 years. The last report I read confirmed that the shrinking has continued unabated on both the north and west sides of the peak. The ice fields and glaciers on the south side remain fairly thick and contiguous, but they, too, are melting and threatened.

Rodrik, about 5 feet 5 inches tall, stands in front of the 70-feet-tall Furtwangler Glacier. It had melted in half at the time and has continued to melt rapidly since.

Scientific Disagreement on Glacier Melt Impact

There is an active argument among scientists about whether or not the glacial melting could have a severe impact on the plants and animals on the mountain and especially on the livelihood of the villagers living on the mountainside and at its base. The ice and snow are supposed to build up during the winter and release melt water slowly during the summer. If the snow is inadequate, less water flows down the mountain streams during the spring and summer to nourish the villagers' crops and to maintain the lush rain forest for the wild animals and plant life. If it rains during the winter and does not freeze, the water runs down the mountain when it is still too cold to grow crops and disperses in the ground or runs off into creeks and rivers beneath the mountain.

Whatever the cause, the fabled snows of Kilimanjaro may disappear during the next half century or sooner. Lonnie Thompson, a world-famous paleoclimatologist and Distinguished University Professor in the School of Earth Sciences at The Ohio State University, believes the glaciers will be gone by 2021. He may be right. (Source: https://en.wikipedia.org/wiki/Lonnie_Thompson)

The contrary, and more optimistic, view, is that the snow and glacial ice melt from Kili is not the primary source of water for the villagers' crops. The montane rain forest is the primary source, according to Wikipedia. (Source: https://en.wikipedia.org/wiki/Mount_Kilimanjaro)

A letter from five scientists to the *Environmental Development 6* (2013) journal stated that if you melted all the glaciers on Kilimanjaro at the same time and poured the water across the mountain, it would amount to no more than about 4 inches deep (13 mm). That's about the same amount that often falls on one day during the rainy seasons from March to May and in November. Instead, these five said, the primary water source is the rain that falls in the montane forest.

(Source:http://lindseynicholson.org/wp-content/uploads/2011/07/Moelg-et--al.-2013.pdf)

The greatest threat to the farmers, they assert, is the continuing clearing of the forest they do to make room for more crops. From my observations, illegal logging and cropland creeping up the mountainside make the farmers themselves their own worst enemies. The same letter to the editor noted that the research shows increased forest clearing has reduced the amount of annual rainfall, so the scientists say protecting the forest is critical to protecting the entire area's water supply. But they also stress that even if the glaciers melt, it will still snow on Kilimanjaro, and the amount and timing of the annual snow melt will depend on local weather conditions.

Regardless of the scientific arguments, the ultimate outcome could mean either a continued good life for farmers next to Kili, the tragedy of failed crops and greater hunger, or major migrations away from Kili.

A Dream Close Enough to Coming True

I felt very concerned about the situation, so I was determined this day to make the most of this unique situation and do my best to fulfill one of my Kili dreams. On another Kili video I watched, I saw two scientists dash down 400 feet from the Kibo Cone at the top of the Reusch Crater to the edge of the Ash Pit—the open crater hole. On the video, they stumbled and careened down the ashy scree to the edge of the crater, but it looked like they had a great time. Since I watched that documentary, I, too, had wanted to get to the edge of the hole and look down; before I began my research for this adventure, I had not known Kili still had an active crater and fumaroles emitting sulfur fumes. But the climb back up to the top of the crater was an additional steep 400 feet on loose scree to the rim at 19,200 feet high in the bright mid-afternoon sun after our very strenuous seven-hour-long breach of the Wall.

As soon as we all got to the campsite, Samia pointed out the crater and asked if anyone wanted to climb it and go into the crater. Although I was very cold and very tired, I immediately said yes; no one else did. They all wanted to crawl into their tents and rest. I had my small dream and a chance to fulfill it, so I volunteered and Samia and Rodrik escorted me to the top of the crater.

By the time we reached the top, I was huffing and puffing very hard. Before I started down the inside of the crater, I used the 20X zoom lens on my video camera to get close-up views of the crater, the smoking fumaroles, the yellow sulfur deposits, and the layers of lava and ash build-up around the edge.

Oh yeh, just as I learned when I visited the Galapagos, beautiful documentary videos are not able to "show" you one critical aspect of the environment: the smell. On the Galapagos, it was the God-awful smell of thousands and thousands of years of bird and seal poop everywhere. At the edge of the crater, it was the rotten egg smell of thousands of years of sulfur emissions that permeated the air.

So, in a dream almost come true, I took many minutes of video of the incredible view around and somewhat inside the crater and the 360-degree view of the blue skies above, the cloud banks below, the ashy gray-white plateau where our tents appeared like tiny specks, the ice-covered summit now less than 150 feet higher than my head, and the glacier split in two. From this vantage point, Furtwangler looked like a climate-changing Moses had split an icepack-white sea in two. I also could see with my eyes—and made a close-up on video of—the sign that marked the actual peak, only 143 feet higher than where I stood—the peak we planned to reach before sunrise tomorrow.

My tough guy Rodrik and I stand on the edge of the Reusch Crater atop the Kibo Cone at 19,200 feet, 400 feet above our campsite on the Furtwangler Glacier plain.

Discretion was the better part of valor this day, as I quickly understood that I would have to descend 400 more feet at a steep angle on loose scree and then climb back up the same 400 feet. I would have added another 800 challenging feet to the 400 feet I had already added to the very difficult 2,800 feet I had just climbed. I also had watched the scientists in the video scramble up the slope, often using their hands to pull themselves up as their feet sank into the loose ash and scree. I made one of my "smart Robert moves" and told Samia that I had had enough, that I was ready to go back down. I told Samia and Rodrik how very grateful I felt toward both of them for helping me see this awesome sight and fulfill a dream.

With all of the memorable views I saw during this journey, I still recall this scene from atop the crater as, if not more, clearly as any of the other amazing views I enjoyed during my climb. It was as stunning as the moon setting beside Lava Tower.

After descending the plateau and thanking the guys again, I rested in my tent for a while until dinner was served. It was a very tired and subdued group in the mess tent as Samia told us that if we wanted to see the sunrise, we were going to get up at 3:30 a.m. and have (another!) light breakfast. We would leave by 4 a.m. to climb the final 543 feet up another difficult trail in the dark for about two and a half hours. If we made it to the summit before 6:30 a.m., we would see one of the most amazing sights in the world. We were all in for this experience; it had been our goal from the beginning, so we finished dinner and went to our tents to sleep. Exhausted and freezing cold, I only wrote three pages in my diary before I fell asleep.

The temperature this night was between 0 and 10 degrees F. or lower, but there was no wind. Thank God! I either slept on or wrapped all of my clothes around me to stay warm. I did sleep soundly for a few hours—exhilarated exhaustion will do that for you.

When I got up sometime around midnight to go to the latrine, I was blessed with even more incredible moonlight on the glacial plateau. The moonlight was so bright that comparing it to daylight does neither justice. I felt like I was alive, somehow incorporated into a three-dimensional black and white photographic negative. While everything else seemed frozen in time and space, I was able to walk around the scene, turn and see everything on the plateau, breathe the crisp air, and look up and see to the end of the galaxy. The plateau glistened with the reflections of trillions of tiny, diamond-bright ashes. The Milky Way stretched across the heavens, still twinkling like a diamond-encrusted wedding band cradling the gigantic precious pearl of the moon. The sharp shadows cast by the tents and the slopes were as dark as those in the afternoon sun of Midsummer's Day. My analogies pale—literally—compared to the reality.

I felt deeply grateful and humbled that I had been granted the gift of the four most beautiful full moon nights anyone could imagine. I thanked my HP, went back to my tent, and slept peacefully for two hours for the first time in days. I was almost there.

Lesson of the Day

Take Steps Nine and Ten as quickly as I can with anyone to whom I owe an apology and amends. Apologize for my mistake, be specific about the nature of my mistake, take full responsibility, discuss only my part in the situation, and state my commitment and my plan to avoid the same mistake. Then, ask the person harmed for forgiveness.

Meditation Musings—On Target Again!

My three daily meditations—again—were filled with apt and ironic advice. The first one stressed that FMG thinks I should do what I can—that is, do the footwork—before He/She gives me more help. Ha! I think I did my "footwork" today—a total of 3,200 feet elevation during the most physically strenuous day of my adult life. Only high school football practice in the 95-degree heat in August in Atlanta, Georgia when I was 15, 16, and 17 years old was worse. Back then, though, I was young and immortal!

Oh—the first meditation also suggested that I do my best to hold my tongue and my temper. I should have listened, but didn't again, darn it! But I also did my "footwork" of doing Step Nine with Humphrey and Samia; I continued to make my living amends with Rodrik during our hike up and down the Reusch Crater.

The second reading urged me to stay calm and peaceful despite the challenges in any situation. I wish I had; I learned that my hair-trigger reactions to the slightest irritation meant that I had much work to do upon my return to the "real world." It also urged me to pay forward my blessings so that the person I blessed would pay it forward and so on and so on in a wave of blessings that would circle the world in unexpectedly delightful ways. It called on me to carry God's blessings and share them. I did my best the rest of this adventure to do this as a living amends for my repeated mistakes.

The last one urged me to meditate outside and experience the energy of the Earth Mother coming from beneath my feet and feel the holy light that shone down from the heavens. It urged me to use my breath and my heart to build a bridge between earth and heaven. I certainly felt an extremely strong connection among all three—earth, heaven, and me—this afternoon as I stood on the edge of the crater and this night as I felt overcome with joy basking in the light of the full moon and the grandeur of the Milky Way.

Humorously, it suggested that I use the warmth of summer days and the soft summer nights to build this bridge. I learned that where and when does not really matter when I want to strengthen that bridge; I built my bridge on strenuous, chilly "summer" days and freezing "summer" nights on a 19,343-feet-high volcano in Africa.

Well, my notes say 3:30 a.m. will be here soon. So, back to sleep. *The Big Day* tomorrow!

MONDAY, JUNE 28

Day Ten, Step Ten

*"Thirty minutes of pure joy at the top as the sun
rose and cast Kili's shadow over Mt. Meru."*
MY JOURNAL NOTE ON HOW I FELT WHEN
WE REACHED THE SUMMIT

Step Ten: *Continued to take personal inventory and when we were wrong promptly admitted it...*and I would add, make amends as quickly as possible.

Boots and Butts to the Summit—And 9,000 Feet Down—In One Day

This day we reached the peak that the Tanzanians call Uhuru— Swahili for Freedom—Peak for very good reasons. (Source: https:// en.wikipedia.org/wiki/Uhuru). It is the highest point in Africa, it is the tallest volcano outside South America, it is an incredible point of national pride, it is a symbol of national unity, it is considered the "Mother Mountain" by the many tribes who live in peace near it, and it was "sanctified" as a special place on Tanganyika's independence day.

A bit of background: After decades of being a German or British colony, on January 9, 1961, what was then Tanganyika gained its freedom from Great Britain as a Commonwealth state. On the same day, Alexander Nyirenda, a leading patriot, carried the Uhuru Torch, an essential national symbol, to the top of Kilimanjaro and lit it. A simple kerosene torch, it symbolized freedom and light for the colonized peoples of the country. Today, a replica sits atop the Uhuru Torch Monument, a white obelisk in a park in the center of Dar es Salaam, the capitol of Tanzania. (Source: https://en.wikipedia.org/wiki/Uhuru_Monument).

The Uhuru Peak Torch and the Eleventh Step Prayer

The torch, a working replica of which is used in an annual race, is said to shine across the country and its borders "to bring hope where there is despair, love where there is enmity, and respect where there is hatred." (Source: https://en.wikipedia.org/wiki/Uhuru_Torch).

Those words sound much like key parts of the prayer of St. Francis Assisi that many people in 12 Step groups have adopted as their Eleventh Step Prayer. I pray my own version of this prayer every day. My version goes something like this:

> *"Father-Mother God, make me a channel of Thy peace. That where there is hatred may I bring love, discord harmony, anger understanding, error truth, resentment acceptance, doubt faith, despair hope, sorrow joy, injury forgiveness...For it is better to love than to be loved, to understand than to be understood, to comfort than to be comforted...For it is in giving that we receive, in forgiving we are forgiven, and in dying to our Selves that we awaken to the eternal life of the Spirit."*

Clearly, I often fail to live up to these spiritual goals. Again, all I can hope is that I make progress, sometimes quickly, sometimes slowly, toward the deeper, richer, more blessed spiritual life that living the 12 Steps promises. Reaching the Uhuru Peak—the Freedom Peak—this day did give me an exhilarating sense of freedom from many sorrows and sins of my past and removed many self-doubts about my courage and my resilience.

Historical Note

Ultimately, Tanganyika and the neighboring island Zanzibar were joined as the United Republic of Tanganyika and Zanzibar on Union Day, 26 April

153

1964. The new state changed its name to the United Republic of Tanzania within a year. (Source: https://en.wikipedia.org/wiki/Tanganyika)

Two Hours of Hard Climbing, 30 Minutes of Pure Joy, Five Hours of Pain

This incredible day was two hours of hard climbing in the dark, 30 minutes of pure joy as we watched the sunrise over the summit, and five hours of pain when I took my will back and hurt myself—seriously this time—when I ignored Samia's direction. It was a day in which I "pole pole" ascended the summit up a steep slope in the dark. I danced with pure joy on the summit. I called my brother from the summit in tears of joy. I stumbled down thousands of feet of scree and jammed my toes badly. I suffered frostbite on all my fingers. Most important, I MADE IT!

With my HP's always laser-like humor, one of the meditations for this day suggested I practice conscious walking today, ask my angels for help, and live in the moment. I guess I practiced all kinds of conscious and unconscious—fearful and fearless, joyful and sad, stubborn and willing—walking this day. I felt the enormous joy of reaching the peak on my own two feet and swing dancing in the sunrise; I felt the strong ego of taking my will—and my daypack—back. And I paid a serious price for once again demanding that I do things my way and ignoring the wisdom and direction of my human HPs. It was a price that my big toes will pay the rest of my life as they serve as constant, though thankfully only ugly, reminders of what self-will run riot will do to me. I got off easy.

Boots and Butts: Final Ascent at 4 a.m. in the Dark

After I was mesmerized by the awe-inspiring heavenly panorama in the middle of the night, I slept only an hour or two in the near-zero-degree cold before 3:30 a.m. arrived much too soon. Samia came knocking on my tent to wake me up for our final ascent. We quickly ate half a bowl of oatmeal and hot tea. We dressed in all our heavy clothes, clamped our headlamps over our heavy sock caps and thick balaclavas—no crash helmets this time!—and started climbing another very steep trail. Fortunately, this time, the trail carvers had "discovered" switch backs, so we went back and forth instead of "stair climbing" straight up.

The final ascent was all watching boots and butts in the glow of my head-lamp to reach the top of the steep 543-foot slope by sunrise. Every step, I put my foot where Matt, with literally his butt-to-my-head in front of me, had just stepped because I knew he hadn't slipped or fallen backward on me!

It was horrifically cold, and my hands, though I had on my heaviest liners and best gloves, grew increasingly cold. I didn't realize then that this was very bad news; it was the beginning of frostbite that I made worse when I took off my heavy gloves during the half an hour we spent on the summit so I could take photographs and videos.

Fortunately, I had only "mild" frostbite. It took *only* a month after I returned home for my fingers to heal and regain normal feeling and func-tion. My fingers only turned deep pink and stayed numb or tingly for days. My fingers never turned black and didn't require surgery or amputation so they are happily typing away as I write this book. There but for the grace of my HP...

Pure Joy at 19,343 Feet

We made it to Uhuru Peak just as the sun began to "peek" (pun intended) over the cloud layer. As the sun rose behind the clouds, they looked like an endless sea of slowly undulating bluish-purple waves. It was a spectacular sight as the first pink-reddish rays exploded like long, slender fingers across the horizon to fill the sky. The Creator began to slowly turn the kaleidoscope of the sky every shade of bright yellow, deep red, pink, aqua, purple, mauve, greyish-blue, and pearl white you can imagine. Then, the slightest edge of the sun's yellow disc poked above the clouds; with every moment, it inched a little higher, and the kaleidoscope continued to evolve into ever-different patterns and colors. A black and white photo could not capture the beauty of this spectacular sunrise, so again, I suggest going to our website at www.recoveryfca.com to see this incredible sight!

I felt overcome with the purest joy I have ever felt. I was 60 years old, and I had made it to the top of this mountain on my own two feet. I just stood there for a few moments watching the kaleidoscope turn, just absorbing the feeling and giving thanks to my HP for allowing me to see this sight. I took off my heavy gloves and took pictures and video to commemorate perhaps the most remarkable morning in my life.

I made it! Subzero temperatures with a glorious new sunrise on top of
Uhuru Peak—19,343 feet! Thank you, Father-Mother God!

Then, the group broke the spell and we all began laughing, hugging each
other, and crying. On my video, I can hear myself sobbing as I described how
I felt. We took pictures of each other and the group standing by the carved,
wooden sign that marked the actual summit.

I wanted to share this moment with someone who meant more to me at
the time than I realized. I used my satellite phone to call my younger brother
in Atlanta, Georgia, seven hours behind my time, about 11:30 p.m. Eastern
time. Again, by an HP miracle, I reached him on the first call. Somehow, the
erratic sat phone worked for a few meaningful minutes.

I told him where I was and what I had accomplished, weeping all the while,
overwhelmed with joy, exhausted and freezing at the same time. Something
just told me to call him rather than my sisters. More sadly than I can express,
he has since died of a stroke caused by symptoms related to his several addictions. Until he died, he always told me that my phone call to him from the top
of Kilimanjaro was one of the most meaningful moments in his life, that he

was so grateful I cared enough about him to do that. It was another great gift from my HP to my brother and to me, as that call brought us closer together than we had been in many years. That call and its long-term blessings were other gifts from my HP that I did not recognize at that moment, but were granted to me because I reached the top of that mountain.

Kilimanjaro "Kisses" Mt. Meru

Just as I ended the call with my brother and stood facing the sunrise in the east, Samia told us all to turn around and face west. Stretching 43 miles west, a perfect triangle of Kilimanjaro's shadow passed slowly over Mt. Meru, embracing all of its sister mountain. Most remarkably, the shadow of Kili's peak "kissed" the peak of Meru just for a moment and then moved on as the sun continued to rise behind us.

"Peak" Swing Dancing

Samia broke the spell that the shadow over Mt. Meru had cast on us after a few moments when he told us it was too cold and it was time to head down the mountain. But I had made myself another promise that I had forgotten in the joy of the moment—until Annie came over to me right then and said, "Are we going to dance before we leave?"

I had literally danced my way into good physical shape by going East Coast swing dancing at least once or twice a week for two years. Two to three hours of non-stop swing dancing with 40 to 50 women—one at a time, of course!—to fast swing music from Benny Goodman to Elvis Presley is one of the best cardio exercises you can do. For a single middle-aged guy like me, it also was the only "moral" way I could get my hands on gorgeous "20- and 30-something" women for 2 or 3 minutes at a time!

On a lark, I had promised myself and told my friends that I would swing dance when I got to the top. When the group got together 8 days ago, I had asked the women if any of them knew how to dance. Annie said Matt and she had just taken some lessons, so she volunteered to dance with me on the summit. I had almost forgotten before she reminded me. Thank you, Annie! Another undeserved gift!

Annie helped me keep my promise to swing dance at the top of Kilimanjaro!

I gave my video camera to her husband, and for 30 seconds, I sang—well huffed and puffed—the first two verses of Bill Haley's "Rock Around The Clock" because it was the only song I could remember. In our heavy clothes and clunky boots, I twirled Annie around for some swing dance steps! I still have the 30-second video, so I have the proof! Actually, it was great fun, another promise kept, and another joyful memory to carry home.

We Lucky Few and the Unhappy Many

When our group got to the top, only a handful of other people had already made it. I have no idea where they came from because we were the only group camped on the plateau. Our group was very blessed because the vast majority of climbers take the shorter, "normal,' 5- or 6-day Mweka Route up the mountain. As I noted, to have an ice ball's chance in hell of reaching the summit by sunrise, most climbers have to start at midnight at 15,000 feet and climb for 6 to 9 hours more than 4,000 feet in the night and zero degree cold.

Only a very few brave and hardy souls—maybe 20—we met at the peak had made it. As we began our descent, we passed dozens and dozens of young people straggling up the trail in small bands. They all looked very unhappy.

Their faces were crunched in frowns and grimaces of real misery. The few we spoke with said that many of their compatriots had stopped and gone back down, or had never started the nighttime climb.

Reversing Our Environment—and Shocking Our System— in Mere Hours

After we enjoyed our brief time on the peak, our goal was to descend as quickly as we could from 19,343 feet to Mweka Camp at 10,170 feet on the edge of the rainforest. It felt like we were reversing in just hours all the time, place, and space we had experienced for the past week, a significant, but welcome, shock to my system.

The first 4,000 feet down to our lunch break at 15,000 feet were very steep and consisted almost entirely of loose bare scree and rock with only a few scrubby grasses. From 15,000 feet to 13,000 feet was a rocky trail; halfway through this area at about 14,000 feet, the mountain marigolds and paper plants began to reappear. From 13,000 feet to the camp at 10,170 feet, the trail blessedly flattened out and became almost entirely dirt, and the highland heather and shrubs reappeared. At first, they were short, but we moved quickly into the very tall heather, some as high as five to 10 feet above our heads. Just as we reached our camp for the night, we entered the edge of the rain forest with its lush plant life and much warmer weather. Well, it was above freezing that night!

The Next Major Rash Robert Regret

As I prepared to descend, my will and male ego reared their ugly heads again. I took my will back, and doing so seriously hurt myself this time. This "small" problem continues to teach me a recovery lesson I was still too stubborn to learn at the peak. My "rash Robert regret"? I insisted that Humphrey give me my daypack so I could make the descent on my own.

Why did I do this? I was overly stimulated, too exhilarated, too full of myself, and too tired of feeling embarrassed that Humphrey was carrying my pack. Did I think, against years of experience, going downhill would be easier than trekking uphill? Who knows all the whys? All I know is that as a recovering addict, I never know which literally ignorant, seemingly minor, decision will hurt me the most.

Humphrey tried to discourage me, but I wouldn't listen (does this sound familiar to my fellow addicts?), so we asked Samia. Samia tried to persuade me, too, but I told him I was fine, so he shrugged his shoulders, looked at Humphrey, and said, "Let him have it." So, I took the pack and boy, did I "get it."

I took the pack, strapped it on, and started down. I raced down more than 2,000 very steep feet of scree slope on the Mweka trail. I ignored Samia's instruction to walk down sideways on the side of my shoes. I started straight down and began jamming my toes into my boot tips, twisting my ankles, losing my balance to gravity, and gathering speed. Samia finally caught up with me, stopped me, and told me that if I didn't give Humphrey my pack, I was not going to make it down on my own feet. Once again, Samia had compassion on me—and let me learn the hard way.

I very grudgingly gave the pack back to Humphrey. As I took it off, I gave Samia my cameras, and he accidentally dropped them. They rolled down the slope about 20 to 30 feet before he caught up to them. I didn't say anything, but I felt angry all morning. At least I didn't say anything; maybe I was beginning to learn from my past mistakes. Fortunately, when we got to the lunch camp at 15,000 feet, I checked out both cameras and they worked fine.

Another real undeserved blessing from my HP! Either or both cameras could have been damaged, and there was no location within dozens of miles where I could have gotten either one repaired or replaced. I could have lost the hundreds of photos I had taken and been unable to take hundreds more photographs during the rest of my trip. If my video camera had broken, I could have lost the breath-taking scenes of the Kili sunrise, and I could not have taken the many more hours of incredible video of our safari on the Serengeti. I am very grateful that throughout this adventure, my spiritual HP protected me when I made so many bad decisions. My human HPs tried to warn me every time, and my spiritual HP saved my undeserving butt every time.

I also never knew which of my bedazzled thoughts would prove false and which I could trust. At the top, I assumed that going down would be easier than going up since gravity would be in my favor. Why would have I thought that at the time when my rational mind knew much better? I had climbed up and down hundreds of hills and mountains, and I knew that going down is always worse than going up. So, gravity dragged me down faster and faster until I almost lost control and couldn't stop myself from running and stumbling down the scree slope. The choice to take my will back at the peak was the worst choice I made during the entire journey and has had the worst long-term physical consequences.

Frostbitten fingers when I climbed up to the peak and took off my heavy gloves to take photos and videos. My silk glove liners were essentially worthless at any temperature below freezing. In retrospect, the short-term frostbite was well worth the opportunity to share my photos and videos with you in this book, through the links in the Kindle version, and on our www.recoveryfca.com website.

My crushed toes and wrecked toenails on my race down the scree slope meant that I was unable to wear regular shoes for a month, and I had to avoid swing dancing for two months while they healed.

One Proud Moment

One proud moment did happen on the way down. At about 15,000 feet, there was a rocky, crowded, dirty, exposed camp called the High Hut. All of those who tried to climb the 4,000 feet from midnight until sunrise stayed there the night before. We passed four 40- to 50-year-olds sitting outside their tents in the bright sunlight. We spoke for a few minutes. They said they might attempt to climb to the peak later in the day; I think they were too busy drinking beer to climb much higher.

After we had seen the dozens of young people going up as we came down, it became clear that our four 60-somethings were the oldest people on the mountain this day. I felt very proud of and glad for the four of us—Matt, Annie, Heinrich, and me. The other three had carried their own packs and made it on their own two feet; all I can—and ever will—say is that I made it on my own two feet. My Creator and my human HPs—Samia, Humphrey, and Rodrik—are the real heroes of my journey.

By the time we got to the camp at 10,170 feet five or six hours later, my toes were jammed and very painful. They remained that way for another week because I had only my sleeping booties to replace my heavy boots. Every morning, I had to cram my swollen, aching feet back into my heavy boots. I had overlooked that one, simple piece of expert advice that Wilderness Travel had put in its list of "be sure to bring items": a pair of sandals or sneakers. Matt and Annie were the smartest; they brought plastic Crocs® that were easy to clean and comfortable both in their tent and for walking around a camp site.

However, this time, taking my will back and ignoring my human HPs' advice hobbled me, jacked up my fear, and triggered my anger response. The thought of my mortality began to worm its way into the back of my mind. In just a couple of days, the certainty of my mortality literally tried to claw its way into my life on our Serengeti safari. This day, I was too full of both exhilaration and pain to bother thinking too much about it.

Mother Mountain Always Exacts A Price

As we left this camp, we saw the emergency, one-wheeled iron "gurney" I had discussed before. It reminded me of a truth about Mother Mountain: No one escapes the peak of Kilimanjaro hale and hearty, if you make it to the summit at all.

For me, the past two days had been the most challenging of my life in every dimension—physical, mental, emotional, and spiritual. For my achievement and joy, I paid with frostbite on my fingers, badly jammed toes, sheer exhaustion, and poor relationships with my fellow climbers. I had repeatedly taken my will back and every time, hurt myself with the simplest errors—failing to bring comfortable camp shoes, failing to follow Samia's instructions, having no hot water to soak my feet, and giving no consideration to proper foot care.

The previous two days had been as bad and as difficult as Samia had "advertised": None of us was truly prepared. Everyone paid a price: Matt's respiratory illness got progressively worse. During the 9,000-feet descent, Annie became very ill. She had to be helped down to the Mweka Camp and recuperate the rest of the day and that night. Jason remained ill and had no appetite for days, losing many pounds. Felicia felt very nauseous most of the time, a bad case of Stage 1 altitude sickness. Scott had been on respiratory medications and antibiotics for days. Heinrich was generally miserable. Of course, poor Etienne had never made it to the top, but she was waiting for us at the Mweka Camp, feeling rested and well. We were grateful she was okay.

All of us paid our penance to Mother Mountain and our tribute for the privilege of ascending this sacred mountain. None of us will ever be the same.

Most Disappointing and Least Ethical Behavior:

In many ways, this journey revealed the best and worst in everyone. On the way down, unfortunately, one of my group showed what I considered the worst. First, it is illegal to take anything off the mountain—even leaves, rocks, feathers, much less live plants, samplings, seeds, animals, and the like. As we were walking down the path and entered the heather/moorland zone, Humphrey pointed out to us some rare plants that grow only on Kilimanjaro.

As I took pictures, I saw a member of the group steal several sets of seeds from these rare plants when that person knew it was both illegal and unethical. The person laughed about it in front of Felicia, the recent college graduate, and Jason, the teenager. When the person had picked the rarest seeds, the person said, "In for a penny, in for a pound," and continued to take other seeds. Why? To find out if they could be grown in the garden at home.

What?!!! Arrogance? Sense of entitlement? Ignorance of the harm being caused? I don't know, but I have a hard time giving the person the benefit of the doubt because rules were known and ignored. Perhaps my self-righteousness kicked in, but I prefer to think it was my concern and reverence for "Mother Mountain," its people, its ecology, and its future.

I don't know if or how the person got them through U.S. customs; if the items were not declared and were hidden in a pocket or in luggage, that act was also a serious federal offense. That person set a very bad example for everyone and showed the crew the kind of behavior that gives tourists from the United States a sometimes-well-deserved bad reputation.

Humphrey was watching, but did not intervene. I went over to him and said quietly, "The difference between XXX and me is that I want to pick up all the trash on the trails and XXX wants to steal the seeds."

Essentially true. Even with my mistakes, my truest, highest motive was to protect Kili's sensitive environment. It was—and is—a very sad commentary that both the climbers—including me—and the crew did nothing about the theft of rare seeds. If there is any solace, Humphrey did tell me that climbers steal fewer plants and seeds than they used to. Some consolation, I guess.

Letdown Leavened with Gratitude

When we reached Mweka Camp at 10,170 feet, I felt a huge emotional letdown after the huge change in altitude affected my breathing, my painful descent, and my disappointment. But I also experienced a wonderful emotional and spiritual sense of gratitude. That afternoon, the sky remained clear so I was able to stand just outside the edge of the forest and look back; I could see our path all the way to the top of Mother Mountain. Nine thousand feet up, the ice and snow sparkled around the summit, and the sky was a bright white-blue with scattered clouds all around the peak.

I felt an enormous, but calming sense of accomplishment. Despite all my mistakes, my fears, and my ignorance, I had kept going, I had persevered, I had made it on my own two feet, and I had completed a goal far more difficult than I had ever anticipated. I also felt a very deep sense of gratitude for the support of my spiritual HP. He/She carried me through the long, bitterly cold, sleepless nights while I tossed and turned, prayed for help, rummaged inside all of the dark thoughts in my head, and wrote my rambling journal. I felt even more grateful because my Creator had put me with my human HPs—Samia, Humphrey, Rodrik, and all 58 other tough guys. They always knew the right thing to do to help me, protect me, and show compassion on me when I needed it.

Extraordinary Lessons in Dependency

That night in my tent, I recounted the many lessons in dependency I learned during this journey. Not only is no man an island; no one is even a "peninsula." Rather each of us is an integral part of something far greater than ourselves. Here are just two vital, yet seemingly trivial ways I depended on others for this success:

- My aluminum walking sticks for balance. Someone or some team designed them somewhere far away. Probably hundreds of people from many different organizations participated in making them, shipping them across the world, and selling them to me at a large sporting goods chain store. Without those sticks, I would have fallen dozens of times and undoubtedly hurt myself badly. They were as important to my physical abilities as Samia's directions.
- Of course, making the sticks doesn't include the thousands of people involved in designing my warm clothes: the farmers growing the fibers, the weavers and textile mill workers making the cloth and fabrics, the operators sewing the garments, the warehouse workers shipping them to the stores, and the store clerks selling them to me. Just to name a few of the thousands of people involved.

- Obviously, I could repeat this gratitude for everything I had with me, every ounce of food I ate, and so much more.
- We spoiled, affluent Americans take so much for granted that the peoples of Africa cannot—fresh water; functioning sewer systems; adequate, healthy food; and modern medicine. We have everything our hearts desire and more than we can ever possibly use and appreciate.
- Two unheralded heroes who had the worst job of all: The two latrine cleaners *and* carriers: Every day, twice a day, these two tough guys cleaned our two latrines (men's and women's), broke down the toilet tents, put them and the latrines on their backs, carried them to the next camp, and set them up. The latrines were clean and ready to go by the time we arrived at every camp site. When we arrived, we were "ready to go" night and day! We left large volumes of waste because we ate and drank so much, and we walked and burned so many calories that our digestive systems worked overtime. Without those two humble men, we would have had to use either "Mother Nature" or the godawful permanent camp latrines that no one appeared to have cleaned out—ever. Those two, who never complained, helped us stay much healthier and enjoy more privacy than would otherwise have been possible.

Reinforced Recovery Lessons

Though focused on correcting current missteps, today's Step Ten lesson does much more: It gives me a way to practice Steps One through Nine every day and in all my affairs. Let me review those steps in the context of Step Ten:

- I was powerless over the mountain in every sense; my life was unmanageable.
- My HPs—spiritual and human—can and will restore me to sanity—if I am willing to follow directions.
- I have to decide to cooperate and surrender my will—one day, one step at a time *pole-pole*—to my Higher Powers.
- The challenge of the "Mother Mountain" revealed every character defect I have, yet the trek and my human HPs granted me just as many opportunities to practice the rest of the steps—if I was willing to take my inventory on the fly.

- I took 5th Steps with Samia, Humphrey, Rodrik, and the group when I apologized and did my best to make amends.
- I prayed constantly for the willingness for my HP to remove my shortcomings. I proved that beyond any doubt, I could not remove them myself.
- Some days He/She did remove my shortcomings, if only for a while. Some days He/She wanted me to keep them and exercise them in some way that though unknown to me at the time, might help someone else. Some days I didn't let Him/Her remove any of them; I needed to hold onto them too much from my fear, lack of faith, and addled thinking.
- Many days, I often had a list of people to whom I owed amends, as I did my best to quickly recognize whom I had harmed and became willing to make amends.
- I made prompt and direct amends as soon as I could after each mistake.
- Step 10 was a daily practice, promptly admitting my mistakes and making direct amends.
- Every night, sometimes for hours, I prayed and had conversations with my FMG about every facet in the "rough diamond" of my life. I prayed that my HP would polish each facet each day so I would make it to the top and become a better person. As I climbed, I constantly prayed and was in awe of the Creator's handiwork that was revealed with every step.
- Although no one ever learned I was in 12 Step programs, I was the message—both for good and for ill. I made several serious mistakes, but I was always willing to apologize and make amends. I will let others judge; I know I did my best each day to practice the Steps and the principles embodied in them.

Meditation "A-musings"

Once again, the three meditations I read today were right on target for the day—remember I am reading these at the end of the day to avoid any influence on my day.

The first said that courage causes change and that I was prepared for change. It urged me to make choices not because I felt afraid of taking a risk, but because I wanted to solve my problems and welcome new ideas. It encouraged me to bring my fears out in the open. Well, I promise you that all my fears have been hanging out there for all to see. I don't claim a lot of courage, just a little willingness to keep going and to work on them.

The second meditation urged me to put my fate in my HP's hands and feel confident that as long as I do my best to do the right thing, good will result. So far, I have enjoyed remarkably good results considering my mistakes: I made it to the top in relative good health, I enjoyed indescribably beautiful blue-sky days and full moon nights, I remained mobile this day, and so much more.

I already mentioned the third—practicing conscious walking outside and trusting my HP.

It also mused on the space between chronological time and the constant present where visions and miracles take place. Well, I certainly did a lot of conscious climbing to the summit in the freezing cold early morning and then walking—well, more like running—down 9,000 feet in one day. This one made me laugh because it was so apt and because I did occasionally, just occasionally, glimpse that space between time and the present and feel incredible joy. My HP's loving sense of humor for the day.

TUESDAY, JUNE 29

Day Eleven, Step Eleven

"I AM WHO I AM…AND IT'S OK!!!"
Diary comment in middle of night at Mweka Camp

"I did nothing but walk and pray, pray and walk,
and keep going, and all at home were praying,
and all 61 'tough guys' carried me."
My comment after we completed our
descent at the Mweka Gate at 6,500 feet

Step Eleven – Sought through prayer and meditation to improve our conscious contact with God, as we understood Him, praying only for knowledge of His will for us and the power to carry that out.

This day—well, really this very early morning—I finally accepted who I am. I felt "okay" for the first time in my life, even with all of my imperfections. It would have been nice, but I cannot say my shortcomings were miraculously lifted in this moment of revelation. Far from it. But I did accept that I just am who I am. I was going to use the cliché, "warts and all," but that would be insulting the warthog, a humorous beast I learned to like on the Serengeti.

Bundled in my tent at the Mweka Camp at 10,170 feet, I woke up at 12:30 a.m. after sleeping maybe three hours. The trials of my wretched sleeping bag and the dreams racing through my mind awakened me. I sat up, turned on my headlamp, and journaled for a long time. I lay down for a while, sat back up, went to the latrine, and journaled some more. The journal entries stopped sometime in the middle of the night, but I stayed awake. The journal entries began again at 5:05 a.m. and continued until 7 a.m. Jumbles of thoughts and prayers and lessons learned and feelings felt floated through my mind for hours.

At some point, I began to jot down a garbled list of all of the many great and not-so-great surprises I had experienced on "Mother Mountain." I wrote about how easily I had fallen back into what I consider to be my unfortunately traditional negative role—the introvert and perpetual outsider. I wrote: "How truly introverted I am—while several members of my group were loquacious about everything, I had little to say…Me—the usual: The questioner, the doubter, the outsider."

I AM WHO I AM—AND IT'S OK!

Then, I wrote in capital letters: "I AM WHO I AM—negative attention getter—Oh well—something to work on. One on one better [for me] than small/large groups. AND IT'S OK!!!"

A later entry after 5:05 a.m. concluded: "I don't like small talk and bab-blers and banals [conversations] and the like. If you want to have a conversation on a serious topic or a truly humorous topic, I'm eager to participate—if you have earned my trust. How [can people] do that? Being authentic and not plastic; being 'abnormal' helps."

I realized I am not very good at making small talk, mingling at a party, or initiating light conversations in groups, at dances, or about anywhere. I don't like it, and I do not have to be good at any of that to be a good human being.

I realized that I had not become friends with anybody in my group be-cause as I learned their stories, I found I just didn't really like them. I did not feel safe with them. I had felt incredibly vulnerable just making this journey by myself. When I started making my mistakes, I felt very embarrassed and even less safe, although I always apologized and made amends. The others in the group clearly became wary of me—my responsibility—and pulled back from me as well.

Yes, Matt and Annie had been kind to me, especially with the swing dance at the top of the mountain, yet most of the time, Annie had a very sarcastic tone and attitude that put me off. Probably because I thought I heard too much of myself in her manner.

I felt safer and closer to Samia and Humphrey despite all the trouble I had given them. They had showered (I use the word deliberately) me with great compassion and forgiveness. They had saved me so that I made it up and down the mountain on my own two feet. But they were also more real, more authentic through the stories they told the group—and more personal ones they told only me—about their lives and families. I had deep respect for them as experts and as husbands and fathers doing a very tough job that took them away from their families for weeks at a time. Their and the whole crew's attitude of compassion, forgiveness, and service made a lasting impression on me. It was far deeper than just the money they earned and the tips they wanted. They were good, kind people who did what they believed to be the right thing for all of us.

I completed my garbled list of surprises with these lessons about myself:

- I believe being "alone" is better than being "with" someone just to be "with" someone who does not have my best interest at heart. This belief harms me when I think falsely that I can't endure being alone, accompanied only by my addict brain. It harms me when I believe falsely that I am not worthy of having a loving partner. I surprised myself this morning when I realized that my "Self," though far from perfect, is OK and I am fine with being me.
- I have very strong fears about survival and vulnerability and a very strong sense about boundaries. They threatened my trip. The "perfect storm" of all three clashed when I yelled at Humphrey on the slick rock precipice at about 18,000 feet. Yet, my cry was setting an appropriate boundary: "Don't touch me without my permission."

Three Simple Boundary Rules

I realized I have three simple rules that I had tried to explain to Samia and Humphrey:

- Ask me to do something, and if it is reasonable, I will do my best to do it.
- Tell me what to do, explain why, and I will probably do it right 99 percent of the time. Unless my fear gets the best of me as it did during my descent at Lava Tower where I banged my head.

- Build trust with me: The problem with Humphrey grabbing me occurred because at that point, I didn't trust him. I came to trust him very soon, but not then.

I believe these are reasonable ways to set boundaries. I learned them the hard way in my marriages and several other meaningful relationships in which I gave away my "self." In these relationships, I truly had no idea how "porous" my personality had become and how little I believed in my "self."

On the plus side, this morning, I realized I had somewhat overcome my fear of heights to climb the precipices and scramble up the steep scree slopes between 16,000 and 18,800 feet.

Doing God's Will and Gratitude—Regardless

In short, throughout the night, I prayed and meditated and rummaged inside my head to seek to understand what the Eleventh Step meant to me:

Suddenly, I realized that every moment of every day during this tremendous trek, I had been doing God's will for me, and He/She had granted me the power to carry it out. I had lessons to learn, fears and resentments to face and let go, mistakes to make, and responsibility to take as well as a depth of willingness, courage, and power I did not know I possessed. I felt deeply grateful for all of it, from the worst moment coming out of the latrine tent to the best moment of reaching the Freedom Peak on my own two feet.

A fitting attitude of gratitude with which to end my "Taking the 12 Steps Up—and Down—Kilimanjaro."

However, little did I know at the time my HP had far more for me to learn during the coming week on our "easy" Serengeti safari.

Getting Ready to Start Our Final Descent

At daybreak, the scene at Mweka Camp was very crowded and noisy as it was a major stop both on the way up for the short-trip climbers and "the last" stop on the way down for most climbers. It had a real "luxury": a concrete block bathroom, such as it was, and an information "center," sort of. It was more like a kiosk with signs and posters. The building was incomplete with concrete blocks and small sand piles scattered all around; no one was working on the building this morning.

Hold this thought—how did they get the concrete blocks up the mountain to this site? You'll read and see the surprising answer when I describe our final descent later this day.

The very good news was that it was relatively "warm" at 10,000 feet, even above freezing this morning. A gorgeous 31/32 full moon shone through the grey-white clouds blowing across the night sky. I actually felt fairly warm with only one layer of clothes—silk long-john bottoms, synthetic long sleeve top, and fleece pullover. I did not need to wear my wool cap and insulated coat except to go to the latrine.

By this morning, I realized I had used three-quarters of a roll of TP for everything from wiping my buns to blowing my nose—not at the same time of course…This is the kind of humor that pops up into a sleep-deprived, exhausted mind scratching notes in a journal at 3 a.m.

Personal Damage Assessment
However, by now, I had serious concerns about my fingers: I had what I hoped—and Samia had said—was mild frostbite on my left hand. My left little finger, left index, left middle, and right index fingers were very sore to the touch and almost numb at the tips. They did not turn white, which would have meant the cells were dying, thank goodness! Or black, which could have meant amputation. They stayed pink, and I could see the lines layering the skin.

I was most unhappy with my expensive, silk glove liners. They were worthless, not even providing the 5 to 10 minutes of protection at zero degrees the manufacturer had promised. Combined with my poor choice to remove my thick gloves at the peak, the poor quality of the liners contributed to the frostbite.

In addition, my left calf was very sore and had a rash. In the past, I had developed a similar rash on that calf when I had let sweat from strenuous effort dry and remain on/in my skin for too long. The rash tends to pop out if I do not immediately clean off the sweat and grime. By this time, it had been nine days since I had had a real shower, so I had been lucky it had taken this long for the rash to break out. Perhaps, the cold had kept the inflammation at bay the previous week. Now that it was a bit warmer...

Much worse, I didn't realize this night how damaged my feet were because they were still thawing out as well. I thought the pain came from that thawing.

Thankfully, this camp was very, very quiet that night. No howling jackals, no loud parties, only occasional noise as people went to the latrines and back. Hardly any animal noises at all. Not even birds, monkeys, or anything! As on our first night, the animals and birds were quiet because they instinctively knew that their night-stalking predators were hunting for them—jackals for the larger rodents, owls for the mice and birds, leopards for the monkeys.

My stomach was finally calming down—I would have killed for a cup of real fresh decaf coffee!!

Oh—and my rock! It had "called to me" by my tent. That afternoon, I had just looked down and spied a small rock that had the exact shape as Kili. In the middle of the night, I remembered I had forgotten about it. At first light, I scrambled outside my tent and found it. To this day, I still have it with me as a reminder of the joys, the pains, and the growth I experienced during this adventure.

Meditations and Step 11 Insights of the Long Night Before Our Final Descent

For this day, the first of the always on-target meditation books essentially challenged me to ask myself: Was I looking for an easier, softer way? If I had been, I had found none. I was—and remain—subject to the same universal cause-and-effect law that governs my own—and everyone's—life.

Actions Have Consequences

I never know which arrogant, mindless—even seemingly minor—choice will hurt me the most. One literally "ignorant" minor decision—to ignore the advice of the travel company to bring sneakers, sandals, or some kind of light shoe to wear around camp—cost me dearly during the rest of my trip. As you will read, this choice made me come face to face with my feebleness, my mortality, and my fear of death for the first time.

Secondly, my choice to take back my daypack and dash down the scree slope rather than leave it with Humphrey and descend *pole pole* hurt my feet. I had severely injured toes that caused excruciating pain throughout my week on safari across the Serengeti. I felt more vulnerable than I had ever felt before. It took my feet more than a month to heal after I returned home; I wore sandals to work every day. More on the sandals at the end of my journey. I also spent two months not being able to do what I love to do—swing dance with beautiful women and hike during the summer and fall in the cool Shenandoah Mountains.

My own prayer from the meditation:

> **Father-Mother God, help me to understand the truth about myself. Help me to ask for the help I need, to accept the help I am offered, and then to use it for what's best for me and for all.**

The second meditation insisted that the only time I have is the ever-present "now." It urged me to release the burdens of my past and step forth in faith. Humorously, it did state that the trail will become "less stony" as I move forward. After I stumbled down the scree slope and reached 10,000 feet, the path did indeed become less stony. Ha!

The last meditation suggested that miracles happen at two points in time: moments when we feel at one with our Higher Power and moments of terror when our brains seize because we have no idea how to react. I had experienced both of these moments during this adventure so far with more to come. My HP's enormous sense of humor again and again! Only because I know He/She loves me.

After I finished journaling, I "dry-cleaned" myself with wipes and got dressed just as the sun came up and Samia came "knocking" on our tent poles to make sure we were awake and ready to eat. Always—after burning thousands of calories a day!

Walking into True Forgiveness

After another phenomenal breakfast, we started the final leg—literally—of our journey. We hiked 3,600 feet down a blessedly easy trail to meet our "Toyotabeasts"—the name the tough guys give their Land Rovers and Toyota Landcruisers—and drivers at the Mweka Gate at about 6,500 feet. Under cloudy skies, we quickly returned to relatively warm, damp, lush rain forest with moss hanging off many of the trees.

My feet hurt so badly and I walked so slowly that the rest of the group quickly got far ahead of me. Humphrey stayed with me, still carrying my pack. If any of you reading this book are avid hikers, you know that going down always causes the most pressure on the feet, ankles, knees, and hips.

As I stumbled very *pole pole*, Humphrey and I talked a lot. I told him how much I appreciated his help and how I could not have made it to the top and down without his help. I apologized man to man for my mistakes.

He looked at me in the eye and said, "I forgive you." I felt a rush of emotion unlike any I had ever felt before. The heavy weight of my guilt for my actions and my shame at being so weak fell away. I felt unconditional forgiveness for the first time in my life. I felt deeply moved by his act of compassion and charity. Even as I write this sentence long after the fact, I feel so grateful and humbled that my spiritual HP put this human guardian angel with me to guide and protect me from myself.

How the Blocks Get to 10,000 Feet

As we continued our slow "stroll" down the path, I—a spoiled American— was startled to see how the concrete blocks reached the site at Mweka Camp at 10,170 feet. Consider this scene: Most of this final leg of the trail was a series of steps made by packing earth behind wood beams or relatively easy descents down well-beaten paths. However, none could accommodate a wheelbarrow, much less a small truck, for very far.

Instead, I saw walking rapidly up the trail in small groups or alone, a line of men, women, and children carrying the concrete blocks on their heads. Yes, on their heads! Fifteen– to 20-pound concrete blocks that they picked up at a dump site at 6,500 feet and carried more than 3,500 feet up the trail to the block building.

Each carrier received the equivalent of $3 US per block—remember they carry the block uphill and come down empty handed to get the next block. Don't call them "porters"! Everyone on the mountain finds the term offensive and reeking of colonialism. Humphrey said the young, experienced men can do an average of three trips a day—$9 US for a hard day's work at altitude.

The best can do four trips a day. Women average two to three blocks a day or $6-$9 US per day.

The children usually only could do one or two blocks a day because, well, they were children. First, they were supposed to be at least 12 years old, but I saw some that looked younger. Second, they were supposed to be in school, so they were playing hooky, I assume, to earn money for their families.

I stopped a group of five young men—they looked like teenagers to me—and asked if I could take their picture. They obviously knew the "tourist drill" because the oldest immediately said, "One dollar each." I looked over my shoulder toward Humphrey who nodded his head, "Yes." So, I smiled at the teen and gave him a $5 bill to split among the group and took an amazing photo of them with the blocks on their heads.

Five young men carrying 15- to 20-pound concrete blocks on their heads 3,500 feet up the trail to Mweka Camp for the new bathhouse and information center.

I did not take the photo shown here as an idle tourist curiosity or with the derogatory thought of how cute the natives were. I took the photo out of sincere respect for their hard work. I wanted to show my friends and readers like you how difficult it is to make a living in that part of the world and how hard they work to do so. Humphrey explained that most of the carriers only did this work either when they could not find other work, or they had family members who could stay home in the village to tend their crops of corn and small herds of livestock—usually goats and cattle.

A tough life indeed. In fact, after they dropped their blocks at 10,000 feet, most of the men jogged or ran down the hill and the women walked as quickly as they could. The children, being children, tended to dawdle. The sight of the steady stream of people going as fast as they could both up and down the one-and-a-third mile round-trip had a serious impact on my thinking.

I have now visited 32 countries and six continents from very rich countries such as Austria and France to very poor ones like Zimbabwe, Namibia, and Cambodia. In the poorer countries, I have always been amazed at how hard most of the people work just to survive and how industrious and clever they are at what they do. My prayer for those people in the poorer countries is for them to evolve into truly democratic countries that free their potential to receive a modern education and enjoy open economic opportunity. What these hundreds of millions of people could accomplish would astonish us "fat, dumb, and happy" Westerners!

Near the end of the trail where a "real" dirt road began, we saw the huge pile of blocks that the carriers used as well as bags of sand and concrete mix. We didn't see anyone carrying the sand or mix, but I assume that they were carried up the mountain on people's heads as well.

The End of the Trail—Age Group, Personal Satisfaction, and Artwork

A short time after we passed the pile of blocks, we reached the end of the trail at the official Mweka Gate. I felt a range of emotions—sad that this deeply moving journey was ending, ecstatic that I was still walking, and overwhelmed that we were back to "civilization" with trucks and buildings and running water and real toilets. It was a strange feeling of great joy and great sadness, the two jostling together inside my heart.

At the gate was a sign-in station, a small emergency clinic, a park ranger station (for rangers who carry automatic rifles to fight poachers), and a gaggle of people selling everything from tee shirts to quality artwork.

Before I started bargaining for the shirts and artwork I wanted, I walked to the sign-out booth where for some unknown reason, we had to include our age. After I signed the ledger book, I flipped through the pages and checked the ages of all of the other people who had come down the mountain during the past several days. There were hundreds of names each day.

I found, and enjoyed with great pride, that of all the hundreds of climbers, only a handful, including the three others in our group, were 60 years of age or older. The vast majority were in their 20s or early 30s with a few in their 40s and 50s. By the grace of my spiritual and human HP and guardian angels, I had made it up and down on my own two feet and celebrated my 60th birthday in style! I felt an enormous sense of satisfaction.

As soon as I stepped away from the station, I was surrounded by the vendors whom I had told I would buy their wares. I decided not to bargain too much because I thought it would be "cheap" for me as a prosperous American to drive a hard bargain. I bought four tee shirts for $10 each—each has a map of all the Kilimanjaro trails on the back—a hat for $10, a Tanzanian flag for $3, and five artworks for $55 total. Each of the artworks is a stylized, almost abstract, scene of Maasai or Chagga women standing in front of their traditional dwellings with Kilimanjaro in the background. All five still hang proudly in my living room. As I noted, two of the tee shirts, my dashiki birthday gift, and bits and pieces of fabric with artwork all were incorporated into my magnificent Kilimanjaro quilt.

Real Showers, Hot Water, and My Bliss!!!

I had to hurry because our Land Rovers or "Toyotabeasts" had arrived, so we all gratefully climbed in for our drive back down some of the world's worst dirt roads with ruts two or three feet deep and all mud. We finally made it back to a paved road and arrived at the epitome of luxury, stunning after 10 days in a freezing cold tent. Called Moivaro Lodge, it is a classic, high-quality African lodge with very modern bungalows. And they full well understand Western prices because the bottle of water in my room cost $6 US!

I raced—well, hobbled quickly—to my bungalow where I found that all the clothes and stuff I had left behind were already there. Just a small example of the superb organization and the excellent customer service we received from Wilderness Travel throughout our trek.

I immediately took a 45-minute shower in hot water! I washed my hair three times and my body twice. After I put on clean clothes for the first time in 10 days, I left my filthy clothes at the laundry; I got them back early the next morning, clean, pressed, folded, and ready to go. Western hotel prices again—$65—but I was happy to pay.

After I got blissfully clean and "creamed" (to repair my beaten-up skin), I hobbled around the grounds filled with beautiful tropical plants, such as Bird of Paradise, in full bloom. Behind the main lodge was a large yard with a swimming pool and a perfect view of the west side of Mount Meru when the peak broke through the clouds.

Another "Weird Robert" Alert

Most happily for me, I found my bliss: A set of playground swings! I LOVE playground swings. I have loved playground swings since I was a child growing up in an Atlanta, GA suburb. Next to my elementary school were a tiny Carnegie library where I learned to read and a large park with a baseball field, clay tennis courts, a recreation center where I learned to jitterbug in the 6th grade, AND a very tall set of metal swings.

In those days, we didn't have rubber mats or inches of thick mulch under the swing set to protect our precious little bodies. Instead, we had real dirt and mud that was hard or wet. It hurt if you fell off the swing, and you got really dirty. We learned to live with scrapes and cuts and bruises. That is where I had a great time just being a kid. I loved the swings best of all, so now, I look for swing sets wherever I go; I once swung on a swing in an elementary schoolyard in Montana that had a perfect view of the snowy peaks of the Rockies.

Another wonderful set is in Bethesda, Maryland, in historic Glen Echo Park. The swings are in a small playground next to the Spanish Ballroom, a 1920s era dance venue with 7,000 square feet of original pine floor. It is the "mecca" for just about every kind of dancing, especially East Coast Swing, between New York and Miami. But as a modern park for today's "precious children," there is a thick rubber mat under the swing set. It does take some of the thrill out of the adventure. By the way, I have invited women from the dance to swing with me on the playground swings to see if they might be compatible with me. If they really enjoyed swinging on the swing set, I knew we could get along. If they thought it was silly or just went along with me, I knew they were not my type. Is that enough "swinging" for you? It never is for me!

Before I began to go "swinging" both on the dance floor in the Ballroom and on the swing set outside in Glen Echo Park, I belonged to a boat club on a river on the Chesapeake Bay. The swing set there was about 15-feet tall, so when I swung as high as I could go, it seemed like I could touch the sky, and if I had jumped, I could have landed in the river.

One of the most glorious settings is a small set of swings—only 4 or 5 seats—in a small park on the edge of the Tred Avon river in the town of Oxford, Maryland. Oxford is a tiny village of upscale, historic homes where wealthy Washington politicians mix with local fishermen and their families. The swing set is literally 10 feet from a small rock and sand beach. When I swing high, it feels like I am swinging over the river and touching the sky.

One of the most poignant swing sets I've ever found is next to a large, old, brick schoolhouse in Stockbridge, Massachusetts. It faces down the main street through the town; about a block away is the town cemetery where the author of the Serenity Prayer, the Rev. Reinhold Niebuhr, is buried. The grave site is a very modest stone cross at the back of the cemetery. Equally interesting for 12 Steppers is that on the other side of Stockbridge is the Norman Rockwell museum; on display is the cover of the March 1, 1941 issue of the *Saturday Evening Post* that published the famous Jack Alexander article that skyrocketed Alcoholics Anonymous to the world's attention.

But the small swing set hidden in the lush tropical garden of Moivaro Lodge outside Arusha, Tanzania is certainly the most exotic location where I have swung on a swing—so far! The swings were small and short, and my feet hurt, so I couldn't swing too high or for too long. I did enjoy a couple of humorous moments, first when one of the lodge workers walked by me, and I asked him to take my picture. He stopped and looked at me like I was a bit strange, but smiled, shrugged, took my camera, and took my picture.

A few moments later, a couple of small local children ran down the path by the swings. When they saw me swinging back and forth, they stopped and gave me a very odd look—like "What in the world is that old man doing on our swings? He must be crazy." I just smiled at them with my goofiest grin, and they ran off. Very funny—and so much fun for me to step outside all of the confining roles of adulthood and enjoy something that has given me great peace and pleasure—and incredibly happy memories—for my entire life.

As I swung at Moivaro, I felt an ecstatic rush of pleasure when I reached the peak of the arc and the pit of my stomach when gravity dragged me down to the bottom of the arc. I don't know how the pendulum motion of the swing jiggles the pleasure chemicals and hormones in my head, but it does in marvelous ways. I always get off a swing feeling much better than before I sat down on it. As I gingerly jumped off the Moivaro swing, I laughed and gave thanks to my Higher Power for the enormous gift of the swing set at this lodge at the end of our very tough trip.

Later that afternoon, I also had one of the best massages ever. A large local woman really worked me over. Every muscle ached and her "tender" ministrations worked out every kink and knot. I felt like a happy "used dish rag" for the very reasonable price of $30 and a well-deserved $20 tip for her delightful hour-long massage.

With my marathon shower, my "swinging," and my massage, I felt like a new man. It was a rapid and strange transition from the cold and deprivation on the mountain back to the luxuries of modern civilization. It felt wonderful to be spoiled, but disconcerting to have disconnected so quickly from the spiritual and physical challenge of "Mother Mountain." I suspect that the tour company wanted to return us to "civilization" as quickly as possible so we stayed healthy and grateful, and they could release the crew members and save money. In retrospect, another night on the mountain with some conversation about our experiences might have given more meaning to our personal journeys and bonded the group better.

Our "Last Supper"

That night was our last supper with Humphrey and next to last with Samia. The next morning, we were going to drive to the Ngorongoro Crater, a 13-mile by 9-mile "Garden of Eden." Samia said after we visited the crater, he would take a day or two off to visit his wife and family; then he would begin his next trip up and down the mountain—it would be his 198th trip in 14 years.

I had been awestruck when Samia told us before we began our trek that our group would be his 197th round-trip in 14 years. This day, I felt even more astounded and humbled after spending 10 days with Samia, Humphrey, Rodrik, and all our tough guys, and facing the challenges that our journey had brought. Ours was fairly easy: We enjoyed four full moon nights and four blue sky days above the clouds when we could have had rain or snow every day. We had only a few drops of rain. Although each of us suffered in our own way, all of us were healthy or well on the way to recovery by the time we reached the bottom. We were very blessed, but Samia just took it all in stride, "saddled up" again, and kept going.

We shared a superb group dinner at the hotel with Samia and Humphrey: salad, pumpkin soup, chicken, vegetables, mashed potatoes, and fruit salad. Just right, and it helped settle my stomach so I began to feel normal again.

The day before I had met privately with Samia and told him how much his wisdom and compassion meant to me. I told him how much I appreciated his "cajoling" me to do what whatever it took for me to make the summit. Also, how exactly right he had been: As he had warned us, when I followed his instructions to the letter, I was fine. When I didn't, I hurt myself.

The same equation works exactly the same in 12-Step recovery. When I do what the program suggests I do—stay sober, clean, and abstinent; work the Steps; use the tools; and follow my sponsor's and other successful examples *one day at a time*, my Higher Power relieves me of the iron grip of my addictions. I get to live a happy, joyous, free, and prosperous life beyond my wildest dreams. I have been at both ends of that spectrum—from abject misery and suicidal thinking to great joy, friendship, love, service, and prosperity. Without knowing anything about 12 Step programs, but having an enormous depth and breadth of human experience, Samia was—and remains, I understand—a shining example of the best in humankind.

After dinner, I went to my bungalow to complete my journal for the day. The day's entry ended, "TY, FMG, FAMMMMMBlssgs!" I climbed into the comfortable bed, pulled my mosquito net around me, pulled the clean, sweet-smelling sheet and cover over me, and slept.

WEDNESDAY, JUNE 30

Day Twelve, Step Twelve Morning

*"Sadly and with grief, I have very little compassion
for most people, especially my own family. I ask
FMG to help me have compassion ON all."*
MY JOURNAL NOTE AFTER READING MARK
5:19 IN THE BIBLE AT 5:20 A.M.

*"….Jesus suffered him not, but saith unto him,
Go home to thy friends and tell them how great
things the Lord hath done for thee, and hath HAD
COMPASSSION ON thee." (Capital letters added)*
MARK 5:19, THE BIBLE

*Step Twelve: Having had a spiritual awakening as a result of these steps,
we tried to carry this message to alcoholics, and to practice these principles
in all our affairs.*

This day, at 5:20 a.m., lying under clean white sheets in a warm, comfortable bed in a bungalow at a luxury lodge near Arusha, I had a truly humbling spiritual experience and again felt my Higher Power's great love. I realized—for the first time—the enormous, and utterly undeserved, **compassion** that Samia, Humphrey, Rodrik, Ely, and the entire crew **had on** me. I am grieved to say I also realized how little that I **have had on** others. And I distinguished the enormous difference between having **compassion for** someone and having **compassion on** someone.

To come to (in the sense of waking from an unconscious state) this awakening, I had one of those subtle experiences that seems like coincidence, but in fact, is a gift from my Higher Power. I awoke early after the first good night's sleep in 10 days. I was restless and could not go back to sleep, so I reached out to the night stand beside my bed and picked up a Gideon bible I had found in a drawer the night before. The Gideons should be pleased to know that their efforts to spread their word have reached into the fancy tourist lodges of Tanzania.

Before I recount my spiritual experience, please understand that although raised as a Christian, I do not believe in Jesus' immaculate birth, resurrection, or divinity. I do have the deepest respect for Jesus and his teachings. His message of mercy and love was an enormous leap forward for mankind. His compassion on society's outcasts (sound familiar to any of you?) and self-sacrifice created a revolution in how people can relate to the God of their understanding.

Love Above the Law; Mercy Above Power

During the time that Jesus apparently lived, the pantheon of gods of most civilizations—Egyptian, Roman, Greek, Persian, Hindu, Buddhist, and many others—were punishing, vengeful, jealous, or indifferent to the plight of mankind. People believed these dangerous deities had to be "bought off" with bloody sacrifices and expensive rituals. Even the worship of Jehovah by Jesus's own people was bound by hundreds, even thousands, of rules the breaking of which brought punishment. The corrupt practices of the Jewish leadership—the Pharisees and Sadducees—had caused great cynicism among their people during the Roman occupation of Judaea about 30 A.D.

To give him due credit, Jesus destroyed this polytheistic pantheon of punishment and rule-bound religions with one simple commandment: **To love your neighbor as you love yourself and to put your spiritual relationship with God first in your life. He put Love above the law; he put Mercy before power.**

He spoke truth to power: He obligated all of us, not only the rich, powerful, and privileged, to use our power to heal the sick, feed the hungry, clothe the naked, and succor the bereaved. These actions make up the Way of Life I can strive to achieve through the 12 Steps and 12 Traditions, one day at a time, with joy and frankly, relief.

So, no, although I don't believe Jesus is the only son of God, I do believe that he created a revolution in the heart of mankind that reverberates for goodness and mercy to this day.

With all that said, I picked up the Gideon bible at 5:20 a.m. As I always do whenever I pick up a spiritual guide "serendipitously," I just let the book open itself. I began to read where the page began—Book of Mark, Chapter 3. I read through Chapter 6. These chapters focus on Jesus' ministry, miracles, and parables, especially his angry retort to the rule-bound, fearful, power-hungry, threatened, and corrupt Pharisees. It's nice to know he had a temper at times—tossing over the moneychanger's tables in the temple and giving the powerful hell for their corruption and thirst for money and power.

All of this should sound familiar to everyone today. I know that for decades, my own ambition, greed, selfishness, anger, and self-pity were driven by fear and emotional instability. They were borne from my addictions, they were intensified by my addictions, and my addictions fed on them in turn. These shortcomings drove actions that harmed me and many others before I began my recovery. Although my FMG has relieved me of many character defects, especially my "anger as my best friend" attitude, I remain far from perfect.

Just as I only claim I made the peak of Kilimanjaro on my own two feet with all the help you have read about, I only claim progress, not perfection, in every aspect of my life. Any progress I have made has been gained because of all the help that my Higher Power, my sponsors, my recovery family, and my fellow members of OA, DA, Al-Anon, and other groups have given me.

The most important quality I have brought to my recovery has been stubbornness, or more politely, perseverance. Long-term recovery, one day at a time, requires perseverance, the courage to keep taking action; it is one of the basic Principles of Recovery discussed in the Overeaters Anonymous book, *12 Steps and 12 Traditions of Overeaters Anonymous*. It correlates with Step 10; it compensates us with a life of continuous recovery.

Remember that my favorite Chinese fortune cookie aptly summarizes my efforts: "Fall Down Seven Times, Get Up Eighth Time." That's all I've done for more than 40 years in recovery: Fall down, get up; fall short, make amends, do better; fail, learn—sometimes—or fail again and again, and maybe finally learn.

Compassion *ON* the Man Possessed of Evil Spirits

I am going to discuss in detail the story in Mark, Chapter 5, about Jesus and the mentally ill man whom Jesus cured during his visit to the land of the Gadarenes by the Sea of Galilee. Jesus met the deranged man, possessed of a "legion of devils," among the tombs near the Galilee shoreline. Many of us in 12 Step programs may relate well to this man. He roamed the mountains and tombs, crying and cutting himself with stones. His rage and his strength meant that no chains could hold him.

How many of you, like me, have suffered grave mental and emotional disorders, frightened others by our insane actions, abandoned our homes and families, and harmed ourselves with physical injuries and mental agony? How many of us have tried suicide, cut ourselves, allowed others to abuse us physically or emotionally, gotten drunk constantly, been arrested and jailed, stolen money, had promiscuous sex for years or been addicted to pornography, lied to our creditors and our families, eaten until we thought we would explode—and then ate some more—starved ourselves, or stuffed ourselves and thrown it all up, or sabotaged our success in our careers and in our relationships? How many of us have been homeless or on the verge of homelessness, felt constant despair, been clinically depressed, or felt so poorly of ourselves that we believed we were worthless and hopeless?

In Mark 5, the deranged man rushed up to Jesus, proclaiming his faith and begging his mercy. Jesus understood the serious depth of the man's illness. It is written that he ordered the "evil spirits" within the man to leave him. The evil spirits complained to Jesus because they feared that if they left this poor man, they would plague another victim. They begged him to cast them into a herd of 2,000 swine grazing nearby.

That is a lot of pigs! These pigs were a critical part of the livelihood of many of the Gardarenes, obviously Gentiles, who lived along the shore and near the tombs.

Jesus "gave them [the spirits] leave"—imagine that!!—to depart from the sick man. The spirits fled the man and entered the pigs. Crazed by the spirits, the 2,000 pigs plunged down the mountain and over a cliff into the sea. The deranged man was healed instantly and restored to sanity.

Compassion on Man and Spirit

Jesus had compassion **ON BOTH** the man and the spirits. The man was apparently known in the surrounding villages as the local "crazy," sort of like the town drunk in Bill W's day or the far-too-many addicted homeless today. The villagers avoided him as much as possible. With Jesus' simple guidance, the man's faith freed him from what was said to have been many years of agony and self-destruction. Do those years of pain and suffering sound familiar? They do to me.

There's also an important question about the spirits: How "evil" were they? After all, they begged Jesus to cast them into the swine rather than allow them to continue to plague the man. They did not simply flee from the man to plague other victims. They begged Jesus to free them, too. They wanted to be redeemed and be made whole. If you are so inclined to believe that "evil spirits" have a life of their own, perhaps you too can have some compassion *on* these spirits.

Of course, granting the spirits' wish wasn't too helpful to the dead pigs and their owners. In fact, the pig herders raced away and returned with a large crowd of owners and villagers. They were terrified and amazed when they saw that the man, whom they had known for so many years as a dangerous crazy, was healed. They were so afraid—and so faithless—that they "urged" Jesus to leave their area quickly and take the man with him. Jesus took the hint, already knowing from many similar experiences that you have to shake the dust off your cloak at those who are unwilling to see or hear the message and move on.

True Perseverance from Grace

As Jesus was climbing back aboard his boat, the man asked Jesus to take him with him. Instead, Jesus told him, "Go home to thy friends, and tell them what great things the Lord hath done for thee, and had ***hath compassion on thee.***" (bold italics added). The man, now sane and whole, did so and apparently became one of Jesus' most vocal supporters among the Gadarenes and in the Greco-Roman city of Decapolis.

Imagine the courage, the perseverance, that the man had to have to live every day after he was restored to sanity. He had to face his family and his neighbors as a living example of how a Power greater than himself could restore, and had restored, him to sanity. He may have lived as an example of that Power; he may have carried the message faithfully, as Jesus asked him to do. We do not know anything else about the man and his future. Did he become a quiet messenger or a fiery preacher or someone in between? Did he live a virtuous life and serve as living proof of the power of transformation? What were the results of his efforts? Did most of the Gadarenes shun him as a weird "one-off," a lucky alien in their midst, and ignore his message. Did a few listen to him, increase their faith, and change their way of life? We don't know the results. Do they even matter?

The True Goal: A Fit Spiritual Condition

Just as our program of recovery teaches us in the 12th Step: If we want to be restored to sanity, we are advised to surrender our lives to a Higher Power, clean up our side of the street, carry the message, and practice the principles as a way of life. Our founders' and our own decades of experience prove that as long as we carry the message—however haltingly—and practice the Principles in all of our affairs—however imperfectly—we strengthen our spiritual condition. As Bill W. stressed in the AA "Big Book," there is only one true goal of working the Steps and living the Traditions: to sustain and enhance a fit spiritual condition so that we stay sober, clean, and abstinent, so that our "evil spirits" remain inundated in the vast ocean of our joy and our abundance.

The Difference between Compassion *For* and Compassion *On* Others

I told this story in detail because it reflects the heart of my deep spiritual experience on Kilimanjaro. As I read the story, I felt very sad and very inspired at the same time. Sadly and with much grief, I realized that throughout my life, I had had very little **compassion for** most people, especially my own family. A wave of remorse and gratitude swept over me as I realized the enormity of the gift of **compassion** that Samia, Humphrey, Rodrik, Chef Ely, and all the rest of the "tough guys" *had on* me for 10 days.

They made sure I had the right foods to eat, enough clean water to drink, and a load light enough to carry so that I could reach the top of the mountain on my own two feet, both physically and emotionally, and with dignity. They carried everything for me, encouraged me when I faltered, refused to criticize but told me the truth, made sure I was healthy enough to go on, and showed me respect and even love. Most of the time I certainly did not deserve their compassion because on some days, as you have read, I complained, cussed, raged around like a lunatic, isolated myself from the others, and made embarrassing mistakes.

Critical Point: The crew did not have to help me; Samia could have sent me back down the mountain at any time for my rude behavior and my mistakes. Instead, Samia and the rest showered me with understanding, forgave me my mistakes, and made my way as easy as I would let them. In short, without knowing anything at all about the 12 Steps, they constantly practiced the principles of service and compassion as they lived the 12th Step.

I realized that a critical difference between the 12 Step Way of Life and "normal living" is the difference between the meaning of the phrase **"compassion for"** and the phrase **"compassion on."** Having compassion *for* someone implies that you feel sorry for the person. It is a passive "poor you" thought that allows the so-called empathizer to avoid doing anything to help the troubled person. The definitions of "for" in *Dictionary.com* imply "purpose" or "intention." How "nice"—with my tongue firmly in my cheek—it is that you might intend to have compassion **for others** in trouble; it does not mean you are going to take any action to help them. You might feel sorry for them, but **"for"** implies you do not feel an obligation to actively help the person.

Perhaps you have said, "I feel so bad for Robert's family because he is a falling down drunk." Did you offer to help Robert or his family, your fellows who suffer the agony of addiction and its consequences? Has your Fellowship ever sent out an appeal for funds needed to sustain its barebones effort to carry the message that saved your life, and you have ignored its appeal? Have you prospered in your recovery, turning your fortunes around to earn a much higher salary, perhaps even become wealthy, yet you still put the same one-dollar bill in the basket that you did 5, 10, even 25 or 30 years ago at every meeting you go to—when you bother to go?

Instead, having compassion *on* someone leaps beyond intention into *action*. That is exactly what Samia, Humphrey, Rodrik, Ely and the crew **had on** me. They went out of their way to help me; they often inconvenienced themselves and the whole team; they gave freely of their time, attention, strength, and expertise to help me fulfill my almost impossible dream. In short, as Jesus honored the mentally ill man's faith and rock-bottom desire to be whole again, the "tough guys" honored my often-grudging willingness to surrender to their will and persevere with my intense desire to reach my goal. Their compassionate actions benefited me in ways I can never repay.

As I lay there reading those chapters in Mark, I felt a wave of humility and gratitude that I had been blessed by these instruments of God's Grace, God's resolve that I should reach the peak and learn the true meaning of compassion.

My Sadness and My 12th Step Prayer
After I completed reading Mark 5, stunned by the revelation I felt, I wrote this prayer in my journal:

Father-Mother God, I ask you to help me have compassion on all—an active caring, understanding, forgiveness, and acceptance of them as they are—for I am that too—an imperfect human being doing the best I can One Day At A Time. FMG—I am intensely grateful for the compassion on me shown by Humphrey, Samia, Ely, the masseuse, Rodrik, the crew—especially the toilet cleaners—so I could reach the peak.

The Ultimate Lesson
The ultimate lesson I realized is this: **I lack compassion on others because I do not have it on myself.** If I do not have compassion on me, I cannot truly have it on others. Without active compassion, my efforts to be "nice," to help people succeed, and to give 12 Step service to other recovering addicts become only selfish manipulations to get what I want or to avoid pain.

As I write this, some time after I returned from Kili, I continue to struggle; I claim some progress in acting more patiently, refraining from criticism, and gaining just a hint of how to give unconditional acceptance to others, especially my family and the woman I love. I do practice having compassion **on** other people when I actively listen to those who need to share, befriend newcomers, carry the message as I can, give generously of my time and resources, live the message by my actions each day, and just have great fun with my recovery family.

As Samia—and my mistakes—taught so well: ***Pole, Pole!***

Slowly, slowly, I grow and change ODAT. I pray the Eleventh Step prayer and only seek God's will for me and the strength to carry that out. God's will is usually simple, and I express it by taking Step 12 each day: Carry the message, practice the principles, and "do unto others as you would have them do unto you." **May God's Will and Mine Be One!**

With this astonishing insight, I knew I had learned the lesson that my Higher Power had wanted me to learn when I began to consider climbing the "Mother Mountain": My deep need to accept compassion from others and to have **compassion on myself and on everyone everywhere**.

Kilimanjaro Completed

Onward to the Ngorongoro Crater and the Serengeti Plains

Mortality Beckons

PART 2

My Mortality Moments
The Ngorongoro Crater and
The Serengeti Plain
Days 12-18, June 30-July 6

WEDNESDAY, JUNE 30

Day 12, Afternoon and Evening
Prelude to My Mortality Moments

After the astounding experience of the past 12 days and my intense surprises from working the 12 Steps, I felt sad, exhilarated, and sincerely moved as I knew that my Kilimanjaro journey had ended. I remained stunned and in awe about Samia's, Humphrey's, Rodrik's, and the entire team's gift of compassion they had on me for the past 10 days. I felt caught between two worlds—the incredible natural world and all its beauty and wonder on the mountain and the "cold plunge" back to the contradictions of civilization. While we stayed in luxury that rivaled any resort in the world and were treated like royalty, the vast majority of the Tanzanians I saw worked very hard to scrape up enough food, clothing, and shelter to live through each day. But this new day promised a new adventure as we headed for our visit to the "Garden of Eden" within the Ngorongoro Crater and our 5-day trek across the famous Serengeti Plains.

Little did I know what lessons my FMG had in store for me during the next six days. When I began preparing to climb Kilimanjaro, my therapist and friends warned me that my adventure might bring me face to face with the idea of my mortality, a topic I had been loath to consider my entire life. I have hated funerals and avoided them since I attended my beloved grandfather's funeral when I was 9 years old. At the time, my overwhelming sense of loss was compounded afterward by months of uncontrolled grieving by my mother. I received very little of much needed comforting at the time from my parents, so I learned to avoid funerals and feeling grief. Until my parents passed away within six months of each other in 1991-1992, I had missed the funerals of my maternal grandmother, all of my many aunts and uncles (22 altogether), my young sister-in-law, and several middle-aged cousins.

As I matured in recovery in my 40s and 50s, I did attend the funerals of my parents after we reconciled, one mother-in-law, and my two fathers-in-law. However, during those times, I was too busy being the "strong" male to grieve too openly or for too long. Even after my parents' deaths, I never truly grieved all the losses of my life. I truly did not know how to grieve.

So, I had never come to grips with my own mortality—the simple fact I am going to die one day. My lifelong prayer/request/goal/wish to my FMG has been to live to be 100 years old. As an erstwhile historian, I am very curious about how the world will have changed from one mid-century to another. Since I have always enjoyed robust health—and still do, thank FMG—I never had any major occasion to seriously contemplate my own death.

Since I had begun thinking of this Kilimanjaro adventure, my explicit aim was to be on the mountain on my 60th birthday and reach the peak. My implicit aim was to prove that despite my divorce and the painful loss of my stepchildren, I was still very much alive. I wasn't thinking about dying, just staying healthy, avoiding altitude sickness, and reaching that peak.

Because of my many years in multiple 12 Step programs, I did expect a significant spiritual experience. I had no idea what it might be—I never do before it happens. Obviously, my spiritual experience—and the lesson—on the mountain was to recognize, accept, and feel grateful for the amazing compassion Samia and the 'tough guys' **had on** me. Of course, I also learned that I lack true compassion and need to follow their exceptional example of compassion and service.

But facing my mortality? It didn't happen on Mother Mountain; it did happen on the Serengeti Plain.

The Ngorongoro Crater

First, let me set the scene for you before I discuss the many mortality moments that I experienced during our safari, because the nearby Ngorongoro Crater and the Serengeti Plains were astounding. Many, if not most, of you have heard about or seen photos or documentaries about the Serengeti and the great annual migration of millions of animals that happens there. Although I missed the migration's high point, I saw many spectacular sights that proved the Serengeti was even more remarkable than I had imagined. As I'll explain below, it more than fulfilled my dream of a lifetime and gave me the spiritual gift of bringing me face to face with my mortality.

However, it is less likely you have heard about the Ngorongoro Crater, 107-square-mile caldera 180 miles northeast of Arusha. It is the easiest way for us "civilized" people to visit a true "Garden of Eden." It is an enormous caldera of a thankfully extinct (we hope!), huge volcano. The Maasai named it El-Nkoronkoro or *Gift of Life*. It truly has been that to the Maasai because it is a wide, fertile plain with a salt lake at one end and many small rivers and streams flowing down its sides into wetlands. It is the natural home to huge herds of small Thomson's gazelles, large Grant's gazelles, a small antelope called a "dik-dik," wildebeests, hippopotami, zebras, and even a handful of very rare rhinoceroses. These plant eaters attract and feed large numbers of lions, leopards, cheetahs, hyenas, and jackals. In turn, the carnivores help sustain the populations of dozens of smaller mammals and bird species, especially the scavenging vultures, storks, and more. They help sustain the herbivores by culling the weakest from the herds so that those with the strongest genes—and perhaps the smartest brains—survive.

The Crater also provides fertile grazing land for large herds of Maasai cattle, the tribe's primary source of food and wealth. Although the Maasai have legal grazing rights, they must take their herds out at night to avoid the predators.

According to Wikipedia, "It is the world's largest inactive, intact, and unfilled volcanic caldera. The crater, which formed when a large volcano exploded and collapsed on itself two to three million years ago, is 610 meters (2,000 feet) deep and its floor covers 260 square kilometers (107 square miles). Estimates of the height of the original volcano range from 4,500 to 5,800 meters (14,800 to 19,000 feet) high. The elevation of the crater floor is 1,800 meters (5,900 feet) above sea level." (https://en.wikipedia.org/wiki/Ngorongoro_Conservation_Area). These facts mean that at its largest, the volcano could have been as tall as or taller than Kilimanjaro.

Even more fascinating, hominids—our ancient ancestors—are known to have lived in this area when the volcano exploded. Can you imagine being a short, naked, stick-carrying, two-legged hominid living in a small family group? Every day, you use your only advantages—your mind, your memory, and your knowledge—to survive against the lions, leopards, cheetahs, and hyenas that are bigger and faster than you, yet just as hungry!

Suddenly one day, the earth under your feet begins to tremble violently. It erupts in an enormous blast and casts scorching hot lava, boulders, and clouds of ash everywhere. It continues to do so off and on for hundreds or thousands of generations, yet somehow, as the famous archaeological digs in the nearby Olduvai Gorge show, you and your descendants survive this incredibly dangerous environment. Amazing!

During this remarkable day, we crisscrossed the Crater's many dirt roads for hours, although unfortunately, we had to share the space with dozens of other "Toyotabeasts" and Land Rovers packed with tourists. The throng of noisy tourist vehicles racing around to see the same animals severely reduced the "Garden of Eden" effect. We spent the night in a camp (back to "luxury" tents!) on the rim above the crater.

It's Good to be the King—a Real King!

Before we reached the crater, after we ate breakfast, and our Kilimanjaro trek ended, the crew packed up our Land Rovers. There, we met our Serengeti guide Kihago, and he drove us across country from the Lodge to the "luxurious" tent camp owned by a real Maasai Mara king. This king was literally the lord of some 3,000 Maasai tribespeople in his clan who lived in an area that stretched many miles around the Crater rim.

As we drove along the edge of this magnificent caldera toward the camp, we enjoyed a vista that stretched across the entire crater. When we turned to look away from the crater, we saw a small herd of cattle being shepherded by young Maasai boys and girls while a herd of zebras wandered near the cattle.

When we reached the king's "village," we learned it is **very good** to be a middle-aged Maasai king: He had a cell phone, an expensive wristwatch, a personal bodyguard of young warriors, a Land Rover, and three wives and many children. He was well-educated and had visited Europe. By the way, this king could be considered relatively "poor": Another village we had passed was the home of a Maasai king with **50 wives** living in dozens of huts. He had so many children that he built his own concrete block schoolhouse to educate them!

The king we visited had tremendous responsibilities: Although Tanzania is a parliamentary republic, in his kingdom, he served as judge, jury, and executioner over all his people's disputes. He served as the area's representative to the national government and as the advocate for his people in the often-difficult decisions that the contending interests (tribes, government, businesses, conservationists) made about how to best protect the Crater conservation area.

That protection requires a delicate balance between ensuring the Maasai can continue their traditional way of life while they and the government benefit from tourist income. Tourism that draws thousands of visitors each year has created hundreds of jobs, but its success depends on protecting the wild animals in the Crater. No easy task when only a small number of government employees patrol a Conservation Area of more than 3,300 square miles—30 times the size of the crater. Fifty to 60 trucks a day filled with gawking tourists are allowed to travel across the dirt roads that crisscross the Crater plain. Fortunately, the "wild" animals are very used to the daily invasion and ignore the trucks and the tourists.

In this king's realm, his first wife and her children lived in a concrete block house with a satellite dish and radio antenna on the roof. About 50 yards away, his second and third wives, including the youngest, a pregnant woman no more than 17 or 18 years old, lived in traditional mud-covered huts inside a traditional cattle corral. This corral consisted of about two acres surrounded by a wall made of very tall, thin, tightly bound saplings or small tree trunks. Every afternoon, the children who tended the herd of dozens of cattle outside in the open fields during the day drove the cattle back into the corral and locked the gates. After all, they have to keep the lions and leopards away from their livelihood—and their main source of food and wealth! The more cattle, the wealthier you are among the Maasai.

Their mud huts were whitewashed on the outside and had short sides and very tall sloping roofs with openings so smoke from the cooking fires could escape. The walls were made of mud layered over thin sticks, like primitive adobe. Imagine a large, mud-covered teepee with circular walls.

The hut's interior consisted of small, dark rooms; a kitchen area with an open fire; small sleeping nooks with wooden beds covered in hides and woven blankets; storage bins; and even a small manger-like area where they fed newborn calves. The floor consisted of packed dirt, and the furniture was made of rough carved wood. They had some modern pots and pans, plastic bowls, metal containers, and cooking utensils; they cooked in small ovens next to, or over, open fires.

The "Goat" of the Day

After we visited the king's village, we drove to our camp and met another group that like us, had just come down from Kili. I mention them only because one man said he had an electronic calorie burning counter; he said he took the Mweka trail straight up the side of the mountain. During his summit morning (up at midnight and the 6- to 9-hour hike to the top), he said he burned *10,000* calories. Of course, we took it much slower and walked shorter distances each day than he did, but we were still burning 4,000-5,000 calories a day at altitude. No wonder I lost 15 pounds in 10 days and then put them all back on in the next week as we sat on our duffs most of the time in our Land Rover!

As for the "goat"—the king invited us to share a goat barbecue and special soup with his young warriors-in-training. The young warriors lived apart from the rest of the tribe and trained to master hunting and warrior skills. All they ate was milk, meat, and blood. They always carried their spears and clubs with them to protect against wild animal attacks as well as to show their status.

Maasai warriors-in-training stirring the traditional goat stew made from goat guts, blood, and bones as well as acacia bark and local herbs. A very different taste!

The barbecued goat leg, cooked over a small, open fire, tasted like gamey lamb, but the special soup was something else! It included boiled goat meat, organs—heart, intestines, etc.—and ribs with herbs and acacia tree bark cooked in goat blood and water. The broth was a dark red, but the meat and organs just turned gray as the mixture was cooked in a pot over an open fire for an hour and a half. The warriors constantly stirred it with a pendulum-shaped wooden tool. They used the tool like a blender blade, twirling it in their hands like a Scout would twirl a stick to make a fire. Of course, we were "invited" to stir the pot, so to speak. It was easy, but the soup had a unique smell—gamey with an oily smell of boiling fat and internal organs and the smell of boiling blood I can't describe.

In a funny "macho" event, the other tourist group included several 20-something guys who hovered around the gorgeous Felicia like bees hovering around honeysuckle. However, when the king invited us to eat the soup, all the "macho" guys shied away, so to prove a point, Felicia smiled, stood tall, stepped up, and drank it first. Only after she said the soup was okay did the guys—the wusses!—try it.

I happily admit I was a middle-aged "wuss" and did not taste it until after they did. Its taste was as unique as its smell: It had a woody taste from the acacia bark and herbs as well as salty, pungent, and meaty. It was neither delicious nor revolting, just very foreign to my taste buds. The goat barbeque tasted meaty, but was stringy and tough.

After that little "ritual," the young warriors started pulling goat ribs from the sticks over the fire and gnawed the ribs. Of course, the guys loved that and joined right in the gnawing. Young men are the same everywhere!

Traditional Dance and Modern Culture

As the sun set, about a dozen Maasai girls dressed in traditional costumes came from the village nearby and chanted and danced into our midst. They wore large, wide collars around their necks and shook the collars as they danced and chanted. After the warriors finished eating, they joined in and began to chant "hoom bi" and to take very high vertical leaps. They would bounce a few times and then leap as high as they could while they screamed war cries. Impressively, a few of them jumped at least three feet off the ground, and a duo jumped together in rhythm as everyone else chanted. Samia told us that the dances were traditional warrior-girl courting dances that they performed to show us some of their culture.

The dance was interesting, but somewhat contrived. It seemed like the young people were a bit embarrassed about doing the dances, but it was part of the "entertainment package" we paid for to stay in the king's campground. Literally, a command performance!

When the dancers left the small open space, I watched as they took off their traditional dresses and revealed that they wore blue jeans and shirts or dresses under their ritual garb. They do not dress in traditional costume much of the time. The men and boys do wear the traditional Maasai cloaks, but they wear shirts, jeans, or shorts under the cloaks. Even more interesting, I saw the chief standing about 50 feet away behind us and out of the group's line of sight; he was next to his Land Rover talking on his cellphone. A fascinating juxtaposition of using tourist entertainment to keep a tribal tradition alive, yet using the tourist income to live as much as they could in the modern world.

After the girls and warriors left, we watched a glorious sunset: a stream of clouds laced in burnt orange, fiery red, bright yellow, sky blue, and deep purple. Then, facing east from the door to my tent, I could see for miles down the long, wide valley of tall grasses that comprised the king's domain.

As darkness fell, I wondered at the astonishing difference a day can make. Two days ago, I was stumbling down from the peak of Mt. Kilimanjaro. Yesterday, I was reveling in the lap of luxury with a hot shower and a soft bed. Today, I am going to sleep on a narrow cot in a thick tent that, thank God!, had its own toilet, sink, and shower. By safari standards, truly luxurious!

Serengeti Plain and Mass Migration Summary

After we toured the fabulous Ngorongoro Crater and enjoyed the king's hospitality, we drove to the world-famous Serengeti Plain. First, before I begin my mortality moments, let me describe the enormous size and natural marvels of the Plain and give you an accurate portrait of the equally famous annual mass migration across the Plain.

The **Serengeti Plain** is a geographical region in Africa, mostly in northern Tanzania with some of it in southwestern Kenya. It annoys the heck out of the Tanzanians because the Western concept is that all of it is in Kenya, because for decades, Kenya's tourist advertising campaigns have claimed it and the massive migration as their own. But we drove for five days and never left Tanzania.

The Plain is just south of the equator and covers about 30,000 square kilometers or more than 12,000 square miles. To give you a better comparison, it is the size of the state of Maryland or about the size of Connecticut and Massachusetts combined.

As noted, it is home to the largest mammal migration in the world. It is one of the Seven Natural Wonders of Africa and one of the 10 natural travel wonders of the world, according to Wikipedia.

Known for its substantial lion population, it is one of the easiest places to observe lion prides in their almost natural environment—I can't call it truly natural when thousands of tourists in hundreds of SUVs traverse the Plain every year, and the tour companies and park rangers work together to tag lions so they can be found easily. I would add that lions are fairly easy to see because unless they are hungry, they spend most of their time sleeping.

However, it is still a very dangerous place. It is home to about 70 large mammals, dozens of small mammals, and 500 types of birds. They are protected in a national park, tribal parks, and private reserves. Except for the occasional Maasai herder or park ranger who works on the plain during the day, no humans stay in the park at night or live there year-round.

Its remarkable diversity derives from its many different habitats, including vast and abundant grasslands, forests that line rivers and streams, swamps, kopjes (small, rocky volcanic hills sticking out of the plain), and woodlands. The best-known plant is the acacia tree, the one you see in all the Serengeti photos and posters; they dot the grasslands in stark relief against the flat plain. As many of the photos show, giraffes do indeed graze on the tender, new leaves at the top of the acacia, somehow avoiding the long and sharp thorns that dot every branch.

Fun Fact: Elephants eat the acacia trees too—all of it, as they tear off limbs and knock over small tree trunks! Their tongues and mouths have adapted so that the thorns do not hurt them.

The most common large mammals are blue wildebeests (actually dark gray, brown, or black), many kinds of gazelles, zebras, and Cape buffalos. However, most tourists go to see the "Big Five" – lions, leopards, elephants, rhinoceroses, and Cape buffalo. Those five are only a part of the large animal story; I have my own "Big Ten," adding cheetahs, hippopotami, giraffes, ostriches, and a very interesting bird hybrid—the owl eagle—to the Big Five.

The great migration happens in phases. As the fall and winter rainy season produces lush grasslands, the migration begins in the south from the Ngorongoro Conservation Area (of which the Crater is only a small part). It moves northeast in January. More than 250,000 zebras lead the way for more than 1.7 million wildebeest, followed by hundreds of thousands of gazelles, antelopes, and other grazers. Of course, tagging along for the "easy, free" meals are several thousand lions, hundreds of leopards and cheetahs, and thousands of spotted hyenas—a particularly nasty, dangerous creature.

The first segment usually lasts until March; the wildebeests have their calves—up to half a million!—within only a few weeks in February. The mass calving causes a frenzy of attacks by the predators, but the mature wildebeests are well equipped with sharp hooves and horns to fight them off. However, as you may have watched in nature documentaries, the lions, leopards, and pack-hunting hyenas are cunning, fast, and powerful. They are experts at taking down unprotected calves or old or sick grazers.

That's how the circle of life continues, regardless of our modern Western hyper-sensibilities. Although today I do not eat much meat because I have thousands of choices for a balanced diet, I can guarantee this: If I was a Maasai warrior in the Serengeti and the choice was to hunt down and eat a Thomson's gazelle or go hungry, I would learn how to stalk, spear, skin, gut, and cook the gazelle as quickly as I could. Humans are born omnivores—we evolved to eat anything because food was so hard to find, catch, kill, and eat many millennia ago.

When the rain ends in late spring in the Serengeti, the animals move northwest to the Grumeti River basin, where they usually stay until late June. The river crossings that start in July attract a lot of safaris for a fairly bloodthirsty reason; the tourists watch the hordes of hungry crocodiles that lie in wait in the water to grab their own free meals of unsuspecting grazers.

A herd of zebras and a few wildebeests drink and cool off in the Grumeti River. Fortunately, no crocodiles laid in wait this day!

The herds reach Kenya in late July and early August and remain there until early November when a short rainy season begins. With the rain signal, they begin moving south again and complete their circle back to the Ngorongoro grasslands in December.

However, the 1,000-mile round trip is extremely challenging. About a quarter of a million wildebeests—more than 10 percent of the total—and tens of thousands of gazelles, antelopes, zebras, and other grazers die each year. Although many become meals for the predators, most of them die in child birth, or of thirst, hunger, or sheer exhaustion. I can attest to the serious problems they have with thirst and hunger. As you'll read in detail later, one of my most humbling mortality moments involved wildebeests and zebras driven to distraction by thirst and the tricks of a selfish lioness.

From Apex Predators to 'Chicken McNuggets' ®

The secret to the Serengeti's rich diversity of grazers and predators is that each type, even close relatives, has evolved a different diet. According to Wikipedia, wildebeests like to eat the shorter grasses; zebras like the taller ones. The dik-dik antelope eats grasses and the lowest leaves on trees; impalas eat the leaves from the middle of the tree; and giraffes graze the leaves closest to the top.

The large, apex predators have a preferred "menu" as well: The larger lions and leopards prefer to attack the smaller Grant's and Thomson's gazelles, and they will attack young or vulnerable wildebeests, Cape buffalos, zebras, antelopes, even elephants. But they shy away from the large and healthy animals because the wildebeests, buffalos, zebras, and elephants can fight back and kill them, and the antelopes can outrun and outmaneuver them.

Cheetahs are extremely fast—up to 60 mph in short bursts. However, as they are much smaller than lions and leopards, they avoid the large mammals and focus on the smaller gazelles and dik-diks.

In a somewhat grizzly, but humorous vein (pun intended), the 'tough guys' call the small dik-diks and Thomson's gazelles "chicken McNuggets" ® because they are the predators' easiest prey. Ouch!

Hyenas tend to hunt in pairs or small packs. They are primarily scavengers and tend to hover around lion and leopard kills, often trying to drive the lions away from their kill. They will also attack lion cubs, so the lionesses are always on alert. In packs, they will attack newborn, old, or sick wildebeests, zebras, and larger antelopes such as elands. Jackals also scavenge when they can, but usually pursue rodents and small mammals, such as dik-diks. In short, the pecking order comes down to which predator is the hungriest and has the strength and numbers to take down the most vulnerable prey.

Close-up of the nasty hyena. Its fierce, tenacious nature is no laughing matter!

It's Even Better to Be the Lion King

By the way, if it's good to be a Maasai Mara tribal king, it's even better to be a male lion. They do not tend to hunt; their jobs are to protect the pride and mate with the lionesses, which they do with enthusiasm. I have watched a male lion follow a lioness in heat and mate every 10 or 15 minutes. The mating lasts about a minute; then the female and male lie down for a while. Then the female gets up and starts moving again, and of course, the male, like any "smart" male, follows. And the process repeats itself, for a mating that, I was told by my guide, might last for **up to two days!** The lion is a better man than I am, for sure! When they are in heat, the lionesses seem to accept it. The lioness I saw did not push the lion away. She seemed quite calm. Whether or not they "enjoyed" it is not relevant, and the question is anthropomorphic—human centered—as their purpose is to reproduce, not have a good time. Thank Goodness, I'm human!

The lionesses do almost all of the hunting; they go through pregnancy with, give birth to, raise, and protect their cubs. Like the argument in the US about the wage disparity between men and women, the "wages" of the lioness are much lower than those of the males. Once the lioness makes a kill, the male "king" of the pride immediately steps in, runs the females and cubs off, and eats the best parts of the kill. When he is "fat, dumb, and happy," he strolls away and lies down. Only then do the females and cubs eat, yet they have to be alert for, and often fight off, the hyenas, jackals, vultures, and storks ready to barge in and fight for their share.

Efficient Mother Nature

Usually, the animals follow a pecking order as they devour a carcass: Males eat first, females and cubs second, hyenas and vultures third, jackals fourth. Mixed in are many kinds of meat-eating insects and flies. Eventually, fungi grow on and eat the horns. Within a few weeks, an entire carcass can disappear. Every ounce will have been "recycled" either as food or fertilizer.

For example, on our safari, we happened upon a Cape buffalo skeleton. Our guide, Kihago, told us about the pecking order I've described. Then, he showed us a streaming fungus—a parasite by definition—that looked like moss growing off—that is, eating—the buffalo's horns. The horns are made of cartilage that softens as it ages, so fungus spores latch onto them easily, unlike bone made of hard calcium. He added that as the carcass ages, the hyenas and jackals return, rip the ribs and other bones off the skeleton, and take them to their lairs to chew to reach the marrow and sharpen and clean their teeth.

Lesson Learned: Mother Nature is thoroughly efficient, nothing goes to waste, and the strong do indeed survive.

Mortality Moments from Real Danger

For the rest of the book, I change my format a bit. Each section focuses on one of the five critical "mortality moments" that genuinely frightened me or astounded me with insight into my mortality. Unlike the detailed daily discussion about my climb up and down Kili, I build from the least frightening or enlightening moment to the most important mortality moment; it is not in chronological order. I do give the day and date of each so you can follow me around the Serengeti.

The key point to remember is that my feet were severely injured and swollen. I could barely walk; there was no way I could run. Each night I took off my heavy boots and put on my warm, lined booties. Each morning, I had to cram my swollen, painful feet into my tight boots and two layers of socks. My feet hurt like hell any time I tried to walk. I felt as physically vulnerable as I have ever felt—with good reason as you'll find out.

WEDNESDAY, JUNE 30

Mortality Moment One
Hungry Hyena Number One

The night we spent near the Crater, I was camped in my luxurious tent—with a real toilet and a shower!—at the edge of a beautiful valley. The 10 other tents were spaced about 40 or 50 feet apart with stands of brush and trees in between. We had our relative "privacy," but the spacing also made us vulnerable. My tent was near the end of the line and among the farthest from the main tent where our guide and the camp staff slept.

The night was windy and cold, with a three-eighths moon high in a cloudless sky. Sounds idyllic, doesn't it? Not exactly. In the middle of the night I had a "visitor." I was awakened by a frantic sniffling and pawing on the "front porch"—a covered canvas laid out in front of my thankfully thick canvas tent. I just laid there. I didn't move for some minutes until the noise stopped, and I heard my "visitor" slink back into the woods. I had a tough time going back to sleep, but I dozed off and on until the horizon began to lighten.

Fortunately, the tents are incredibly well designed to protect you. They consist of thick canvas; the "doors" are thick flaps with industrial-scale zippers. Each tent is a "box" with all six sides, especially the floor, stitched tightly together, impervious to rain and water, and thank God, hungry, frantically scratching hyenas.

As soon as I could see outside, I got up, put on my clothes and my boots, and unzipped the door to my tent. By the zipped door and all over the "front porch" were muddy paw prints. I quickly—well, actually slowly and painfully—got Kihago to look at the prints. He told me that they were either hyena or jackal, but most likely hyena because of their large size.

"Shit!" I thought. A hyena tried to rip my tent open to get at me. I must have smelled like one of the easiest and tastiest meals the hyena would ever find. No one would have heard my screams in time to save me. "Shit and double shit!"

At breakfast when I told everyone else about my "visitor," there were a lot of hesitant chuckles. Kihago and the camp staff assured me that all I had to do was yell at the hyena and it would run away. I did not feel reassured; I kept my mouth shut, but I felt more afraid because of their nonchalant response. Not exactly a response that would encourage me to think they would help me if I got into real trouble. At that moment, I began to feel fairly concerned and a bit more mortal than I had before.

FRIDAY AFTERNOON, JULY 2

Mortality Moment Two
The Lioness, the Cub, and the Carcass

During the afternoon of our second day on safari, we drove across the Serengeti plain under a bright blue sky. We saw several children, no more than seven or eight years old, in bright red Maasai cloaks herding about 200 cows. Later, we saw numerous herds of zebras, wildebeests, and the ever-present Thomson gazelle "McNuggets" ®. About 30 young ostriches raced across the road in front of us. Kihago told us that we could tell they were young because of their grayish-brown color and their relatively small size. Mature male ostriches are the ones with the bright pinkish white head and neck and dark black feathers. Mature females are grayish-brown and larger than the young ones.

Bad Joke: Why did the female ostrich cross the road?
Answer: To answer the "male" on the other side.

We also saw large numbers of giraffes, including a major family group with nine calves of different ages and sizes, grazing in a large stand of acacia trees. There were about 20 giraffes total, a sizable grouping as giraffes tend to be more solitary as they mature. Large Grant's gazelles clustered around the giraffes and ate from the same stand of trees, again sharing the wealth by eating the lower leaves.

Trick, but True Question: What do you call a group of giraffes?
Answer: Obvious when you think about it—a "Tower."

A "tower" of almost 20 giraffes, including nine calves, grazes in a
thicket of young acacia trees on the Serengeti Plain.

In mid-afternoon, we joined a "herd" of about 30 trucks that circled a
lone leopard lazing on a large tree branch. Dozens of idiotic "touristas" were
yelling at each other and pointing at the leopard. Their cameras were clicking
and whirring, making quite a racket. Obviously not the "Garden of Eden,"
because the poor leopard "knew the drill" and was probably annoyed every
day by hordes of tourists, so it did its best to ignore us and sleep. As we
watched it for about 30 minutes, it did occasionally raise its head to sneer at
us. Otherwise, it slept as we gawked at it.

About 20 minutes later, I had my second mortality moment. Again, with
trucks parked everywhere, a lioness carried a Thomson's gazelle carcass within
a few feet of our Rover and walked toward a cub sitting on a small rock farther down the road. The cub had been straining its neck and looking anxiously down the road, watching and waiting for "momma" to bring him (her?)
dinner.

Where's Momma? A months-old lion cub anxiously looks for the lioness that is bringing "home" a Chicken McNugget *—a Thomson's gazelle—for dinner.

Before this moment, we had seen lots of bones and flocks of vultures hovering around dead animals, but we had not seen a fresh kill in the mouth of a lioness. Reality is that the "food chain" means beautiful animals that eat only plants must die to feed other beautiful animals that eat only meat. That harsh fact of life hit me very hard. Like almost all other Americans, I have never butchered a hog, a cow, or even a deer; I buy my meat chopped up prettily and wrapped up neatly in plastic. In my whole life, I have shot and killed only one living creature: One rabbit when I was 12 years old. After I looked into its open, lifeless eyes, I could never kill another animal.

As an adult and a confirmed city dweller, I never gave the natural order of the food chain any real thought; however, on the Serengeti Plain, finding a fellow mammal to eat is all that carnivores and omnivores like me think about—except sex once in a while. With any luck, I will die peacefully in my bed and not be one of those "happy meals" for a hungry carnivore when I am old. But I came closer than I ever expected within the next three days.

FRIDAY MORNING, JULY 2

Mortality Moment Three
Hungry Hyena Number Two

That Thursday night (July 1), we had camped on the plain in a copse of trees near a stream. It was laid out much like the previous camp with individual tents 30 to 50 feet apart, separated by bushes and trees. Early Friday morning, I was awakened by another night "visitor," another hyena. This middle-of-the-night visit was more frightening than the first because this hyena scratched and clawed at the side of my tent, trying to dig under it or rip out the stitched seam along the bottom.

However, this time I was more prepared when I woke up. I grabbed my camera, turned on the flash, and quickly flashed the bright light at the side of the tent several times. I then turned on the lights and yelled. The hyena was startled and ran away.

I did not feel particularly brave. I felt scared and lucky. I felt glad I had been "educable" and had learned that bright lights and noise might startle an animal trying to get into my tent. After all, the hyenas—and most wild animals—prefer to take the path of least resistance to a good meal. The hyenas especially prefer to scavenge. I still must have smelled like a juicy morsel to the hyena. Thank Goodness, there was only one! A smart pack might have ripped open the seams.

Since that didn't happen this time, I was able to go back to sleep. When I mentioned the hyena the next morning at breakfast, Kihago told me I had done the right thing. "Well, duh", I thought, "I'm still alive."

SUNDAY, JULY 4 INDEPENDENCE DAY??? – AFTERNOON

Mortality Moment Four
The Wildebeest That Wandered *Toward* the Lions

Independence Day! Except for the Injured Wildebeest

Although today was U.S. Independence Day, I learned this day more about the extraordinary "interdependence" of every living thing than I ever had before. I felt humbled and understood that my life, though valuable in its own right, is just another infinitesimal cog that keeps the Great Circle of Life perpetually moving.

I learned this awe-inspiring lesson during this day's drive through the Serengeti. I witnessed two of the most remarkable examples of 'life and death' behavior I have ever seen. Both occurred during the same amazing incident. By the way, these events did not include the sight of dozens of vultures, a Kori bustard (huge bird with eagle-like head and beak), and a huge stork—yes, a stork—scavenging the carcass of a dead wildebeest. We had been watching scavengers for several days now, and the sight was "old hat." How easy it is to become used to gruesome sights as soon as you accept them as "normal" or as "nature's way" (in homage to the late Crocodile Hunter Steve Irwin)! But the sheer number and variety of scavengers this time shocked me.

A Nasty Lioness Harasses Thirsty Grazers

About 11 a.m., we came upon two huge herds of wildebeest and zebras, more than a thousand wildebeest and hundreds of zebras all standing on one side of the dirt road we drove along. On the other side of the dirt road were a small, algae-green pond and a small stream of water, practically a dry river bed. Across the small stream was a large clump of bushes and trees. We parked our Land Rover "beast" within a few feet of the carcass of a recently killed Thomson's gazelle, scattering several vultures as we drove to within 50 yards of the herds.

The wildebeests and zebras were milling around in groups, looking very thirsty, but not crossing the road to the stream. We asked Kihago what was going on, and he said a lioness was hiding upstream and the animals knew it was there. They were too frightened to cross the road.

But Kihago then said something that amazed me, and I realized that the lions are much nastier and even more conscious and thoughtful than I had ever considered. He explained, "The lioness is just messing with them. She's eaten recently and is just sitting by the stream so the wildebeest can see her. She knows they are thirsty, but she doesn't want them to drink at her watering hole."

When he said this, I could not see the lioness sitting more than a hundred yards upstream, yet Kihago could see her clearly. I had to use the super zoom on my video camera to finally spot the lioness. She indeed was sitting out in the open on her haunches. Her belly protruded with whatever she had killed and gorged on recently, apparently the other half of the gazelle we were parked next to. She indeed was staring at the herds milling about and pawing nervously across the road. (Note: You can experience these amazing sights by watching the video clips available through the links in the Kindle version of this book, or go to our website at http://www.recoveryfca.com.)

For the next two hours, we watched the wildebeests and zebras grow thirstier and thirstier. Every 10 minutes or so, one of the wildebeests would either get so thirsty, or gather up enough courage, that it would walk out of the herd alone and move slowly toward the beckoning water. Then, it would either see or smell the lion, and it would turn and race back to the herd.

Either from abject fear or a strong sense of survival—maybe the same thing—the zebras never took the lead. They waited, either mixed in with, or mostly behind, the wildebeests. The zebra "master" males, each of whom protected a small "harem" of females and young, barked or whinnied loudly in unique, high-pitched calls that sounded like the strained bark of a small dog. The males dashed around the edges of the herd, barking loudly both to warn their "harems" of females and young about the danger and to chase away any "unattached" males who wanted to encroach on their harem. The large zebra herd was an unusual grouping that came together at the watering hole to protect themselves from the lions. Normally, the zebras we saw were in relatively small groups of 10 to 30 when they fed on the open plain.

A Pecking Order at the Water "Fountain"?

I don't know why the wildebeest drank first. Maybe a natural pecking order had evolved over millions of years. At numerous watering holes I have parked or camped near in five African countries, I have sat for hours and watched species after species take turns or share different sides of the same watering hole. Troops of baboons and herds of elephants, wildebeests, zebras, many species of gazelles, Cape buffalos, and more seem to work on a natural rotation and co-operate to take turns drinking. Except the baboons, all of these are herbivores, and the baboons do not pose a threat to the herbivores and vice versa. The predators—lions, leopards, cheetahs, hyenas, and jackals—rarely drink during the day and visit the watering holes at night. I've heard their roars on the far side of a watering hole in the middle of the night. A very scary sound, indeed.

However on this hot, dry day, time after time, a single wildebeest would walk across the road toward the water. Every now and then, a few more would straggle slowly behind it, borrowing the thirsty courage of the leader to buck up their own will or using the leader as a shield from the lion.

The hot sun rose higher and higher into the mid-day sky. The herds grew increasingly restless, milling about, pawing the dry dirt, raising dust that made them even thirstier.

"You Go First!"

Some of the larger, presumably "more senior" male wildebeests even used their heads and horns to butt "less senior" wildebeests toward the water. Their actions made me feel an intense kinship with them. I remembered that when I was a child, we would do virtually the same thing when we were afraid to do something new—like cross a stream, jump into a pool of water, walk through a cemetery at night, or worse. We said the same thing the wildebeests were "saying" to each other:

"You go first."
"No, not me. You go first."
"What's the matter? Are you afraid? Fraidy cat, fraidy cat!"
"If you're so brave, why don't you go first? So, who's the fraidy cat?"

And on and on until one of us would either feel enough courage or enough shame to go first.

I suspect that you, my reader, often felt and did the same thing, not only when you were a child, but as an adult. I worked for many years in a large bureaucracy that discouraged risk-taking; one of our (the worker bees') favorite expressions was: "The pioneers are the ones with the arrows in their backs." I can say that on occasion, I took what I hoped were prudent risks. Most of the time, I avoided the arrows when I had good bosses who wanted to actually get things done. Sometimes, I took the arrows and suffered unpleasant consequences when my bosses feared change or were jealous of my success.

Among the wildebeests, when the younger ones were pushed, most of them scampered away from the others and ran back into the middle of the herd. I could almost feel them thinking: "Are you nuts? There is a freaking lion over there! If you're so thirsty, you go first."

At the same time, dozens of ugly vultures crowded the trees, perched virtually hidden among the limbs and leaves, across the stream and watched the show. They knew one small meal—the half of the small dead gazelle near us—was waiting; I suspect they were "hoping," if they can feel such a thing, that the lion would attack and kill a much more satisfying meal, like a wildebeest.

The average Blue Wildebeest, the most common in the Serengeti, weighs between 8 and 15 times more than the average Thomson's gazelle. The smallest female gazelles may weigh as little as 33 pounds while the largest male wildebeests may weigh 550 pounds or more. By the way, both can sprint at about the same speed—50 miles per hour—for short distances. Another reason their predators go after the young, the old, and the sick. They would waste too much precious energy chasing a healthy animal that will simply outrun it. (Sources: https://en.wikipedia.org/wiki/Thomson%27s_gazelle; https://en.wikipedia.org/wiki/Wildebeest)

Once in a while, a wildebeest "leader" would reach the water. As soon as it would begin to drink, dozens of wildebeests would rush toward the water in a melee and gulp greedily at the dirty water. Each time, the lion would make a quick dash toward the small group, and they all would scatter and race back across the road to the herd.

Finally, the lioness either got sleepy, or bored, or had had enough "fun" teasing the herds, and wandered into the bushes on the other side of the stream. Still, it took about 15 minutes for the herds to realize the lion was gone. Tentatively, a few wildebeests crossed the road and began to drink. When the rest of the two herds saw nothing happened, they first slowly crossed the road and reached the stream.

The Dam of Fear Breaks, The Melee Surges

Then, the dam of fear was broken by their intense thirst and the courage of the bold few, and hundreds of wildebeests and zebras raced to the stream. Sometimes they slammed into each other, but the surge took on a flow of its own. The animals formed a living river as they followed well-worn trenches down the muddy bank into the stream.

They jammed the small dirty pool in front of us and filled the even smaller pools upstream where the lion had been. Many pushed and shoved their way through the others to reach the pools. They gulped the water quickly, still fearing attack, and raced back across the road as soon as their thirst was sated.

This chaotic surge and retreat lasted a long time as the melee played out across a 100-yard-long stretch of the stream. We could not count the numbers as individuals and small groups raced into the stream at different entry points. The animals mixed and mingled, some satisfied with one drink, others going back for more. On our side, our view was also obscured by clumps of small trees and bushes along the stream bank.

Interesting Observation: There were few small or "baby" wildebeests because the birthing season had been about six months before so the survivors had reached the yearling stage. The younger, smaller wildebeests drank last and alone, but the young zebra colts and fillies stayed close to their mothers.

By mid-afternoon, the melee began to subside as the last members of the herds had drunk their fill. For a short while, they appeared to wander around our side of the stream, but then the herds regrouped and moved slowly back into the shade of a small grove of trees about 75 yards away.

Extraordinary Act of Self-Sacrifice?

As the herds moved away, I experienced this day's second mortality moment, the most remarkable act of instinctive or deliberate self-sacrifice I have ever seen. I am deeply puzzled by this wildebeest's action.

After the melee at the stream, a large wildebeest limped out of and away from its herd, dangling its right hind leg. The spindly leg appeared to have been kicked or stomped during the melee. It appeared to be broken at the joint between its hoof and pastern and fetlock (joints connecting the hoof and the rest of the leg).

Blood dripped from a wound at the break. As the wildebeest staggered slowly down the dirt road, it left a thin trail of blood.

The injured wildebeest, with blood dripping from its back right forelock, wanders away from its herd. It limped toward where we last saw the lioness. Was this an instinct to protect the herd, or a deeply subconscious act of self-sacrifice? I don't know, but it was one of the most remarkable actions I have ever watched an injured animal make.

Now, consider this question: If you were in a large group of people, and you had broken your leg and could barely walk, what would you do? If you are like me, you would scream for help and limp as quickly as you could back to the group to safety and care. Right?

Not this wildebeest. It began to limp *away* from the herd *toward* where the lion had been. It "instinctively"—whatever that word means anymore—left the herd because somewhere in its brain, it knew it was severely injured. It knew that if it stayed with the herd, it would endanger them. It literally walked toward its death. Kihago said that it would be killed and eaten by lions, leopards, or hyenas within a few hours.

What caused that wildebeest to walk toward its death? Millions of years of herd "memory" or instinct? "Knowledge" that its inability to run meant its imminent death? "Knowledge" that its injury would never heal properly so it would die soon anyway? Did it have a "choice" in the way we understand the word?

I don't understand why it walked toward its death. All I know is that I saw it choose to walk away from the herd toward the lion.

What Drives Animals and People to the Ultimate Sacrifice?

That wildebeest's action has troubled me ever since. At the time, it made me feel very sad and very vulnerable. It goaded me to ponder how I would act or react in dangerous situations that called for the ultimate sacrifice. Soldiers and warriors willingly go into battle, knowing they may be killed. First responders race into burning buildings and jump into raging waters to save people. They are trained to do so, but of course, there is something more within them, some source of courage, that compels them to risk their lives. They often say they are just doing their jobs, but what compelled them to seek out such dangerous jobs in the first place?

What about the vast majority of people who are not trained to take such risks? Parents, from love or instinct or both, risk their lives to save their children. Some people will knowingly rush into burning buildings, pull strangers out of burning cars, or jump into raging rivers to save others. It happens every day somewhere in the world.

Perhaps we all think we know what we would do, but no one knows for sure. More people panic and run away from a burning building, or stand on a riverbank and cry for help, rather than race toward the danger. Remember the broadcasts of the September 11, 2001 attack on the World Trade Center and the Pentagon. Most people fled in fear and panic while some civilians and hundreds of first responders raced into the buildings and died. A handful of people on American Airlines Flight 93 deliberately sacrificed their lives and the lives of everyone on that plane to crash before the plane reached Washington.

Do courageous people who sacrifice their lives want to die? I doubt it. But they are willing to do so for the good of others. A deeply thought-provoking attribute of human beings that few other animals seem to share. I believe that many mammals, elephants for one, do work for their mutual good, as I discussed, as they appear to feel severe grief when a member of their herd dies.

Individual mature wildebeests, zebras, elephants, and Cape buffalos, to name a few, also are ferocious defenders and have been known to kick, butt, and stomp predators to death. However, if a female wildebeest fights a predator to save its calf, but loses it, the female will run back to the safety of the herd, abandoning its child. After all, if she lives, she can have more calves; she can't if she's dead. They must realize this at some incredibly deep level and act accordingly.

However, many groups or herds will join together and fight off predators. Before a united group gives up and scatters to avoid predators and leave an injured member to its fate, they first do their best to take defensive positions. In these positions, the groups can warn each other and set up protective cordons to prevent attacks. I have seen a herd of zebras, each standing at a slightly different angle, so the herd as a whole had a 360-degree view of the plain. I have seen a zebra herd all turn toward a cheetah less than 50 feet away and stare it down.

I have watched a pod of hippos react when they became aware we were standing near their river. When they suspected we posed danger, the largest males and females in the pod formed a line across the water, facing the danger head on. The younger, smaller "teenage" hippos formed protective flanks to the sides. They kept their young safe behind the line. It was an impregnable line because the larger hippos weighed up to 4,000 pounds. They have enormous mouths with huge tusks that could crush me to pieces.

I have seen baboon troops of 50 or more form a defensive, moving rectangle, which looks disorganized, but is actually highly structured, as they scampered across open spaces. The largest males—troop leaders—formed the front line, younger males and females without young formed the top, bottom, and rear lines of the rectangle. The nursing females and their babies stayed inside the rectangle, protected from predators.

Do the Wildebeests and We Share Something Primeval?

How does all this pondering relate to my memory of the self-sacrificing wildebeest? I wonder if that wildebeest and we *homo sapiens sapiens* don't share something in common—some deeply ingrained response to protect others like ourselves.

It may be uniquely human that many people willingly put themselves in danger to help other species. Tens of thousands of people devote their lives to protect endangered species, to help injured wild animals, and to fight poachers. Many hundreds of these people have died at the hands of poachers across Africa, trying to prevent the poachers from killing rhinos for their horns, elephants for their ivory, leopards and zebras for their skins, as well as destroy many more precious species. Despite the best efforts of many governments, park rangers, soldiers, and civilians, thousands of rhinos, elephants, and big cats are killed each year, threatening their existence.

Which kinds of protective behaviors are only animal instinct and which happen from some kind of rational choice? I have no answers, just a deep awe at the sacrificial behavior of supposedly "dumb beasts" I have witnessed. I have never faced a similar choice, so honestly, I hope I would have that kind of courage, but I am not sure.

Why Didn't We Help?

I'm sure one question has come to your mind: Why didn't we help the injured wildebeest? Why did we sit there and watch it walk toward its death? The reason is as simple as the natural order. Kihago told us that we could not save it. It would be very difficult to catch. If we did catch it, we had no way to anesthetize it, fix the leg, or carry it. The closest veterinarian was hundreds of miles away. Lastly and perhaps most truthfully, it was dispensable: there are millions of wildebeests, and the predators, scavengers, insects, and fungi have a right to survive, too.

The truth of the wild may seem harsh to our "civilized" sensibilities, but dying patients and their doctors and families make similar choices every day—who lives and who dies.

Perhaps it is my "Pollyanna" anthropomorphism—ascribing human traits to other animals—but I prefer to believe that the wildebeest understood in some way what it was doing, that its action was a perhaps noble, necessary act of self-sacrifice to protect its herd. For the greater good?

SUNDAY, JULY 4 – EVENING, AND MONDAY, JULY 5 – MORNING

Mortality Moment Five
The Last and Worst

O n the afternoon of July 4 and the morning of July 5, I had my most terrifying mortality moment. This one made me realize that I could die at any time, that I was eventually going to die, and that my body—but I hope not my soul—will return to the dust from whence it came.

First, in the late afternoon after we watched the injured wildebeest wander toward the lioness, we were driving down a long sandy track to our last camp. To our right, we saw a herd of about 50 elephants. Then, we drove up to a medium-sized tree that the elephants had knocked down across the road. Kihago said—and I believe—they did it deliberately be-cause they did not want us in their territory. We had to drive around the tree.

To our left, as we neared the camp, we saw a herd of more than 200 Cape buffaloes (I counted), grazing across a small stream. I knew from experience from both of my safaris that the buffalos could easily wander into the camp. Worse yet, there is no large African mammal that is dumber and meaner than a Cape buffalo. So, on one side, we have what seemed to be a good sized herd of irritated elephants and on the other, a large herd of unpredictable buffaloes.

A herd of dumb, mean Cape buffalos watches us closely as we
drive through its territory to our last camp.

By the way, after we arrived at the isolated camp, we left our bags in our "luxury" tents—a shower and a toilet inside my tent 100 miles from the nearest small town is indeed the height of luxury! We had dinner prepared by the two locals who manned the camp. Exhausted as usual, we returned quickly—well, I limped slowly—to our tents and tucked in for the night. I wrote in my diary for a while and surprisingly and gratefully, fell asleep quickly and slept soundly. It's amazing what being at a normal elevation will do for your sleep! And no hyenas tonight! I learned why early the next morning.

Lion Bait!

The next morning, when I limped up the trail toward the cooking tent, the two locals waved at me excitedly and called me to them. When I reached the edge of the ashes from the previous night's fire, they pointed at them and said, "Look, lion tracks!"

I saw a trail of enormous lion paw prints through the cold ashes that disappeared into the grasses. I freaked out! At least one large lion had wandered through the camp that night.

An enormous lion paw print in the ashes of our camp fire. I am lion bait!

Startled, I looked at the locals and asked, "What is going on?"

They said nonchalantly, "Oh, we're in the middle of a lion pride."

I thought, "What! Holy shit!! Elephants, Cape buffalos, and lions!"

Instead I asked them, "Do we have any guns?"

They said, "Oh, we don't need any guns. They're not going to bother you."

Then I lost my temper, scared to death because I could barely walk and was the most vulnerable person in the camp. As the old joke goes about when a group of people is being chased by a predator: "I don't have to be the fastest runner; I just need to be faster than you." By far, I was the slowest person in that camp. I was the proverbial lion bait.

I yelled, "Are you out of your minds? I've been on another safari. The guides had two 30-30 Winchester rifles because they will take down buffalos and lions. But we don't have anything at all to defend ourselves?"

I ranted to Kihago, "Just tie me to a stake right here because I'm dead if anything happens."

Of course, my complaints did no good because there was nowhere to buy a gun for more than a hundred miles, and they had no intention of buying one anyway.

They tried to reassure me that all I had to do was make a lot of noise and any lion, elephant, or buffalo would go away. But I was livid because I knew the risk was very real. During my other "less adventurous" safari, one night a herd of elephants had foraged through the camp, tearing down small trees and grazing on large plants literally within inches of my tent that was perched on five-feet-high stilts.

Another night, the guides had had to fire warning shots to frighten away several buffalos that had lain down across the stone pathway that led to our tents. They had refused to move when the guides approached them. It was cold that night, but the stones still radiated warmth from the day's sun. Would you want to leave a nice, warm spot to sit on the cold grass? Me neither. So, it took some serious persuading—like gunfire, which they feared—to "encourage" the buffalos to get up and leave.

I had never been more vulnerable and felt less safe in my life. And I grew up in the constant fear that comes from living in a very dysfunctional, addictive family where I rarely felt safe. Tension ran through my family like vibrations from a tuning fork.

At that moment, I realized that I was utterly defenseless if any animal decided I looked like easy prey. Because I was.

My mortality stared me in the face. I lost the illusion of safety that I had felt driving around in a large Land Rover for five days. I felt lost and enraged at the thought of dying, while the rest of the others seemed non-plussed by our real predicament.

A Reasonable Fear?

How real was it? As I reviewed my notes, photos, and videos of the day before and the day we saw the lion tracks in the ashes, I found that the morning before, we had seen a large lioness, with an empty belly, wander down the road 100 feet in front of us; she showed no fear of our truck at all. A short while later, we saw an eagle standing on the ground picking a rodent apart, having "breakfast."

Later, we saw a crocodile hidden in the shallows of a muddy river, its eyes and snout barely sticking out of the water. It watched a young monkey sitting on its haunches by the edge of the river. The monkey leaned forward to drink quickly and then raised its head to peer nervously all around it. Even Kihago was scared for the monkey. When the monkey scampered away without being attacked by the croc, he said, "Lucky monkey. No croc attack."

A little later down the road, we saw a lion and a lioness sitting by the side of the road, watching dozens of zebras downwind from their scent. The zebras knew the lions were there and had taken their classic 360-degree defensive position. The lioness stood up, staring at the zebras. The zebras slowly began moving away, leaving five males as a rear guard.

Moments later, we saw another lioness hiding in the grass, watching an impala herd. Nearby, a fish eagle, which looks much like our bald eagle but has more white feathers down its back and chest, was "snacking" on a fish while perched (pun intended) on the branch of a tree. In the middle of a broad plain, we watched a female cheetah with three cubs as they chowed down on the carcass of a Thomson's gazelle in the shade of an acacia tree.

Later that afternoon, we watched a lioness and two healthy springboks—a male and a female—"face off" about 100 feet away from each other. For some minutes, the lioness just sat on its haunches, observing, and I suspect, comparing its odds of success to its degree of hunger. It began walking slowly toward the springboks with its head up. Fifty feet apart, the lion stopped for a moment.

A lioness stalks a springbok, but the springbok is too healthy, too alert, and too quick. It leaps away, and the lioness saunters away, looking for easier prey.

As it began to move again, the female springbok ran toward the lion and then darted to the side to divert its attention. The lion stopped and sank into the deep grass out of sight. The springboks stayed on high alert, standing tall with their heads and noses sticking into the air. When they saw the lioness again, the female springbok turned and leaped a short distance away. The male stayed for a few moments, watching the area where the lion was hidden. The grass rustled and the male springbok turned and leaped away from the lioness. She stood up and began walking slowly in the opposite direction. She gave up on pursuing the springboks—she had an empty belly, but they were too fast for her. Too much trouble, and somewhere in her mind, the lioness knew her odds of success were low.

In short, for days, I had been watching the natural cycle of life and death, of prey and predator, of the stalkers and the stalked. I had seen very closely that only the fastest, smartest, strongest, most alert, and most skittish survived for very long. I saw that ultimately, every living being becomes vulnerable, either from age—too young or too old—illness, or sloppy mistakes, and dies.

For decades, in my youth and naivete, I had prided myself that I, a poor Southern boy from Georgia, survived living in New York City as a fresh-faced, broke young writer. I withstood dozens of reversals, including bankruptcy, repeated self-sabotage, and relapses into food binges, debt, and alcohol. I stayed in two difficult marriages for a total of 35 years. I had always been told—and I knew in my soul—that I was a classic "survivor" of an addicted family and the classic overachieving child, nephew, and grandchild of relatives with multiple addictions.

Working and living the 12 Steps through more than 35 years of recovery, however marred by relapse, depression, and despair, had given me the strength to maintain my illusion of immortality and secretly nurture my pride.

Yet, a trail of tracks in the ashes of a campfire devastated my pride and shattered my illusions. At that moment, I knew I was the slowest, dumbest, least alert, and most naïve person in that camp. I felt terror and hid it with my rage and incredulous hostility. I believed that I could not trust anyone in that camp to save me. I believed I was alone in a foreign and hostile world. I was a mere mortal, just another potential tidbit for a faster predator.

I had never felt so utterly powerless over my life. When I joined OA in 1976, I felt desperate and miserable, but not on the verge of death. I have often felt depressed, even felt suicidal once and went into treatment. But in those days, I was surrounded by program friends and professionals in the heart of civilization. I could go to meetings, make phone calls, go to a treatment center, hang out with program friends, read literature, exercise, and see my therapist to help me work through the tough spots. I always—well, eventually—have grown in my recovery and as a person any time that I have faced an "AFGO," as some of us call it—Another Fucking Growth Opportunity!

At that moment on the Serengeti Plain, however, I was shocked and terrified that I could die at any moment. Perhaps you felt that way when you joined your first 12 Step program, or maybe you feel that way now as you seek a solution to your struggles with addiction. For me, it was the first time I truly faced death alone, and I felt devastated.

It was the most complete challenge to my faith in my Higher Power I had ever known. It was very difficult that day because I was gripped by fear and rage. My core issues of betrayal and abandonment were roaring in my head; there was no human power I believed I could trust at that camp. I was wrong, of course, as I now feel sure that Kihago would have protected me. The tour company can't have the clients eaten by lions, now can they! Actually, everyone at Wilderness Travel treated me extremely well.

However, during the rest of that day, after everyone had "pooh-poohed" my fears, I felt more alienated and more alone from that group than I had during the past 16 days.

That afternoon, I used my sat phone to call another very close friend, Tim. Miracle of miracles, I reached him too on the first try. I ranted and complained about the lion tracks and my "lion bait" status. Tim, being one of the funniest and most sarcastic people I know—and I mean that in the best possible way—merely said: "Well, that's what you signed up for."

I was flabbergasted and very annoyed at the time. Didn't I deserve some sympathy? Poor Robert!

You know what: He was absolutely correct. I did not consciously know it, but facing my mortality was exactly what I had signed up for when I decided to climb Mt. Kilimanjaro. I was warned to expect the lesson on Mother Mountain; instead, my FMG had better in store for me on Kili and a much more potent lesson in mortality for me on the Plain.

MONDAY, JULY 5 AND TUESDAY, JULY 6

End of Mortality Moments, End of the Safari,
Completing the Circle

As I still seethed in my fear that morning, we ate quickly, packed up, left that campsite, and drove back down the same track with the same elephants and the same Cape buffalos watching us. Later that evening, we returned to civilization with paved roads and noisy, crowded, dirty towns.

Finally, when we reached our last camp—an amazing luxury lodge, I began to calm down because we had reached a safe place. My ever-humorous HP played another perfect "trick" and sent me another perfect message in my meditation books. As I lay in bed and read them late that night, one meditation told me to realize that my HP is with me **all the time** and waits on me to ask for help. The daily prayer was for strength and wisdom to accept my HP's direction for my life.

Next to the prayer, I wrote, "OK, FMG, this is my condition. Use it for your purposes. It's OK with me."

At that time, the direction in my life was very unclear. As you will read shortly in the Epilog, God chose for me a direction I would not have chosen for myself—and resisted mightily—until my HP crushed my resistance with more pain. Now, some time after I climbed and learned to have compassion on others on Kili, and I faced my mortality on the Serengeti, I am living a life beyond my wildest dreams.

The last night, spoiled as we were, we stayed at a famous lodge that dated to the height of the British Empire in the late 19th century. Surrounded by a huge coffee plantation, it was a beautiful sight; the lodge rested on top of a small hill and with large colorful plants and trees all around it, it blended into its environment. I looked out the main door and I saw perfect rows of coffee bushes stretching across low rolling hills for what seemed like a mile.

There is no doubt I had it better than Queen Victoria or Prince Edward ever had: I had both an indoor and an outdoor shower, running hot water, large dual sinks, an indoor toilet, heated bathroom floors, and a multi-room suite that was larger than my condominium at home. Humorously, I had a glorious view of a lush garden outside the glass wall of the indoor shower. It was very elegant and quite a shock to so quickly leave the danger of the wild and feel safe again.

Best of all, the lodge had an on-call doctor. They called him as soon as we arrived, and I explained I needed help. He arrived within 15 minutes and examined my feet and hands. He confirmed mild frostbite on my fingers and said they would take several weeks to return to normal—which they did. He confirmed my toes were battered and bruised, but nothing was broken. He trimmed my damaged toenails, gave me antibiotics and painkillers, and advised me to stop walking in the boots as soon as possible. I couldn't have agreed more!

Fortunately, a small town was nearby, so Kihago drove me to its "shopping district." It was a stretch of wide dirt road with shops that were little more than tin shacks crammed side by side along each side of the road. After we tried several "variety" stores, we were directed to the only "shoe store" in the village. It sold what looked to be used sneakers and strapless sandals made of recycled auto tires. None of those fit. The owner dug out from behind the counter a new pair of sandals with straps that fit across the top of my foot and the back of my Achilles heel. They didn't touch my toes. Sold!

At $20, I knew the price was outrageous, but I didn't ask Kihago to haggle. It was a price I was more than happy to pay. I wore those sandals for the rest of trip and for a month after I returned home. It took that long for my toes to heal before I could wear regular shoes to work and return to swing dancing. I still have them in my closet, and I wear them when I go wading in shallow streams along hiking trails.

My big toenails were wrecked and remain so to this day; only one of them eventually fell off, but the regrowth is thick and heavily ridged. Every day I get to see these permanent "souvenirs" of my pride and arrogance on the mountain.

After the pain in my feet was relieved, I began to feel calmer. I suppose I was more open to suggestion because that night's meditations continued my HP's theme and humor: One reading suggested that recovery means I must completely change my way of life; I must do whatever I have to do to stay clean, sober, and abstinent. It also urged me to ask for direction and clarity from my HP and any trusted source. After days of pain and misery, I finally was in a position to ask for and receive the help I needed from the doctor and Kihago.

This reading's prayer for the day urged me to forsake my arrogance and pride and pray **only** for God's will for me and the power carry that out. The 11th Step anyone?!

A second reading reinforced the essential need to ask for help from other people and to ask for, be willing to receive, and put to good use my ability to know and do their will. In other words, replace fear with faith, pride with humility, anger with acceptance; that is, live the St. Francis of Assisi prayer.

Coming Full Circle

The last day, July 6, was somewhat anti-climactic. Early in the morning, we left our luxurious digs, drove to a hotel near the international airport, and had a day room while we waited for our flight. It took me about 30 minutes and two disposable razors to shave off my 17-day-old beard—if the scraggly mess could be called that. I finally put on some wonderfully clean clothes that were waiting for me at the lodge. Another superb service by Wilderness Travel; they kept my belongings safe and sound throughout the entire trek, especially when they were stored in one hotel and moved to another many miles away.

As I lay on the comfortable bed, I read the final meditations. They stressed that my journey up and down Kilimanjaro had been a time of testing to prepare me for my future mission. One warned that the answers might feel painful for a while as I worked on my shortcomings and became willing to have my HP remove them. So, it proved to come true in spades.

The meditation reinforced what I had experienced for the past two weeks. The prayer asked that I be ready to persist through a time of testing, the duration of which I could not—and did not!—control. It urged me to have faith in the results that my HP was arranging for me.

So, at the end of this incredible 12 Step adventure, I came full circle. I began powerless and I ended powerless. From start to finish, I had to believe in powers greater than myself—from people like Samia, Rodrik, Humphrey, Kihago, and the 58 other tough guys to the awesome forces of Mother Nature. I had to surrender my will and my life to the care of those Higher Powers. I had to keep the focus on me and my actions, take my own inventory, and make amends when I was wrong. I had to do my best every day—one day at a time—to pray for God's will and the strength to keep climbing up the mountain and keep walking on damaged feet. Especially, I had to practice these principles if I wanted a positive result; sadly, I cannot claim to have been very good at applying the principles, but I did often express my deepest gratitude. I hope I was a positive example of "progress, not perfection."

In short, I took the 12 Steps up and down Mount Kilimanjaro and across the Serengeti to the best of my ability—one day at a time.

I'll end my journey with the same quotation that began this adventure: "*If an ass goes traveling, he'll not come home a horse.*" This ass was still an ass, definitely not a horse; I hope that as the Epilog shows, I have become a more compassionate, more humble, and somewhat improved ass.

EPILOG

The Ass Is More Like the Ass He Is Meant to Be

As I write this epilog many months after I returned from Kilimanjaro, I sit here at my computer. I wonder how I am going to sell a story without a "happy ending"? Is it enough for me to simply have limped down the "Mother Mountain" safe only because of the enormous compassion others had on me? Is it enough to have meandered through the Serengeti hobbled with injured feet and too-tight shoes only to come face to face with my mortality? Since then, I know I have become a little older, but have I become any wiser? How have I changed as a recovering addict and a man—for the better and for the worse?

For some time, I have pondered what to share and how to share the challenges and changes in my life since I returned home from Kili and the Serengeti. One word has kept coming to me for a long time: humility. I do not claim to have gained, been granted, or learned "humility" on my trek; to do so wouldn't be very humble, would it?

I have no fairy tale "happy ending" to share because my journey through life as a recovering addict continues One Day At A Time. I continue to take Steps 1, 2, and 3 every morning. I do my best to live all the Steps ODAT. When I pray, I pray for myself and others, and always end with "Thy Will, Not Mine, Be Done." I do my best to be prepared to gladly accept from my FMG better outcomes than the ones I think I want.

As I have learned so very painfully, my best thinking got me into every difficulty—drinking to excess, eating compulsively, falling $100,000 into debt, forming unhealthy relationships, and committing episode after episode of self-sabotage. So, it is much better if I get out of my own way and let my FMG call the shots. I am dedicated to practicing the 12 Step Way of Life.

Yet, I continue to feel many mixed emotions—gratitude, disappointment, accomplishment, and self-sabotage—all roiled around inside my head and my heart. For one, since I returned from Kili, many people have looked at me with something like awe when they learn I climbed the mountain. I say thank you, but I make sure I tell them two things: First, it was the hardest thing I have ever done at every level—mental, physical, emotional, and spiritual. More importantly, I always tell them about Samia, Humphrey, Rodrik, Kihago, and the other 58 "tough guys." I tell them how the "tough guys" ran up and down the mountain in tattered clothes and sandals and took care of our every need. I tell them how short, skinny Rodrik carried my 50-lb bag for 10 days for this spoiled, cantankerous American without complaint. I tell them how Humphrey carried my day pack as well as his own for five days so I could make it to the peak and down. I give the "tough guys" all the credit for making it possible for me to have reached the peak and survived the Serengeti. I just put one foot in front of the other "pole pole."

My friends have told me that although I had so much help from so many, I still have the right to feel good about my achievement. Very few 60-year-olds even consider, much less start or finish, this challenge. Rather than feel pride, though, I feel deep gratitude toward the tough guys, my fellow climbers, my recovery family, and especially my Higher Power.

Didn't Know What to Say, So I Asked for Help

I was having serious trouble writing this Epilog, so at the suggestion of my significant other (L.T., thank you!), I asked some of my closest friends to tell me how they have seen me change since I completed this adventure. One close male friend, J.Da., who fought tank battles in the horrible oil fields during the first Iraq War in 1991, said the mountain indeed changed me. "I saw a man who went from closed to open, open to self-examining and vulnerable. You kept the courage that it took for a man in his late 50's to climb one of the world's highest peaks. I saw you apply that to slowly changing the things in your life that were of no value to you. I saw the vulnerability of a man struggling to redefine himself. I saw a brother working through change, sometimes with great angst and tribulation, but never surrendering to good enough."

I am truly grateful for his praise because he is one of the few men with whom I would trust my life and go into any battle. He has had his own share of angst and tribulation as he has recovered in his 12 Step programs. He now lives a wonderful life with his second wife, his own and her adult children, and multiple grandchildren.

Critical Change: Vulnerability

J.Da. hit precisely one of my greatest challenges since I returned: my deep feelings about, and fear of, vulnerability. My recovery quest—and my halting steps forward and backward—have largely been allowing myself to feel vulnerable, yet turn to my Higher Power for protection and to buck up the courage J.Da. says I possess. I have strived, always imperfectly, to go through the fear and open myself to the most vulnerable feeling of all: unconditional love and acceptance for, and from, my family, my recovery "family," and my beloved L.T.

I come by my deep-seated fear of being vulnerable honestly: As an adult child and relative of multiple addicts, I never felt safe in my own home. Critical punishments, secrets that led to severe losses and abandonments, and crushing expectations taught me to protect myself with anger most of the time. As a child, I hid my fear of vulnerability behind many masks: I was the smartest kid in the class, the biggest kid in the class, a bully at times, and an isolated, voracious reader of as many books as possible as often as possible.

All that anger, frustration, and isolation protected my soul, my true Self, when I was a child, but they harmed me for decades as I strived to become an adult. Most of my adult years, I struck out at others when I felt threatened, I scowled constantly at the world, and I isolated myself from others. I had no clue how to have friendships or intimate relationships with women not based on giving myself away to others or demanding what I wanted when I wanted it.

I had also learned as a child how to turn my teachers into my protectors and my role models by being the best student and frankly, "sucking up" to them. Making excellent grades protected me because it was my parents' greatest expectation and constant demand.

Consequently, as an adult, I was very good—most of the time—with impressing my bosses and clients. I was very good at my work first as a reporter/bureau chief and later as a freelance writer and instructor of professional writing at a prestigious public university. I could isolate and work 12 hours a day for days and weeks on end to complete projects. In my first marriage, we were always behind on our bills and missing deadlines, so I felt in sheer terror of failure much of the time. I used that terror and my life-long anger, sexual frustration, and isolation to generate enormous energy to publish more books, articles, essays, and reports in 11 years than most writers complete in an entire career.

But truly vulnerable—not on your life! In my marriages, my "I want when I want it" attitude and expectations always led to frustration and resentment. Neither my wives nor I knew how to be truly open and honest with each other in a kind, loving way that would nourish the relationship, enhance our intimacy, and build a healthy, happy marriage.

Since I have come down the mountain, I have experienced a huge amount of pain—and ultimately joy—by opening myself up to those long-suppressed feelings. In my case, it has meant being vulnerable enough to feel more grief than I can describe at the permanent loss of my stepchildren and the chance to have my own grandchildren.

On the bright side, that loss has meant a great gain with my family, from whom I was alienated for so long—emotionally since I was about 13 and physically as much as possible between the ages of 18 and 40. I have grown closer to them and been able to help them more than I ever dreamed possible. I have been more caring for my family members—my late brother before he died from obesity-related diseases and my two older sisters. I now take special care to serve as a positive support and role model as the uncle of my late brother's son and daughter and his son's family—my two great nieces. My nephew, his wife, and my great-nieces suffer, too, from obesity and food disorders, although recently they have learned about their food allergies and have changed their food plans quite a bit. They seem to be doing better.

My nephew and niece have lived several decades of serious pain since they were orphaned as children, ages 6 and 10, when their own mother died of lung cancer at age 34. After her death, my brother made awful, addictive choices in remarrying three times, each time to someone worse than the previous wife. His chaotic marriages made it all the more difficult for my nephew and my niece as they grew up and became adults. From what I understand, their home life was constantly unsettled and unstable, and my brother made unwise financial decisions that cost the family a lot of money. Each of his wives had either addictions, severe mental illnesses, or both. Extramarital affairs were also involved.

Given their upbringing, which I know was much worse than mine, I am doing my best to **have compassion on** them and their families as Samia, Humphrey, and Rodrik taught me on the mountain.

The Greatest Gift of Love

Since I came down from the mountain, my quest to be a better person has meant being vulnerable enough to enter several relationships that did not work out. I had to feel the pain of repeating some serious mistakes in those relationships as I continued to learn the hard way. I must have learned something though, because two of those three lovely women still consider me a good friend, and the third I hear has only good will for me. An utterly radical difference from the reaction of my two ex-wives.

I attribute the difference to my slowly learning to make better choices, treating all of them with respect, taking responsibility for my mistakes, and learning that breaking up as a couple did not mean we could not be friends. I had to practice the thoughts and actions that create a happy, healthy, loving relationship.

One Enchanted Evening, I Met A Stranger

Finally! In my 60s, I am learning how to give and receive unconditional acceptance, the heart of true love. I have received that gift from my relationship with L.T. We were brought together by an enormous gift of God humor by a chance meeting on a dance floor. The song "Some Enchanted Evening" describes just about how it happened, but not in a mansion perched on a mountain in tropical Bali Hai! When I saw her across the room, it was across the linoleum dance floor in an old German dance hall where a rock-and-roll band was playing. It wasn't love at first sight, but it was an amazingly strong reaction. We love to dance together and have a permanent agreement to dance until we can no longer move.

A few months into our relationship, L.T. gave me perhaps the greatest gift I have received as an adult—the gift of learning to smile. Now, I can share the joy I feel with others when I laugh and smile with them. One day, she called me on a contradiction in my behavior and appearance that confused her. Again, from my fear of vulnerability, I was hiding behind my well-practiced scowl. How I acted was not matching how I appeared; how I appeared did not match what she considered important to her in a relationship.

During our early months, I was being very romantic. I emailed her links to love songs on YouTube almost every day. I brought her flowers and sent her hand-written notes. I said what I thought were all the right things. I definitely loved to dance and be with her.

Then, she "blew my cover" and asked, "If you really feel this way, why don't you ever smile?"

I replied cautiously, "Huh? I'm not smiling? I don't do that very easily. I don't like to show my crooked teeth. I think I look goofy when I smile." My usual excuses for hiding my vulnerability.

She told me that the few times she had seen me smile a real smile, she had loved them. She had seen in me a much different, happier, more honest person. She said my smile lit up my face. My smile meant to her I truly cared about her and enjoyed being with her.

Today, I still think my smile looks goofy, but I do my best to smile most of the time. When I do, everyone around me feels better and I feel happier. When L.T. smiles back at me, her glorious smile melts my heart as I know it is always authentic and truly meant.

The Most Important Question for a Healthy Relationship

Being vulnerable in our relationship has meant that when I am with L.T., I always ask myself, "How Important Is It?" when something irritates me, I fear a boundary has been crossed, or my addict brain is kicking my butt out of fear. Compared to my love for L.T., the answer is almost always: "IT IS NOT IMPORTANT!"

When I feel even the least bit confused or "put off," much less annoyed, I do my best to stop before I react. I check what I am feeling and why; then, I let go of the little things that can erode a relationship drip by drip, that are just excuses for ignoring any real issues. It's "my stuff," so I manage it on my own.

Because L.T. and I trust each other, if I find an issue is important to me, then I sit down with her, and, God forbid! (tongue in cheek), we talk about it. If I begin the conversation, I ask for permission and for her attention. We listen to each other carefully. I feel free—and safe enough—to be honest about how I feel. I tell her how I am willing to change. I ask for her permission to offer suggestions for new ways she can approach the situation. I respect her right to agree or disagree or offer another path. I feel safe enough to ask her for help. In turn, she feels safe enough to bring up her concerns and ask me to change what I do.

Usually, when she brings something to my attention, she is correct. I'm not quite perfect at this vulnerability stuff yet; for example, L.T. sometimes has to remind me that rather than listen, I will take her concern and make it all about me. (Whaaatttt? The world doesn't revolve around poor, victimized Robert anymore?? Hah!)

Sometimes, I assume I know what she is talking about when I don't, and I "step all over" what she is saying. She feels free to point out my error. If I disagree or need clarification, I ask questions and we discuss it. Since her feelings and views are as valid as mine, I apologize for any specific mistake and make a firm commitment to change. As I have said throughout, I only claim progress, not perfection.

Furthermore, my willingness to feel vulnerable has meant that I can be my real "self" with my men friends. Until I became single again after my second divorce, I had had very few men friends since I played high school football—and that was a long time ago! I had been "joined at the co-dependent hip" to both wives for a total of 35 years. In each marriage, we only had her or "our" friends; I really didn't have any of my own friends outside of my 12 Step meetings.

Since I joined Al-Anon and began to attend men's Al-Anon and OA meetings regularly, I have learned to feel safe among men for the first time. I can share with them in all honesty my most painful struggles with my addictions and my recovery. Outside meetings, in our social life (Wow, I even have one with the guys! What a gift!), I can be my funny, serious, sarcastic, caring, vulnerable Self. Above all, I can be honest with them, and I can ask them for help when I need it.

From Acting Out the Worst in Me to Working toward Better

However, despite all this progress, I sometimes feel sad because the more I reviewed my journals and written notes to prepare this book, the more I believe Kili revealed my human nature to make mistakes. However, all of the mistakes you have read about turned out to be the best things that could have happened for me and my long-term recovery. My Higher Power gave me the enormous "gift" of driving me to come face to face with my shortcomings. FMG then, and now, has given me many opportunities to surrender those defects and practice the 12 Step principles in all my affairs. After many years of thinking I was worse than others because I made mistakes—when I was supposed to be perfect!!!—my Kili adventure taught me that it is natural to err and just as natural to correct those errors.

The only principle I claim I practiced very well on Kili was the principle of accountability—Steps 8, 9, and 10. I was always willing to take responsibility for my mistakes and make the best amends I could when I offended the crew and my fellow climbers. I continue to do my best—ODAT—to avoid mistakes, but apologize and make amends when I do, since making them is simply part of being human.

I was raised to believe in "original sin" and feel terribly guilty about my "sins," which were supposed to be so bad to deserve harsh punishment from my parents and God "Himself." That belief helped contribute to my sometimes overwhelming sense of worthlessness—and my constant belief I was "lesser than." Both helped cause, derive from, and strengthen my addictive behaviors in an awful circle that reinforces itself.

I thoroughly disagree with the "original sin" concept because of my experiences everywhere from 12 Step meetings to the savannahs of Tanzania and the jungles along the Amazon River. In 12 Step meetings, I believe almost every member has a serious problem with believing they are "lesser than." (Why I strongly dislike, and avoid, the overused concept of "self-esteem" is a subject that could make up another book!)

Their core belief is simply wrong: Almost all of the people I know in 12 Step groups (thousands over the years, so it's a pretty good sample size) are smarter than average and have a greater capacity for love, compassion, and empathy than "normal" people. My bias? Fine, I accept that, but experience has convinced me it is true.

But there is no bias in how I have seen baboons, chimpanzees, and other primates act in the forests, savannahs, and jungles. Within their troops, they bicker and quarrel, young ones irritate their parents and elders, and one troop will attack another troop to gain territory and food or protect its own. AND they protect each other from predators, the mothers feed and take care of their babies with an innate sense of responsibility, the ones bickering quickly end their quarrels, and they abide by a social structure that has clear lines of responsibility and authority. Almost human, I'd say, and they are perfectly imperfect creatures of God. Just as I believe you and I are, too. Am I too anthropomorphic? I am just sharing what I have observed.

In short, I believe mere imperfection—or our perception of it, biased by our belief systems and backgrounds—is "baked in the cake." We were simply born imperfect, not because we have to redeem ourselves to avoid punishment by some harsh God, but because that is just how we evolved from our primate ancestors.

Sense of Satisfaction

Since I have returned, those observations have helped me to forgive myself for my past mistakes. I have come to accept I am always going to make mistakes, and I have relieved myself—most of the time—of the heavy burden of feeling lesser than others because I have ingrained problems. Perfectly imperfect, as each of us is, and that is fine with me! It creates so much more room in my heart and mind for understanding, patience, forgiveness, and compassion for others.

About my 12 Step adventure up and down Kili, I have felt satisfaction—but not pride—that I set and achieved this incredible goal which I had only a small chance of achieving. The strenuous trek up Kili and the painful hobbling in the Serengeti taxed every resource, irritated every character defect, cost a substantial portion of my financial resources, incurred a serious physical price, drained every emotion, challenged my faith, and threw me headlong into facing my mortality.

I believe I faced all this with courage, but perhaps only perseverance (or stubbornness—what is the difference?) and willingness. Above all, however much I resisted Samia's direction, complained, and self-isolated, I was willing to experience what my Higher Powers wanted me to experience.

Since I came down from the mountain, I have experienced a series of significant fits and starts—very much Steps forward and Steps back. As soon as I arrived home, I had a major self-sabotage reaction, binging off and on for weeks afterward and gaining 11 pounds. Perhaps these binges were only the physical reactions to the weeks of unusual, though abstinent, foods I had been eating.

However, this reaction was predictable. Many times in the previous 35 years, I had always had varying degree of "kickbacks" from other major positive steps forward. This time, I knew that the powerful strength of my reaction to my achievement showed me that my addict brain was terrified of the major leap forward in my recovery that I had made by climbing Kili. My addict brain—my terrified childhood memories hard-wired in my brain cells—believes that only my addictions—eating primarily, but also drinking, debting, damaging relationships, and sabotaging my good—can protect me, can save me, as they did in my childhood. Wrong!

That episode convinced me to work my OA program more diligently and take it more seriously than I had in many years. Unfortunately, although I remain sober, clean, and debt-free, I continue to learn quite often the hard way what my priorities must be in my OA program. One of OA's key words, of course, is BINGE. As a program slogan, it stands for "Because I'm Not Good Enough." As I've stressed, "not good enough" has been one of the, if not the most important, false belief I have carried inside me since I was a child.

With the "up and down dance" I have been doing with my weight, I once got close to the highest weight (233 pounds, about 60 pounds too heavy) I reached in 2002. Just for today, I have a healthy nutrition plan that works when I work it. After all, how much "fun" is it really to binge on nuts and seeds instead of bread, booze, and bon-bons? Seriously, I know that my cunning, baffling, powerful, subtle, devious, insidious addict brain sometimes just acts out because it wants—and finds—any excuse to do so.

Triggers, Resentment, and Response

The "excuses" that drive my slips and short-term relapses with food have almost always been caused by the following "triggers":

- Feeling deep grief, such as
  - When I lost contact with my stepchildren, and the opportunity to be the grandfather to their children, after my second divorce.
  - When my brother—the youngest of the four of us—died unexpectedly at age 60 from his addictions, while I had climbed Kili at age 60;
  - When I reclaimed and released the grief, shame, and blame for my many years of anger toward, and alienation from, my parents; and
  - When a number of friends, relatives, and loved ones died soon after I came home from the mountain.

- Feeling incredibly vulnerable, such as when I clashed with my supervisors in two jobs I was unsuited for and in which I felt betrayed and abandoned;
- Feeling angry and resentful at my parents, ex-wives, and former stepchildren;
- Feeling "not good enough" or vulnerable in my relationship with L.T. when my old thought of "I want what I want when I want it" reared its ugly head; and
- Allowing my always fearful "addict brain" to convince me that it is "just fine" to take that first compulsive bite. That thought means my self-sabotage is lurking beneath the surface, ready to leap out and bite me when I bite into any unhealthy kind or amount of food.

One of the critical tools I use to respond to and work through my resentments and my subtle self-sabotage is the "resentment prayer." You can find the suggestion for how to do this prayer on page 552 in the 4ᵗʰ Edition of *Alcoholics Anonymous* (the AA "Big Book"): To quote:

> "If you have resentment you want to be free of, if you will pray for the person or thing that you resent, you will be free. If you will ask in prayer for everything you want for yourself to be given to them, you will be free. Ask for their health, their prosperity, their happiness, and you will be free. Even when you don't really want it for them and your prayers are only words and you don't mean it, go ahead and do it anyway. Do it every day for two weeks, and you will find you have come to mean it and to want it for them, and you will realize that where you used to feel bitterness and resentment and hatred, you now feel compassion, understanding and love."

For many years, I have prayed this "resentment prayer" for anyone I have felt angry or resentful toward. I ask my HP to grant them all the blessings of this life that I want for myself. I have prayed for them daily, sometimes for weeks and sometimes for months, but the prayer eventually does work.

As the prayer says, sometimes I even mean what I am praying. Many times, I just grit my teeth and pray for them anyway through my anger and resentment. Sometimes, four-letter words are involved in my prayers. None of that matters as long as I just pray and leave the results up to my FMG. I also discuss my resentments at my meetings, with my therapist, with my sponsors, and with my friends. I pray for God's will to be done, for what is best for everyone in the situation—whether I like it or not.

In fact, on several occasions, I have been told to stop praying this prayer for others after a time because continuing to pray for them means I am still holding on to my resentment. I get to "play with" my anger and keep it in the front of my mind. For example, I prayed for months for several bosses, who I believed were treating me unfairly. I complained about this situation to my therapist off and on for months, always adding I was doing the resentment prayer for them. Finally, one day, he just said, "Cut it out. You really just want to hold onto your anger and justify not doing your best in the job."

Oops! He was right. I felt constantly angry with them; I wasn't truly turning my will over to my FMG. In addition, by my standards, I was doing a lousy job and putting onto my teammates the work I didn't want to do.

God humor again—when I stopped praying for them and really surrendered them and the problem over to my FMG, the situation dramatically improved within weeks. The bosses I didn't like gave me what I considered a "dream job": teaching hundreds of people in our agency to improve how they wrote the complex budget justifications they had to draft for my department. It was win-win-win; the bosses got me and my bad attitude out of their hair, I got to do what I love to do, and the workshops did improve the quality of writing we received, thus reducing the amount of time we had to spend editing their drafts. Eventually, that assignment led some months later to my working directly with the head of the department. Within a few months after that, the department head volunteered my editing services to the head of my agency; the agency director liked my work so much that I was made the chief speechwriter, the apex of my long career.

So—I did not pursue any of these great opportunities. Every one was a gift from my FMG because I had released my resentment and surrendered to my FMG's will for me. FMG's will—and His/Her path—has always been far, far better than what I wanted for myself.

As this example shows, sometimes quickly, sometimes slowly (when I insist on my way!), as in all recovery, I am freed from my resentment. Some people change their attitudes toward me as I change my attitudes toward them; others do not. Not my problem. My blessing is that I no longer harbor the intense grudges that harm my recovery. Remember the Program saying: ***When you point a finger at someone else, three fingers (and a thumb, I would add) are pointing back at you.***

One of the Best HP Jokes—and Gifts—of All

I also believe that my HP has played a huge joke on me since I came down the mountain and off the plains. I believe that for some time after, as I struggled through the old grief, the new deaths, the bad jobs, and more, my HP's message—that I did such a poor job of hearing at the time—was:

> "No, you can't have what you think you want. It's not best for you. I know what's best. For now, I need you to stay where you are and do the best you can for yourself. I've surrounded you with all the 12 Step meetings and tools, friends, and resources you need to get through this trying time. You need to learn some lessons. And I'm arranging circumstances that will bring you far better than what you want for yourself. Patience."

At least, that is what I heard in my heart of hearts when I could hear anything at all.

I believe that FMG has five answers to prayer: "Yes, no, maybe, not now, and I'm rearranging the chessboard to bring you what's best for you."

During those difficult months, I was given a large dose of "rearranging the chessboard" in every way. I had to take a huge leap of faith, amid bouts of faithlessness and doubt, through my recovery work. I had to sustain my belief that FMG was moving the pieces on the universal chessboard to my ultimate benefit, not only in my work, but also in my personal life and my recovery.

Of course, and as always, my HP has had the last laugh. After many months of grieving, praying the resentment prayer, working resentfully yet successfully, binging, AND doing intense and dedicated recovery work, my HP brought me two enormous gifts: my relationship with L.T. and the peak job of my career I described earlier.

Both times, my therapist gave me the same excellent piece of advice: "Don't fuck it up," when my addict brain tempted me to do so, as it often did during the early days after I received both gifts. I succeeded in the challenging, yet highly rewarding speechwriter position, close to the director of a large federal agency, so that I was able to retire with honor, integrity, and the deep respect of those with whom I worked. As I've stressed, L.T. remains the love of my life and becomes more so each day.

The Great Benefits of Al-Anon

The success of my relationship with L.T. has been due largely to my recovery work in Al-Anon—and her unconditional acceptance and love. To repeat because it is so valuable, the most powerful statement about relationships I have ever heard is "The Three Cs" of Al-Anon to which I add a fourth:

> I didn't **cause** any alcoholic to drink—or my family to consist of generations of multiple addicts, my parents to be obese smokers, and my wives to be as clueless as I was. I cannot **control** the addict or how anyone in life acts or reacts. My addition: I cannot **change** anyone else. And the third Al-Anon "C"—I certainly cannot **cure** any alcoholic, addict, or anyone in my life.

I had joined Al-Anon, as I mentioned, about the same time I began prepping for Kilimanjaro. Before my trek, I had taken Steps 1-3 with one sponsor: I had admitted

- I was powerless over my cross-addicted family history, my divorce, my stepchildren, and my bosses;
- My life was undoubtedly unmanageable;
- I knew only a reimagined and loving Higher Power could restore me to sanity; and
- I had decided that at the very least, the members of men's Al-Anon groups were far more sane than I. I wanted their serenity, wisdom, and fellowship more than I wanted anything else at the time.

After my return from Kili, I changed my Al-Anon sponsor and diligently worked Steps 4-9. My Fifth Step, in which I revealed "the exact nature of my wrongs" to my FMG, myself, and another person, in this case, my sponsor, was a powerful experience during which I released many mistakes.

After working Steps 6, 7, and 8 to prepare the way, I took the Ninth Step with my former wife and stepchildren—I apologized in writing several times and made the best amends I could. They rejected or ignored my overtures to do a face-to-face Ninth Step amends, and they made it clear they did not want to see or hear from me again. As painful as their rejection felt at the time, I also felt at peace with how I had done my best to be courteous to them and to offer my heartfelt amends. Their choice was theirs. I chose to respect them and let them go. It still hurts, but it is now merely a dull pain. It no longer sears my soul, and I don't use it as an excuse to eat as I used to.

Since they never responded in any way to my overtures, my friends called them rude. Agreed, but I know my stepchildren. I know that my leaving their mother abruptly agitated their own unresolved issues and caused intense feelings of betrayal. My therapist and friends also stressed: 'Blood is thicker than water."

If and until their HPs change their mother's anger and resentment toward me, they will choose to side with her. As much as I hate to admit it, that is the right thing for them to do.

In fact, I asked for it: When I separated, I told my stepchildren to take care of their mother. They have. So, it has been another huge HP joke at my expense and another painful lesson in the universal principle of unintended consequences.

Facing the Family "Demon"

In therapy, I finally confronted another dangerous demon—the utterly damaging belief that somehow, I was responsible for—and should be punished severely and fail miserably because of—all the bad things my parents said and did to me and my siblings. It comes from my age-old, core addict belief, learned from my parents, that I am not good enough. To do what? To live a healthy, happy, prosperous life filled with love and joy.

Through the months of post-Kili emotional pain and food slips, guided by my therapist, I spent several weeks in mental, emotional, and spiritual "confrontation" with my long-dead parents. They died within six months of each other in the early 1990s; both died of lung cancer from an addiction to nicotine and smoking. Both also were obese; my father had serious Type II diabetes he didn't manage well and a host of other long-term illnesses. My mother was only 68, my father 75.

During the weeks of my mental and spiritual confrontation with them, I cursed them, I threw figurative cow manure at them, I dropped them into black holes in space, I yelled at them, I howled at them how angry I have always felt. I screamed that they were utterly wrong to punish me by hitting me with switches and belts when I was a child for what I know now were only simple mistakes every child makes. I shrieked that when I was born, I did not become, and never was, responsible for what they did, who they were, what happened to them, and what they so unreasonably demanded of me. I roared at my HP that my parents needed to take responsibility for what they did—the constant emotional turmoil, my father's rage, my mother's victimhood and martyrdom, the unsafe environment they created, the family secrets and lies, and their failure to make it safe for me to be who I was and to reach my potential.

I believe that their spirits remain and heard me. I believe that wherever their souls are, they received my message and have taken spiritual responsibility for their actions.

Thanks solely to FMG's grace, after months of rage and grief, one day all of that rage toward them and hatred toward myself was lifted. I forgave them as Samia, Humphrey, and Rodrik had forgiven me. I felt amazingly free. Today, I feel more at peace with myself and who I am than I ever have before. Sixty-plus years were much too long to carry such an enormous amount of angry, addictive "ballast." I feel deeply grateful I was—and continue to be—willing to let my HP pry all of it from the tight grip of my pain, blame, and shame.

From Deprivation to Prosperity

In other recovery steps related to releasing my self-destruct demon, my challenge in my Debtors Anonymous program has been to overcome my false belief in deprivation—again, because I'm not good enough—and live in prosperity. For decades, I had difficulty reconciling the *appearance* of living in great prosperity with failing to take simple *actions* that put my needs first. I find it very easy to take three-week trips to foreign countries. But I procrastinate for a long time before I buy both simple things, even new underwear for God's sake, and more expensive things that make my life easier and more convenient, such as a new sofa, a new chair, and quality office furniture.

Guy Moment—When I separated from my wife, I did buy a new TV! Years later, I still have it and the audio is getting fuzzy. Time for a new TV?!

For a long time, I have treated my condominium—in a beautiful area of Northern Virginia—as a way station, a temporary stop on my journey to return to some mythical place where I am supposed to belong, to my "real home." To again cite the late, lamented, and very wise "philosopher" Yogi Berra: "Wherever you go, there you are." Oh yes, absolutely true. After so long, since I am still here with me, it is long past time for me to accept that wherever I am, I am home. I need to bring "home" with me within my heart, though a nice condominium in an upscale neighborhood works, too!

Thanks to my HP's gradual removal of my urge to self-sabotage; a flat real estate market; my retirement; and my terrific men's Al-Anon, DA, and OA meetings, I am taking small steps each day to put my needs first. Let me explain: In DA, one of our critical actions is to take care of our basic requirements first: nutritious food, adequate shelter, appropriate clothing, adequate transportation, needed medical and dental care, enough sleep, and even enjoyable entertainment. For example, driving a quality used car so you can get to and from work on time is very different from leasing a Mercedes you cannot afford to impress the neighbors and make yourself feel better than other people—which my first wife and I did. These days, I drive affordable cars that I keep in good shape for at last 5 years.

As for myself, I am making my condo into my home. Thanks to my years of recovery in DA, I have not had any debt--and **NO** credit cards--except my mortgage and a car loan for a long time. So, since I returned from Kili, I have moved into a much nicer condo. Over time as I could afford them comfortably, I have bought a new sofa, a new handmade dining room table (half price from a friend) and four chairs, a new computer, a new office chair, and new office furniture. My closets overflow with more clothes than I will ever need in my retirement—even after I have given much away to charity. I have nine Hawaiian shirts I go dancing in—a few bought new for $35, a few bought from Goodwill for $1 each, and a few given to me by L.T.! I have even bought enough socks and underwear, a miracle indeed—LOL!

No Longer Want—or Expect—To Become A Horse

To sum up, I went up Kilimanjaro an ass hoping desperately to come down a horse. I came down the mountain and off the plain still an ass. I hope I have become—and become more each day—an improved ass.

Best of all, I no longer want to become—expect to be, demand to be, or try to change myself into—a horse. I am happy and content to be the 60-plus ornery AND caring, disdainful AND concerned, and irritable AND loving bundle of recovering contradictions I am.

I ask my HP each day that I be granted many more years to carry the message, to BE the message, to love unconditionally, and to accept life on life's terms. In short, to live the 12 Step Way of Life happily and healthily according to my Higher Power's will for me, one day at a time. Life is very, very good this way.

APPENDIX

Ultimate Lessons in 12-Step Recovery from My Kilimanjaro Climb and Serengeti Safari

Step 1 – From the beginning of my thought about climbing Kili, I admitted I was powerless over doing that. I accepted that as a given. I knew I could not get up the mountain alone. I researched the adventure travel companies with extensive Kili experience. I chose the best one I could find with the most sensible route for my age and physical condition at the time. I admitted that my life was unmanageable about climbing that mountain. I also surrendered to my two trainers—Adam and Darryl—and their exercise regimens that helped me get into shape. Unfortunately, during my 18 months of preparation, I often took my will back and did not exercise as much as they recommended and would have been best for my physical condition. And I had the two weird accidents that set me back. So, when I got to Kili, I quickly found out I was not in good enough shape, and I paid the price. Mother Mountain is what she is and no one is going to change that, and one had better be as well prepared as possible. I wasn't.

My life was unmanageable despite what I thought was a wonderful façade and all outward appearances. My Al-Anon "brothers" have since disabused me of my false beliefs—they thought I was, as my dear friend Eric vS told me, "a raving, disoriented person that had a tremendous problem with women." True at the time. Without doubt, I am a recovering cross-addict. On my own, I am now, and always will be, powerless over my addictions. Despite my best efforts to put up a stable, healthy façade, my life without recovery is unmanageable, or quickly becomes that way when I stop taking the steps ODAT.

Step 2 – Before my climb, I had believed for many years in a Higher Power that could restore me to sanity. He/She had done so with alcohol, compulsive debting, and when I allowed Them and the OA program, compulsive overeating. On the very first day I arrived in Tanzania, I knew only a power greater than myself could get me up and down that mountain. As soon as I met Samia, I believed in him as my most important human Higher Power—and my greatest blessing. I believed not only because it was his 197th trip up and down the mountain, but also because of whom he was as a man, how he acted, what he asked us to do first, what he said, and how he said it. I learned that Samia, Humphrey, Rodrik, and all the tough guys would indeed be my higher powers. Only their compassionate actions and sane advice enabled me to overcome my negative reactions to the altitude and my distrust of my fellow climbers.

Step 3 – When I turned my will and my life over to the care of Samia and crew, the climb was simple, if not easy, and I was safe. When I tried to do it my way and resisted their instructions, I hurt myself every time and almost sabotaged my trip. In recovery, it means I must make an absolute surrender to my Higher Power. Without that, I will always swing back and forth, taking my will back and giving it back only after I make enough mistakes to feel enough pain to surrender again. On Kili and in my life, I have always paid a heavy price for my self-will. On Kili, over my bitter protests, but based on my primary goal, I did surrender my pack to Humphrey so I could achieve my goal. That goal was more important to me than my foolish pride. In recovery, if my goal is to stay sober, clean, abstinent, sane, and healthy, I must surrender my "backpack of worry, weakness, and pride" to my HP every day.

Step 4 – Climbing the mountain caused every character trait—defect *and* asset—to erupt like the active volcano Kili used to be. It was up to me to face my defects fearlessly. On Kili, I spent every long, cold night journaling, thinking, praying, and taking my inventory about how I acted during the day. With regard to recovery, my actions and my thinking were much like a Step 4 inventory because I had to identify and describe every shortcoming and face it. As the Step says, you must make a "searching and fearless moral inventory." It takes a special kind of desperate courage to do a thorough inventory, AND every addict has that courage within him or her to take this Step.

Step 5 – I did my Fifth Step on my character defects in several ways. I admitted my errors, took responsibility, and was accountable for my actions before all my fellow climbers and the crew. More like a direct Fifth Step, I spoke privately with Samia each day to admit my deteriorating physical condition. Similarly, I had a long conversation with Humphrey on the last day of our descent, admitting my mistakes as well as apologizing and offering amends for how my defects affected him. See Step 9 for my amends to all. In recovery, taking the Fifth Step is a giant leap toward self-forgiveness and relief from years of shame and self-blame.

Step 6 – "Pole-pole," slowly, slowly, one foot after another, I became more and more willing and ready to have my HP remove my defects as they increasingly caused me more pain and threatened my goal. I can never be "entirely ready" to have my HP remove my shortcomings. But I can be more and more willing to be ready each day. On Kili, the worse conditions became and the more exhausted I felt, the more willing I became entirely ready. We can choose to pray for the willingness each day and avoid the suffering that comes from a simple lack of willingness. How do you gain the willingness? See Step 11.

Step 7 – On Kili, I expressed my honest willingness to "humbly" ask my HP to remove my shortcomings when I became willing to—and allowed—Humphrey to carry my daypack. At least, I was willing enough to allow my HP to remove my defect of pride and self-will so I could climb the mountain. True awe and gratitude began the second day when I learned it would take 61 "tough guys" to take care of us. I knew I would need every one of them to make it to the peak. In recovery, again, how do I ask humbly? Again, see Step 11. I need to practice daily prayer and understand that my weakness, not my strength, is the secret to my recovery.

Step 8 – On Kili, this Step was much too easy. I made too many mistakes before the entire group and crew. It was immediately and abundantly clear whom I had harmed and needed to put on my daily list. Interestingly, I was far more willing to make amends to the crew than I was to apologize to the members of my group. I felt the worst of my character defects about the group because I defaulted to my false belief that I was "lesser than" they. I quickly fell back into my much-too-old role of "being different from" and "lesser than" and expressed those feelings through resentment and isolation. In recovery, I must be willing to list *everyone* I have harmed and become willing to make amends to them all. Again, how do I become willing? See Step 11. My only Eighth Step action was to make the daily list.

Step 9 – During my climb, I did my best to make the amends on the spot—the appropriate amends whenever my mistakes affected the group as a whole or individuals within either the crew or our group. One important aspect of making amends was to gratefully accept the generosity and help that the crew and certain group members, including Annie and Matt, were willing to offer me. My Ninth Step amends to Samia, Humphrey, and Rodrik included much larger than normal tips and a note of high praise for each to his Adventure Travel managers. Publishing this book and sharing how incredibly good and compassionate these men are may be the best Ninth Step amends of all.

Step 10 – As should be clear by now, I practiced this step daily during my trek. In recovery, I had learned from my decades in 12 Step groups and my years of work in a large bureaucracy that people tend to be flummoxed when you admit your mistakes, apologize, and offer amends. I have made friends from enemies and gained the respect of many people who previously did not like me by my willingness to take Step 10 with them as soon as I made a mistake. It is especially important for me to do so in my relationship with L.T. and with my friends and family.

Step 11 – During my trek, I often climbed "pole pole" in constant prayer and in awe at Mother Mountain. At night when I couldn't sleep, I journaled, I prayed my litany of six daily prayers over and over, I had conversations with my HP, I listened to the wind outside my tent. During the day, I appreciated the magnificence and awesome beauty of the Creator's work. I was in awe of the strength and determination of the plants and animals that survived the harsh conditions on the mountain. In recovery, the key to Step 11 and the true answer to how to work Steps 6, 7, 8, and 9 is simply this: Pray *only* for knowledge of God's will for you and the power to carry that out.

My approach is simple: I have a list of things to do each day. I take Step 11, and I go about my business. If my FMG changes the plan, then however grudgingly at times, I shift gears and change my plan. My HP always has something better in store than what I planned for myself. If He/She doesn't seem to create something better, and I waver from my positive plan, I can experience trouble, failure, and pain. They happen either because of my resistance, because my HP has given me something very important to learn, or because my difficulty is part of a much larger plan that my HP is developing to bring more good to me and others.

Step 12 – I do not claim to have been struck by a lightning bolt of the "Holy Spirit" awakening me on Kili. Rather, the awesome gifts of four blue sky days and four full moon nights overwhelmed me with a sense of the true power, majesty, creativity, and Love of our Creator. The beauty and natural order so evident throughout my journey contrasted sharply with the poverty, chaotic disorder, trash, and grime I saw in so much of the "civilized" world in Arusha—and so many other cities I have visited around the world. The incredibly crowded and unhealthy conditions in most of the world's urban areas demonstrate the epitome of "self-will run riot," that is, mankind's mistaken attempt to control everything, in my opinion.

Rest assured I am neither a Luddite who opposes modern technology nor a utopian who believes we should all live on organic farms, grow our own food, and make our own clothes. I am deeply grateful for my blessings; most mornings when I sit down to breakfast, I give great thanks in prayer to my FMG for all of the incredible natural—and man-made—processes, technologies, and systems that bring my food to my table from around the world. Blueberries from Chile in winter time; almond milk from California; quinoa from Bolivia; rooibos tea from South Africa, and a variety of healthy supplements blended with ingredients from who knows where. I give thanks for the workers who plant the seeds, nurture the crops, and harvest them. I give thanks for the packers, the shippers, the factory workers who process the food and products, and the truck drivers and dock workers who deliver all of these products to a grocery store—with thousands of choices—I can walk to in 5 minutes. I use electricity from a coal-fired power plant in West Virginia, natural gas from Texas, and clean water from a nearby river connected to a treatment plant. Every product, every energy source—all of them—come to my condo in perfect order through the brilliant technologies developed by, and the hard work of, tens of thousands of people. Don't get me started about where all the parts of this computer I am using come from and how the global elements of the Internet allowed you to buy this book—either as an "eBook" or a softcover. All of these people take all of these actions so I get to enjoy all the "necessities" of modern life that 95 percent of the rest of the world cannot imagine. In return, their companies earn a profit and their workers make a living—both marvelous results of very smart people creating innovative ways to help and serve people better.

In such an amazing world—both marvelous and terrible—the best I can do is to serve as the best living example of Step 12 I can be. Step 12 advises me to use what spiritual awakening I have and use it for the good of all people. It directs me to carry the message to other suffering multiple addicts—of whom there are hundreds of millions across the world and in my neighborhood alone, many thousands—and to practice these principles in ALL my affairs. "All my affairs" means just that; I need to base every action I take on one or more of the 12 principles.

I am charged by my HP with paying forward and practicing the gift of the **compassion bestowed on me.** Samia's, Humphrey's, and Rodrik's compassion on me changed my life forever. Whereas I used to be "hell on wheels" with store clerks, wait staff, and others over whom I had power, since I came down from Kili, I have done my best to treat everyone with courtesy and kindness. I continue to learn—pole pole—to practice these principles in all my affairs.

What are the principles that form the foundations for the 12 Steps? The OA *12 Steps and 12 Traditions of Overeaters Anonymous* book summarizes them better than any other source I have read. Starting on page 103, it correlates each step with a principle:

- Step 1 – Honesty
- Step 2 – Hope
- Step 3 – Faith
- Steps 4 and 5 – Courage and Integrity
- Steps 6 – Willingness
- Step 7 – Humility
- Steps 8 and 9 – Self-discipline and Love
- Step 10 – Perseverance
- Step 11 – Spirituality
- Step 12 – Service, the foundation for all the other Steps and the action that brings me a lifetime of happy, joyous, and free recovery.

Samia and his team of "tough guys" lived these principles every day because of the nature of their culture and the kind, generous, and compassionate men they are. By literally following the footsteps of the trail guide up the mountain and Samia's directions, I was practicing the principles, except when I took my will back through my fear.

As my friends and loved ones helped me realize, I have been charting my own deeper path through recovery since I returned from the mountain. In my own way, I carry the message. By admitting my foibles; by sharing my joy and my pain honestly; and by being a calmer, more patient, more compassionate person than before, I live the message and share it with others. I pay my blessings forward so others have the chance to find and create their own unique path to recovery. Then, I encourage them to pay it forward as they grow stronger.

Index

The Twelve Traditions of Alcoholics Anonymous

(SHORT FORM)

- Our common welfare should come first; personal recovery depends upon A.A. unity.
- For our group purpose there is but one ultimate authority—a loving God as He may express Himself in our group conscience. Our leaders are but trusted servants; they do not govern.
- The only requirement for A.A. membership is a desire to stop drinking.
- Each group should be autonomous except in matters affecting other groups or A.A. as a whole.
- Each group has but one primary purpose—to carry its message to the alcoholic who still suffers.
- An A.A. group ought never endorse, finance, or lend the A.A. name to any related facility or outside enterprise, lest problems of money, property, and prestige divert us from our primary purpose.
- Every A.A. group ought to be fully self-supporting, declining outside contributions.
- Alcoholics Anonymous should remain forever nonprofessional, but our service centers may employ special workers.
- A.A., as such, ought never be organized; but we may create service boards or committees directly responsible to those they serve.
- Alcoholics Anonymous has no opinion on outside issues; hence the A.A. name ought never be drawn into public controversy.
- Our public relations policy is based on attraction rather than promotion; we need always maintain personal anonymity at the level of press, radio, and films.
- Anonymity is the spiritual foundation of all our Traditions, ever reminding us to place principles before personalities.

About the Author

Robert P. has been in recovery from multiple addictions through 12 Step Fellowships for more than four decades. He is a recovering compulsive overeater, his primary addiction, and has been an active member of Overeaters Anonymous for more than 40 years. He has been sober through Alcoholics Anonymous for more than 30 years. He owes his current prosperity to more than 27 years of recovery from compulsive debting and spending through Debtors Anonymous. His nine years of recovery in Al-Anon Family Groups have enabled the healthiest and happiest relationships of his life. In addition to Kilimanjaro, Robert often hikes in the Rocky Mountains, the Shenandoahs, the Blue Ridge Mountains, and the Great Smokies. He also has hiked on the Galapagos Islands, Machu Picchu in Peru, on a separate African safari, on the Amazon, and in other amazing places. In his professional career, he has been a journalist, author, editor, professional writing instructor, and speechwriter for more than 45 years. He gives thanks to his Higher Power for every moment of his recovery. He does his imperfect best to live the 12 Step Way of Life ONE DAY AT A TIME! For obvious reasons, in keeping with 12-Step Traditions, the author's anonymity is being protected in public forums.

Reach Robert through his website at www.recoveryfca.com, Twitter @Robert-Recovers, Facebook www.facebook.com/pleasant.oliver.1, Instagram at Robert-Recovers, or email at recoveryfca@gmail.com. Robert is eager to conduct 12 Step workshops or speak at 12 Step meetings.

Made in the USA
Lexington, KY
16 February 2018